Praise for *Married at Fourteen*

"Told with self-lacerating honesty and unvarnished prose that rises on command to poetic intensity, *Married at Fourteen* is the absorbing memoir of a young woman who struggles to find storybook romance and a purpose in life beyond it—and, against cruel odds, succeeds. Lucille Lang Day, only child of an obsessive-compulsive mother and an indulgent but passive father, was gifted with brains and beauty but grew up an unguided missile, willful, reckless, and impulsive in her choice of lovers. Her autobiographical quest transports the narrator across badlands of emotional chaos on her improbable route to domestic serenity and high accomplishments in both the arts and sciences."

— Richard Kluger, Pulitzer Prize–winning author of *Ashes to Ashes*

"Lucille Lang Day gives eloquent voice to the teenager she once was— precocious, hungry for love and adventure, disrespectful of conventions, adept at getting into serious trouble. She transports us into worlds of intense experience—having a baby at age fifteen, partying with Hells Angels, dropping mescaline. As Day begins to comprehend her calling to be a writer and a scientist, we watch the development of a fine intelligence and a wise heart. Along the way we meet a bestiary of male chauvinists and a variety of psychotherapists—some helpful, some less so. Those of us who work with young people and their families can learn much from Day's story. It challenges the conventional wisdom that a teenage mom and dropout has no future and reminds us that rebellious kids who defy authority may become—as has Day—the innovators and creators that our culture needs."

— Naomi Ruth Lowinsky, Ph.D., M.F.T., author of *The Motherline*

"*Married at Fourteen* catches a social class that is uniquely American but resonates with what I know of working people worldwide. Although the rebellion against mothers is universal, Lucille Lang Day carries it to a new extreme. And yet the tone is calm, upbeat, and humorous, and she emerges a confide[...] tested and clarified in this exceptiona[...]

author of *The Medic*

"In this compelling memoir, what propels Lucille Lang Day to break free of constraints, internal or external, can be found in a telling insight: 'I sensed there was something just beyond my consciousness that I needed to know about my life.' Her illuminating story tracks the search for that expansive terrain just beyond the *No Trespassing* signs. *Married at Fourteen* is a testament to the independent spirit and indomitable will of a woman whose reinventions show the way to transformation and hope."
—Toni Mirosevich, author of *Pink Harvest*

"*Married at Fourteen* is the story of the late and somewhat surprising discovery of genuine family by someone who was—in her own terms—'a bad girl.' She survives *les bas-fonds* to become a respected poet, scientist, and educator. The book tells us that a restless, not easily satisfied, constantly questioning intellect may, in the right situation, pull us away from Dropout City towards love, satisfaction, a world—these are the last words of the book—'alive with offerings.'"
—Jack Foley, KPFA literary host and author of *Visions & Affiliations*

"The saga *Married at Fourteen* is many things: both a cautionary tale and a tale of redemption, a multigenerational account of the passing of an era, a parable of the Prodigal Daughter, a gripping narrative rendered from a tenacious memory, a scientist's precision, and an artist's sensitivity. Parents should read this book, teachers and counselors, dreamers and seekers, anyone who wants to read a book that once you pick up you'll find hard to put down. While you will not condone all of Lucille Lang Day's actions—she does not expect you to—you will understand, sympathize, and perhaps sometimes see yourself more clearly."
—Adam David Miller, winner of PEN/Oakland's 2011 Josephine Miles National Literary Award for Lifetime Achievement and author of *Ticket to Exile*

Married at Fourteen

Lucille Lang Day, 1967

Married at Fourteen

a true story

Lucille Lang Day

Heyday, Berkeley, California

Also by Lucille Lang Day

POETRY
The Curvature of Blue
Infinities
Wild One
Fire in the Garden
Self-Portrait with Hand Microscope

POETRY CHAPBOOKS
God of the Jellyfish
The Book of Answers
Lucille Lang Day: Greatest Hits, 1975–2000

CHILDREN'S BOOK
Chain Letter

SCIENCE EDUCATION
*How to Encourage Girls in Math and Science: Strategies for
    Parents and Educators* (coauthor)
*SEEK (Science Exploration, Excitement, and Knowledge):
    A Curriculum in Health and Biomedical Science
    for Diverse 4th and 5th Grade Students* (editor)
Family Health and Science Festival: A SEEK Event (editor)

For my daughters, Liana and Tamarind
And my husband, Richard

Library of Congress Cataloging-in-Publication Data
Day, Lucille.
Married at fourteen : a true story / Lucille Lang Day.
   p. cm.
ISBN 978-1-59714-198-7 (pbk. : alk. paper) -- ISBN 978-1-59714-214-4 (apple e-book) -- ISBN 978-1-59714-208-3 (amazon kindle e-book)
  1. Day, Lucille. 2. Authors, American--20th century--Biography. I. Title.
PS3554.A965Z46 2012
813'.54--dc23
[B]
                              2012008020

Cover Photograph: Courtesy of Lucille Lang Day
Cover Design: Lorraine Rath
Interior Design/Typesetting: Rebecca LeGates
Printing and Binding: Worzalla, Stevens Point, WI

Orders, inquiries, and correspondence should be addressed to:
        Heyday
        P.O. Box 9145, Berkeley, CA 94709
        (510) 549-3564, Fax (510) 549-1889
        www.heydaybooks.com

10 9 8 7 6 5 4 3 2 1

Contents

Preface

All of the events described in this book are true, but I have changed the names of many people to protect the guilty. Part I tells the story of my teen years, 1960 to 1967, from my adolescent point of view: I have tried to recapture what I was thinking and feeling then and reveal how, bit by bit, I matured. Part II consists of nine self-contained stories that focus mainly on events in my adult life.

The details of my experiences are unique and personal, but the themes are universal. This book is about men and women, parents and children, how they communicate with each other, and how they fail to do so. It is also about adolescent rebellion and how it can give way to self-discovery, hope, survival, and love.

Acknowledgments

Many people helped make this book a reality. Special thanks go to Cyra McFadden for providing much invaluable advice and criticism; Herbert Gold for his longtime support of this project; Marcia Falk, Molly Giles, Frances Mayes, and Steven Rood for their insightful feedback on early versions; and Gayle Wattawa of Heyday for helping me identify the weaknesses and build on the strengths of the manuscript. I am also indebted to my daughters, Liana Day-Williams and Tamarind Fleischman Pease, who read earlier drafts and helped me to remember events more clearly and understand them more fully; my father, the late Richard Lang, who believed in me as much as is humanly possible; and my husband Richard Levine, whose love and wisdom are my bedrock. Richard has enabled me to finish what I started long ago and has inspired me to make this into a much better book than it started out to be.

Portions of this book have appeared in the following publications, sometimes in slightly different form:

Excerpts:
Cadillac Cicatrix: "The White Swan Motel"
Eureka Literary Magazine: "Visit to *David*"
The Gihon River Review: "The White Swan Motel"
The Hudson Review: "Worse than a Dozen Kids"
Passages North: "Time-Out!"
Pennsylvania English: "Will I What?"
River Oak Review: "Angel on 24 East"
Waccamaw: "Married at Fourteen"
Willow Review: "Stalked"

Poems:

    The Curvature of Blue (Červená Barva Press) and *Blue Unicorn:*
       "Color of the Universe" and "A Blessing in Beige"
    Psychological Perspectives: "Birding: A Love Poem"
    Wild One: Poems (Scarlet Tanager Books): "To an Artist"

"Stalked" received the 2009 *Willow Review* Award for Creative
    Nonfiction.
"Time-Out!" was cited as a Notable Essay in *Best American Essays*
    2010.

Part 1

Left: Dick and Evelyn Lang on their wedding day, July 6, 1940.
Right: Lucy at the skating rink, 1961.

chapter 1

"*Worse Than a Dozen Kids*"

I own a switchblade knife. It has a black plastic handle with two
brass buttons. One button is the lock. When you slide this button to
its uppermost position, the knife won't open (a handy feature that
prevents it from opening in your pocket). But when you slide the lock
button all the way down, then press on the larger brass button in the
middle of the handle, the blade pops out with a click, in less than a
second, making a clean 180-degree arc.

There is a special way to hold a switchblade so that you won't cut
yourself when it opens: you cradle it in your palm with your thumb on
the large button, the tip of your index finger pressed behind the base
of the blade, and your remaining fingers curled beside, rather than
around, the handle, so as not to interfere with the opening blade. Bill
Arthur taught me this when he gave me the knife. He was nineteen, a
blueprint delivery boy; I was thirteen, in eighth grade.

I almost had to relinquish the knife not long after acquiring it. I was
smoking on the way home from school, and a boy named Ken followed
me and threatened to tell. I pulled the knife from my purse, holding
it just as Bill had shown me, and pressed the button. When the blade
popped out, I waved the knife at Ken and said I'd cut him up into little
pieces if he finked on me. He called my bluff and fink he did—not
only for my smoking but also for threatening him with a switchblade.

The next day I was called to the office of Mr. Louis Ferry, principal of Piedmont Junior High School, and told that Inspector Lamp
wanted to see me at the Piedmont Police Department, across the street

from the school. I stopped on the way to put the switchblade in my locker.

"We have a report that you threatened a boy with a switchblade knife yesterday," said Inspector Lamp.

"That's crazy. I've never even seen a switchblade."

"Why do you think the boy said that?"

I pulled my key chain from my purse. On it, I had a fold-out nail file in a unit that also included a tiny knife, less than one inch long. I held the handle and flicked my wrist. The little knife popped out.

Inspector Lamp said, "You'd better give that to me," and I took it off my key chain and handed it to him.

Then he asked me to empty my purse, which was close to the size of a suitcase (all the better for shoplifting), but only my makeup, brush, comb, wallet, tissues, pencils, pens, chewing gum, cigarettes, matches, and a Hershey bar came tumbling out. He took the cigarettes and matches, then asked if I'd like to see his collection of switchblades.

His were much finer than mine. Some had bone, wood, or mother-of-pearl handles; many had much longer blades. "They're illegal," he said. "We don't give them back."

Nevertheless, I kept mine, which was tucked safely behind my math and history books in my locker. I wasn't about to hand it over to any cop. It was a symbol of who I was. It meant I didn't play by the rules; it meant I made up my own rules. It meant I was a rebel. It meant I was bad.

I've had my switchblade now for over fifty years. For two decades I kept it in my desk with other childhood mementos in a pink box with My Treasures stamped on top. Now I keep it in my bedroom in a drawer in an antique oak dresser with other special things, like my gold charm bracelet, my children's milk teeth, and my Phi Beta Kappa key.

...

I started seriously looking for a husband when I was twelve. I'd had enough of being a child, enough of being told what to do. I was unhappy at school; I resented homework; I didn't get along with my mother. Having seen movies like *South Pacific, Sayonara,* and *A Summer Place,* I believed in true love. More than anything, I wanted Rossano Brazzi, Marlon Brando, or Troy Donahue to come rescue me from my childhood. I wanted to be an adult, to be free, and to be loved.

The grown-ups always warned that getting pregnant as a teenager would ruin your life, but I didn't believe them. I felt that in truth my life would be ruined if I had to live with my mother much longer: her nagging would drive me crazy. And my sanity would benefit even more if I could be freed from boring math drills and stuck-up classmates. A high school diploma? I didn't need one. I already knew everything I'd ever need to know.

My thoughts on all these things began to crystallize in the summer of 1960, after my sixth-grade graduation from Egbert W. Beach School in Piedmont, California. That summer I went to Camp Augusta, where Piedmont Blue Birds and Campfire Girls rode horses, swam, wove key chains from long strips of colored plastic, and painted daisies on salt and pepper shakers for their mothers. On the bus, which took us from the Piedmont Community Center to the Sierra foothills, we sang "Ninety-Nine Bottles of Beer on the Wall" and "A Hot Time in the Old Town." But my fun was to be short-lived. Singing on the bus, I had no inkling that once at Camp Augusta, I would spend my time figuring out how to avoid the broom treatment, and that having accomplished that, I would dive headlong into a turbulent adolescence.

The campers were assigned to groups called Tents, each of which included about ten girls. Every Tent had a real tent—a large sturdy canvas one where we kept our belongings, changed our clothes, and slept when it rained. Most of the time, we slept in our sleeping bags on cots outside, under the Douglas firs, sugar pines, and glittering constellations.

Every Tent also had a broom for sweeping the tent. Only this isn't how the girls in my Tent used it. After breakfast my first morning at camp, I found out how the broom was really used. When Marlene and I, the only beginning swimmers in our Tent, went back to change into swimsuits for our lesson, the rest of our tent mates followed. As soon as Marlene, who was beginning to get breasts and curly black pubic hair that matched the hair on her head, was naked, one of the girls grabbed the broom and ran after her, threatening to swat her unless she ran outside, which she did, as everyone laughed and cheered.

The broom treatment, as the girls called it, was administered whenever someone was changing her clothes and no counselors were near. My refusal to chase anyone with the broom and my strategies to avoid nakedness in the tent (changing my clothes in my sleeping bag or in the lavatory, wearing my underpants beneath my swimsuit) did not win me any friends, nor did my decision to wear shorts and blouses instead of cut-off Levi's and sweatshirts like everyone else wore, even when the temperature was over one hundred degrees. I spent a lot of time sitting on my cot, watching the squirrels and jays clean up the peanuts and sunflower seeds dropped by the campers and trying to figure out how to get out of Camp Augusta.

On the fourth day I limped to the infirmary, threw myself writhing onto a cot, and moaned, "I have a terrible stomachache. I want to go home."

"What kind of stomachache?" asked the nurse.

"The kind that hurts here." I put my hand on my abdomen.

"Is there anything special about this stomachache?" she asked, leaning closer.

"No."

She sent tan, freckled Janet Driscoll, the favorite counselor of the campers, in to see me.

"Hi kid. How're you doing?"

"I feel sick."

"You don't look very sick to me."

"I have a stomachache."

"Listen, I know it's hard sometimes to be open with people you don't know very well," she said, sitting down beside me on the cot and leaning so close I could count the flakes of peeling skin on her sunburned nose, "but believe me, we're all your friends here. You have nothing to be afraid of. All of us know how it feels to...." She paused and looked at me knowingly before continuing, "...to have cramps."

I started crying. "I'm not afraid; I'm just sick. Please call my mom and dad. I want to go home."

An only child, I usually got my way. My parents arrived the next day. I had no intention of telling them about the strange puberty rite I had witnessed. If I told my mother about the broom treatment, she would tell the camp director, who would confront the girls. I did not want to be a tattletale.

As we pulled onto the highway in my father's blue-and-white '55 Oldsmobile, my mother, who had argued against my going to camp, said, "Lucille, I told you that you shouldn't come here. You should've listened to me. This was an awful drive for your father and me." She wiped her forehead with a handkerchief, brushing back her brown hair, which was starting to turn gray. "You're worse than a dozen kids," she added emphatically. "You don't know what a nuisance you are."

"Are you feeling any better?" my father asked. His face was flushed, his hair matted with perspiration. He was forty-two, seven years younger than my mother, but he wasn't holding up any better in the heat. My parents were overweight and always had a hard time in hot weather.

I was about to say, "I'm feeling okay now," when I realized that I actually did have cramps. "No, I'm feeling worse. I'd like to stop at a gas station."

Several miles down the road, when we pulled into a station, I was feeling quite uncomfortable. No acting was necessary as I walked, slightly bent over, to the restroom.

Back in the car I tried to sound casual as I said, "We have to stop at a drugstore. I need some Kotex."

My mother looked at me disgustedly. "You made us drive all the way up here for that! I knew it! That's what everyone at the camp said it was." She rolled her eyes and raised her voice. "That's nothing, you hear me, nothing! You didn't need to come home for that. Lucille, sometimes you just don't use your head."

This was mild criticism from my mother, who had been telling me ever since I could remember that I was nothing but a troublemaker and would be sorry when she was ten feet under and pushing up daisies. I was sick of it. I didn't want to listen to her nagging anymore, nor did I want to wear the Piedmont Junior High and High School uniform—a black or white pleated skirt, a white blouse with sleeves and a collar, and bobby sox with saddle shoes, tennis shoes, or oxfords—with the girls from Camp Augusta for the next six years.

I'd heard many times that my Aunt Liz's cousin met her husband at Dimond Roller Rink when she was eighteen. Maybe I could find a husband there too. "I want to go skating at Dimond," I told my parents when we were almost home.

My mother said that I absolutely could not go roller-skating and break my neck, but my father and I talked her into it. So it was that on a Friday night, I put on pink-and-blue plaid pedal pushers and a white ruffled blouse, tied my long golden hair back with a pink satin ribbon, and took a long look at myself in the mirror, wondering if I looked like a woman someone would want to marry. My best friend, Eileen, who was coming along, said, "Hurry up! Don't be so vain."

After skating around the rink a couple of times, I asked my father to leave. I continued to glide around the rink, surprised I could do so without falling, since I'd never been skating before, until the lights went dim and the announcer said, "Couples only." Everyone cleared the floor except one boy, who remained at the center of the rink, practicing leaps, spins, and figures. By far the best skater there, he was either totally oblivious to everyone else or showing off for us. I was awed. "Couples only," the announcer said again. The skater, who was in midair, landed, spun around on one foot, and skated directly toward me. I did not attach any significance to this until he held out his hand and said, "Would you like to skate?"

The world turned in the palm of my hand. I had never imagined that finding a man would be so easy. He was tall and slender, with a high forehead, brown hair, lively brown eyes, and a terrible complexion. The complexion didn't bother me: I was sure it would clear up in time.

"My name is Woody," he said. "What's yours?"

Could I tell him my name was Lucille? I'd hated the name even before the kids in elementary school started calling me Lou the Seal. He was waiting; I had to think quickly. I said, "Lucy."

He would be a senior at Oakland High School in September, he was an artist, and he hoped to win a scholarship to the California College of Arts and Crafts. Could I tell him I was twelve years old and starting seventh grade? "I'm fourteen and going into ninth grade at Piedmont High," I said.

Woody asked me to skate every time the announcer said, "Couples only." At the end of the evening he asked, "Are you coming back?"

"Yes."

"When?"

I didn't pause a nanosecond. "Tomorrow night."

Eileen kept muttering, "You lucky bum," as we changed into our shoes.

I went skating every Friday and Saturday night for the rest of the summer. During the week I spent most of my time making skating skirts with felt, corduroy, and floral-print cottons. For some skirts I simply cut the fabric in a circle, made a hole for my waist, and added a waistband; for others I stitched together multiple panels that were narrow at the top to make a snug fit across my abdomen, but flared at the bottom to make the skirt full.

I felt like a woman and I wanted to look like one. I started curling my hair (no more pink ribbons!) and wearing green or purple eye shadow, bright pink lipstick, black eyeliner, and black mascara. My mother, who didn't wear makeup, screamed, "You're a disgrace. You look like a flapper!" every time I left the house.

Woody and I were a couple. We always skated together during "couples only," and sometimes even during "all skate." When we weren't skating, we sat under the high windows on a scratched and stained wooden bench on which many couples before us had carved their initials. As we drank Coke and watched the other skaters, he always put his arm around me, and sometimes I turned my head just to admire his hand resting on my shoulder. After skating, he walked me back to meet my parents at my Aunt Ethel and Uncle Dick's house, two blocks away. I didn't want my parents to talk to him, though. I was scared to death my father would say something embarrassing like, "You know, she's only twelve years old."

One night toward the end of summer, when the last "couples only" period was announced, Woody said, "Let's leave."

"Why?"

"So that we can have some time alone before I have to get you home."

I led him to my cousin Jan's playhouse in my aunt and uncle's backyard. He wanted to sit on the floor, but I didn't want to get my skating skirt dirty, so we stood in the middle of the room. He put his arms around me and pulled me close. I knew he wanted to kiss me, so I looked up at him and smiled.

His mouth felt very hard against mine. This wasn't at all what I'd imagined kissing a boy would be like. I remembered reading about a girl's first kiss in a Beverly Cleary novel: "She had never thought a boy's lips could be so soft."

"Your lips are soft," I said, because I wanted this moment to be like the one in the book.

"Well, what did you expect?"

"I didn't know what to expect. I've never kissed a boy before."

He leaned forward to kiss me again.

•••

On a Saturday in August, my father took Eileen and me to the Santa Cruz Boardwalk. We rode the Ferris wheel, the roller coaster called the Giant Dipper, and the Wild Mouse, which felt at every turn as though it would fly off the track. Then we entered an arcade where there were rows of rectangular red fortune-telling machines the size of toasters. You put a penny in, asked a question with a yes or no answer, then pulled a lever. The answer popped out on a little card. I put my penny in, asked, "Will I marry young?" and pulled the lever. The answer popped out: "I will be truthful—signs say yes. Genius may have its limitations, but stupidity is not thus handicapped."

All too soon, summer ended and I entered the dreaded Piedmont Junior High, the only public school I had ever heard of that required girls to wear uniforms. That year the uniform had been updated: tennis shoes and blouse styles other than middies were now allowed. To the best of my knowledge, these were the only changes that had ever been instituted. Except for the tennis shoes and blouses, the uniform was no different from the one my mother and her twin sister, my Aunt Ethel, wore in the 1920s. But it wasn't only the appearance of the uniform that bothered me. I was also angry that girls had to wear this awful costume, while boys didn't have to wear any uniform at all. They could even wear shorts in hot weather.

I splashed Coke and orange juice on my skirts to keep them at the cleaners as much as possible. I cut holes in my tennis shoes and complained that oxfords hurt my feet. One morning I wore a black blouse and a tight green-red-black plaid skirt with a fringed hem underneath my uniform, and on the way to school I peeled off the hated garments and threw them into a Dumpster in front of a typical Piedmont home: a Jacobean mansion, complete with guest cottage, swimming pool, bathhouse, greenhouse, rolling lawns, and a Greek pavilion overlooking the tennis courts.

My family wasn't rich. The school and mansions were up in the hills, but I lived in "lower Piedmont," in a nondescript three-bedroom, one-bath white stucco house near busy Grand Avenue. I had strong mixed feelings as I walked past the mansions each day. Sometimes I was simply disgusted that anyone should have so much. Other times I felt that the people who lived in these houses weren't important or real, that the real people were the families living in crowded apartments in nearby Oakland. Still other times, I fantasized that I would be rich and famous someday, not just rich enough to buy one of the mansions for Woody and me, but rich enough to buy three or four—maybe even a whole goddamn street—and share them with our friends from the skating rink.

I had already begun to get detention for coming to school out of uniform, and now I had gone too far for Mr. Ferry. He took one look at me and ordered me into his office: I would not be allowed to be seen in my V-neck blouse and tight plaid skirt in the halls of Piedmont Junior High.

"It isn't fair," I said, "that the girls have to wear uniforms, but the boys don't—and girls at other schools don't. No other kids at public schools have to put up with this." (I had a point: a dozen years later Title IX would make discriminatory dress codes illegal at public schools, and the uniform would be abolished.)

Mr. Ferry was a sturdily built man with the broad shoulders of a football player, a round face, and a gray crew cut. "Without the uniform," he explained, "the wealthy girls would have wardrobe competitions and the other [middle-class] girls would feel shabby and excluded."

"That doesn't show much faith in the character of any of the girls," I argued.

"Well, it's a tradition," he said sternly, "and traditions should be respected. Without them, society would fall apart."

Try as I might, I couldn't convince him that the fate of twentieth-century society did not hinge on Piedmont girls' wearing black or white pleated skirts and white blouses with sleeves. After the bell rang and the other students were safely in their classrooms, where they couldn't see me leaving in my nonregulation attire, a counselor escorted me out and drove me to the Little Daisy, where she told me to select a new uniform and charge it to my mother's account. I called my mother and begged her to say we couldn't afford it, but she refused.

I was a nail in Mr. Ferry's shoe. Not wanting the same old schedule of classes everyone had always taken, I begged him to let me take shop instead of home economics.

"Absolutely not. It's against the rules." (Again Title IX would bring change.)

"Why?"

"Girls might get hurt using the tools."

"Boys might get hurt too. Besides, girls can burn themselves on the ovens in home ec."

"Those are risks that society is willing to take."

Mr. Ferry, who had encountered a lot of kids, could see that my rebelliousness ran deep. He asked my parents to get professional help for me.

They first took me to see a psychotherapist at Kaiser Hospital in Oakland. A lean man with intense eyes, he looked at me searchingly when we spoke. During our first session he said, "Suppose twenty people are on a spaceship, on a long voyage that will require their being together for many years. Supplies are limited; decisions must be made regularly. How will the people make decisions? How will they get along?"

"They'll need rules; they'll need leaders." I was exasperated already. "I know what you're saying: the Earth is a spaceship. I want you to know I don't object to *all* rules, only stupid ones."

He raised his bushy eyebrows in an expression that showed more surprise than disapproval. Then he smiled. "That sounds reasonable," he said.

Four or five visits later, he began by saying, "This is our last session. I've told your parents that you're a normal adolescent and I see no point in continuing to waste my time, your time, and their money."

Next my parents, who were more intimidated by Mr. Ferry than I was, took me to a corpulent psychiatrist with a full black beard. He asked me what I thought the other kids thought of me. Why did the ones who were my friends like me? Why did others dislike me? Was I sure they disliked me? And so on. I thought I gave reasonable answers, but at the end of the session, he gave me two prescriptions: one for a pill to calm me down, the other for a pill to pep me up. The pill to calm me down made my tongue so heavy I could hardly speak. The one to pep me up kept me awake when I was taking the one to calm me down. It also made my heart race and my hands tremble.

A few days later my mother's friend Phyllis, our next-door neighbor, invited me over. She showed me a magazine article that told how psychiatrists had started using drugs to control the criminally insane. I recognized my two pills in a photograph of these drugs, which were already, the author said, producing excellent results with prisoners and parolees.

As soon as I got home, I emptied all my pills into the toilet. The tablets sank to the bottom, but the capsules floated. I flushed, and as the water swirled down, I was pleased that all of the pills disappeared. Then I went to the kitchen, where my mother was washing dishes, threw the empty pill bottles onto the floor, and screamed, "I'm never going back to see that crazy psychiatrist again!"

My parents asked Dr. Joseph Presant, our family physician, for his advice. He told them that counseling teenagers was one of his specialties and he would be happy to start meeting with me. Fiftyish, with thin, graying hair and a kind smile, he turned out to be a good listener and seemed genuinely sympathetic to my point of view. When we discussed the rules I didn't like at Piedmont Junior High, he said, "Lots of things in this world don't make sense, Lucy, and we need people like you to change them. Just wait until you grow up. Then pick your battles carefully and fight the ones you think you can win."

A few months later I met his son, Bobby, at a party. "My old man is pretty cool," Bobby told me as he swept his straight dark hair away from his eyes between swigs of beer, "and he knows a lot about delinquents, all of which he learned from me."

At school I was placed in accelerated math and English and an honors French class. I didn't want the French class, because it meant extra homework; I wanted a study hall, so that I could do my homework at school and spend my time at home on the more urgent task of designing skating skirts. I asked my mother to write Mr. Ferry a letter saying that the French course was too much work for me, that I needed more time to study, and would he please put me in a study hall instead.

Mr. Ferry called me into his office. Sitting behind his desk, he shook my mother's letter at me. "Baloney," he roared. "You have a good mind. Unfortunately, instead of putting it to work, you use it to get out of working. Do you know that I get several phone calls a day from parents begging me to put their son or daughter into that French class?"

"It's too hard for me. I need the time to study."

"You mean you want the time to play. You can fool your parents, but you can't fool me." He shook his head. "What a waste. I wish I had your mind; if I had your mind, nothing would stop me."

"What would you do?"

"I'd be a doctor or a nuclear physicist. I certainly wouldn't be sitting here arguing with kids like you."

I was startled. It sounded like a compliment. I knew I'd scored high on standardized tests, but I was not convinced that this had any implications for real life. I had no idea whether I could really be a doctor or a nuclear physicist, but I felt flattered and began to suspect that deep down somewhere, Mr. Ferry liked me.

In the days that followed, I thought about what he had said. My parents had never suggested that I think about going to college, perhaps because they hadn't gone to college themselves and just didn't think about it as something that a person, especially a girl, ought to do. My mother frequently told me her dream for my future: "I hope you marry a rich man. I hope you find your prince." The only college graduate in my family was my Aunt Liz, my father's brother's wife, who took night classes at UC Extension and graduated when she was almost forty. Our neighborhood, too, was short on college graduates. Phyllis's husband was a florist; Mr. Meisner, our other next-door neighbor, an elevator operator; Betty Sink, who lived on the other side of Phyllis, a bookkeeper; and Mr. Zenner, across the street, a retired contractor. Carole and Hal Mickens, also across the street, were a beautician and a merchant marine. I think the only college graduates in our neighborhood were Mr. Meisner's second wife, Dorothy, a hospital lab technician, and Betty's sister, Bobby, a nurse. It seemed that Mr. Ferry expected me to go to college, so I told Phyllis, whom I admired and trusted. She said, "The only reason a girl goes to college is to find a husband," and warned me not to get bigheaded because

I'd scored 100 percent on Mr. Swartzell's entry exam for accelerated math. "Girls aren't as good as boys at math," she said. "You'll find out when you get to high school."

Phyllis also offered the following advice: "Never ask a boy out, beat him at tennis or chess, or let him know that you're better than him at anything."

I didn't want to believe everything she said, and I had a feeling I would someday break her rules, but because she had admitted to me that she got pregnant by having sex with her husband, I considered Phyllis a more reliable source of information than my mother, who boasted the second immaculate conception. I'd first asked my mother about sex when I was eight, after my friend Nancy told me what her mother had told her about where babies come from: that a woman gets pregnant when a man touches his penis to her privates. My mom started screaming, calling Nancy's mother a liar. "That's nothing but an ugly lie," she yelled, making a face to show her disgust. "I'd never do a dirty thing like that!" But I knew instinctively that she was the liar.

Mr. Ferry gave me the study hall, but I didn't use it to do my homework. I used it to draw skaters and pass notes to anyone who would correspond with me.

Every day I wrote in my diary: "I can't stop thinking about Woody. Now I know what love is really like." "I'm madly in love with Woody. I hope we can get married when I'm sixteen." "I feel like the luckiest girl in the world because Woody loves me." Woody had never said he loved me, but I assumed he felt the same way I did.

Because I was taking seventh grade classes, not ninth grade ones, Woody knew that something was amiss. I admitted the truth, rather than letting him think I was a remedial high school student. His interest in me waned, but another boy at the rink started giving me a lot of attention. His name was Barry, but everyone called him Lucky. He didn't know as many jumps and figures as Woody, but he could do a perfect waltz jump and win at limbo. He had wavy jet-black hair, a clear complexion, and a mischievous grin. All the girls thought he was cute. Moreover, he was fourteen years old and in the eighth grade. He knew I was twelve, almost thirteen now, and thought that was fine. Could I love him instead of Woody? Yes.

I started smoking, although Woody and Lucky, both smokers themselves, advised me not to. I did it because it made me feel like an adult and because it was a way of being different from my parents, neither of whom smoked.

Soon Lucky and I were going steady. The only thing that could possibly be better, I thought, would be to marry him and have his baby. I knew we could get married if I got pregnant, but we never even talked about sex. The closest we ever came to discussing it was a conversation that went something like this: "Did you ever do it with Woody?" "No." "Good, I'm glad you're no whore."

Dimond Roller Rink closed its doors for good at the end of the year to make room for the MacArthur Freeway, and the skating crowd moved to Chimes Skateland on the other side of town. Since this rink was nowhere near either my aunt and uncle's house or my own, I now needed a ride home every time I went skating. My father would have been happy to pick me up, but I preferred to get rides with the other kids. One time I accepted a ride from an older man who was a regular at the rink. I didn't think there was anything wrong with this, because he was driving several other kids home as well. But after taking everyone else home, he said we needed to talk and took me to a little diner on Broadway, about a mile from my house. We sat on stools at the counter. He ordered coffee and I ordered hot chocolate. While we waited for our drinks, he took my hand and said softly that he loved me. He also told me he was sixty-three years old and his wife didn't love him. Back in the car he kissed me, fondling my breasts, and said he wanted to take me to the hills to look at the view. I was terrified. I told him that if I didn't get home soon I'd be in a lot of trouble and my mother might even call the police, but I'd go to see the view with him some other time. "Do you promise?" he asked. "Yes," I lied.

I didn't tell my mother about this incident, because I knew it would mean the end of skating for me. My mother, the nagger, now focused a lot on my friends at the rink. "You're in with bad company," she told me every day. "Those kids at the skating rink are no good: they all smoke. They're not your type of people. If you keep friends like that, you'll come to no good end. You're putting me in my grave." How could I tell her I'd met a genuine child molester? She was letting me go skating; I decided to leave well enough alone.

One night Lucky brought a friend to the rink. Steve Labate was part Italian, compact and muscular, with olive skin and dark hair. When Lucky introduced us, Steve smiled with mock flirtatiousness and said, "I'm in love." Lucky said, "You're too late. She's already taken."

I immediately liked Steve, not the way I liked Lucky and had liked Woody, but the way I liked Eileen. I wished Eileen were here at the rink to meet him, but her mother rarely let her come skating anymore, because she thought we were too young to be involved with boys.

Lucky, Steve, Woody, and I often talked about going somewhere after skating, but we needed transportation. One possibility would be to take my father's Oldsmobile (he had given me a key and started teaching me to drive, but so far, he had only let me practice at empty factory parking lots on weekends); another would be to take Lucky's grandparents' car (he knew that his grandmother kept a spare key in a little box on her dresser). We talked about these options every week, until we finally talked ourselves into acting.

First we went to Lucky's grandparents' house, and while they slept, Lucky tiptoed into their bedroom and took the car key from the little box. We feared that the sound of the engine might wake them, so I steered while the three boys pushed the Ford to start it rolling down the driveway. As an extra precaution we let the car roll a full block away from the house before starting it.

Lucky insisted on driving, although Woody had a license. We turned the radio on full blast to hear Neil Sedaka sing "Happy Birthday Sweet Sixteen." Lucky drove fast, tailgating cars that didn't speed up or pull over for us and barely missing the cars we encountered at intersections.

We headed for my house, having decided that two cars would be more fun than one. The porch light was on for me. I had no idea if my parents were asleep or up watching television. The boys and I used the same strategy that had already worked once: I steered while they pushed the car down the driveway. Woody insisted that I ride with him because he was a better driver than Lucky.

We went bowling, and after I'd demonstrated all my techniques for throwing gutter balls, we went cruising, with Woody and me in the lead in the Oldsmobile. We sped through the deserted streets until about two o'clock, when we came to a red light. Woody stopped for it, but Lucky didn't. There was a screech of brakes, a sudden jolt, the sound of crunching metal. Ours were the only two cars on the street, and we had crashed.

We all got out to examine the damage. My father's car had a pretty good-sized dent in the rear fender, but what really worried us was that the front end of Lucky's grandparents' car was a jumble of twisted metal. The engine was practically on the front seat. Thankfully, Steve and Lucky were alive and talking to Woody and me, but it was obvious that no one would ever drive that car again.

Woody shook his head. "You totaled it."

"What the hell did you stop for?" Lucky asked, pretending indignation.

"The light was red."

"What difference does that make? There weren't any other cars around. You could've gone right through."

"I didn't want to get a ticket."

"A ticket! You've been doing double the speed limit for the last two hours. What made you so concerned about a ticket now?"

A squad car arrived. The officers radioed our names to the police station, and all of our parents were called. Because Woody had a driver's license, he was allowed to drive Steve and me home, but Lucky's father told the police to put him in jail.

•••

Lucky lived in Hayward, about twenty miles away from me, so it had never been easy to get together during the week. To compensate, we'd started writing letters early on in our friendship. This correspondence really blossomed after the car wreck, because Lucky was on restriction and wasn't allowed to go skating. (My own parents were angry but forgiving. They didn't even take away my car key!) It was in these letters that we started plotting to run away together.

"I can't stand living with my mother anymore," I wrote. "She says I'm trash and my friends are trash. She hasn't stopped yelling since the night of the wreck. We should dye our hair, take my father's car, and go to Mexico or Canada."

"My stepmother hates me and sometimes I think my father does too," he wrote back. "If you can get the car, we will go away. I don't know where, but I think we will go to Los Angeles."

When we finally saw each other again, running away was all we could talk about. Lucky wanted to go to Los Angeles. His mother and sister lived in Southern California, and he thought his sister would be able to help us.

On a sunny Thursday morning in late spring, we rendezvoused at a prearranged corner in downtown Oakland. I took off my uniform skirt, under which I was wearing Bermuda shorts, and I threw both the skirt and my schoolbooks into a trash can, because I figured I wouldn't need them anymore. We went to the parking lot where my father always left his car when he was at Bank of America, where he worked as a loan officer. The attendant didn't give us a second look as we got into the Oldsmobile and drove away.

Our first stop was in San Leandro at the boxy tract home of John, one of Lucky's friends, who was cutting school to help us. He had offered us food and a blanket from his house, as well as a tank of gas, which he planned to siphon from the car of one of his neighbors. I expected to stop only briefly, but two other guys that Lucky knew were there, and all the boys started talking. John took a six-pack of beer from the refrigerator and opened a can for each of us.

"Won't you get in trouble for taking that?" Lucky asked.

"Not as much trouble as you'll be in for taking the girl and the car."

"I don't plan to get caught."

After a couple of beers, we all decided to go for a ride. "Show me what this thing can do," said John as Lucky revved the engine and I opened my third can of beer.

"Not here. I know a place where it's safe," Lucky told him.

He took us to a dirt road near the San Mateo Bridge. A large sign said No Trespassing. He drove past the sign, stopped the car and revved the engine, then floored it. We were off, flying over bumps and spilling our beer.

"Man, this thing's got more power than you'd think," said one of the boys.

We were about halfway between the No Trespassing sign and Highway 92 when Lucky said, "Don't look back." The rest of us turned around to see a police car, red light flashing, coming past the No Trespassing sign. Lucky kept his foot firmly on the gas pedal, turned right when we reached Highway 92, and made another quick right into a restaurant parking lot. We laughed as the police car whizzed by, light still flashing and siren screeching, on its way to the bridge.

Lucky said, "I've been on that road a hundred times and never seen a cop around."

When we pulled out of the lot, no cops were in sight. But instead of going back to John's house, we circled back to the road with the No Trespassing sign. Lucky drove past the sign and floored it, just as he'd done earlier.

Halfway down the road, John said, "This is just where we were when we saw that cop coming after us."

"Shit! He's after us again," Lucky yelled, looking in the rearview mirror, "and this time he's closer!"

Again we turned right onto 92, then right into the restaurant parking lot, and watched the police car fly past us toward the San Mateo Bridge. About a minute later another police car followed at full speed.

"Dumb fuzz," Lucky snickered.

"This shows why bank robbers get away," I said.

"Yeah," Lucky agreed, "the dumb fuzz are all busy chasing kids."

"And they can't even catch *us*," John added.

"Do you think they got our license number?" I asked.

"It doesn't matter. Your parents are going to report it anyhow," said Lucky.

"Maybe we should steal some license plates," I suggested.

"That's not a bad idea," said one of the boys. "The broad's got brains."

The boys decided to wait until after dark to steal the license plates and siphon the gasoline, so we went back to John's house to drink more beer.

When Lucky and I finally pulled onto Highway 17 to begin our journey to L.A., the moon was shining softly through a veil of clouds. The only clothes we had were the ones we were wearing: jeans, a plaid shirt, and sweatshirt for Lucky; a white blouse, sweater, and Bermudas for me. We had a can of tuna, two apples, a half loaf of bread, a quart of milk, and some cookies, as well as a blanket, from John's house. I counted our cash and found that we had three dollars between us, but this didn't worry me, because I'd done some financial planning for the trip: in my purse was my Bank of America savings account passbook, which would give us access to my life's savings, about seventy-five dollars.

We sped down the dark highway, leaving the lights of Hayward and San Leandro farther and farther behind. As we passed the farms between Hayward and San Jose, the car filled with the stench of fertilizer, and I checked to make sure all the windows were tightly closed. They were, but the car stunk anyhow. From San Jose, we took 101 through the Santa Clara Valley, past cherry orchards, garlic farms, and the oak-dotted foothills of the Santa Cruz Mountains. In the low, flat farm areas, stands of eucalyptus had been planted as windbreaks. Before long we could pick up only static on the radio, but I kept thinking I heard music: Elvis Presley, Jimmy Clanton, Dick and Dee Dee. I searched for a station, struggling to tune in the ghostly music playing far off in my head. The static grew louder; the static grew softer. The radio crackled and hummed, but I knew it was trying to make music for me.

"It's trying," I said.

"It's very trying," Lucky retorted. "Turn that damn thing off!"

I turned the radio off. I didn't want to argue now, when I was on the verge of a new life. I envisioned both of us finding jobs in Los Angeles. After we started working, I'd get pregnant. Then we'd get married. A thrill ran through my body as I thought about it.

Ravenous, I took out the food and discovered we didn't have a can opener for the tuna. Well, so what. We'd had tuna sandwiches earlier at John's house. By midnight we'd consumed everything else from John's house except the blanket.

In Salinas we left 101 to head for the coast, having decided to take Highway 1 for the rest of our journey. I'd always loved that highway winding above the Pacific. When we reached the ocean, there were no other cars to be seen, but Lucky drove carefully for a change. The road was narrow, the cliffs steep. Opening the window to hear the surf pounding the black rocks below us, I felt fortunate to be a Californian. I would hate to live far from the sea.

Sometime in the middle of the night, we pulled into a town that consisted of a gas station, a gift shop, a restaurant, and a few houses. Lucky said, "We're almost out of gas. I think we should stay here until the station opens in the morning."

"I feel like sleeping, anyhow," I said.

We turned around and drove a couple of miles back up the highway to a turnout overlooking the ocean. "Do you want the front seat or the back?" Lucky asked.

"I'll take the front."

He kissed me gently, barely touching his lips to mine. Then he kissed my forehead and went to the backseat, and we both fell asleep well before the car grew cold.

When I woke, the sky was uniformly gray. The sea too was gray, but with a slight metallic sheen and whitecaps to break the monotony. Shivering, I reached to the backseat to take John's blanket from under Lucky's feet. This woke him, and he climbed into the front seat and started the car as I wrapped myself in the blanket.

The Oldsmobile had hubcaps with spokes that flashed when the wheels were turning. My father had told me that these spinner hubcaps were very expensive. "Let's try to sell the hubcaps to the attendant," I said as the Oldsmobile came to a stop at the pump block of the dusty two-pump station. "My dad says he paid a lot for them."

"I'll talk to him," said Lucky.

"Okay, try to get at least twenty-five dollars. I think they're worth more than a hundred."

Lucky was smiling when he came out of the little office. I thought he'd gotten over twenty-five dollars.

"Well, how much did you get?"

"A tank of gas."

This was the first time I'd ever been really mad at a man, but I didn't want to start a fight. "Next time let me do the bargaining," I said.

Our next stop was a café in Santa Maria, where we sat in a purple-and-orange vinyl booth and consumed pancakes, sausages, scrambled eggs, orange juice, and coffee. I felt good after eating, as though we would soon find jobs and a nice place to live, as though nothing bad could ever happen to a girl with a full stomach.

We reached Santa Barbara before noon. Palm trees swayed in the wind, white sand stretched in a crescent along the sea, and purple hills overlooked Spanish-style buildings with red tile roofs. I thought it was the most beautiful city I'd ever seen.

It was time to go to the bank. I was worried that my parents might have thought of my bankbook and told the police, who would have alerted the bank officials, who would now report me when I tried to withdraw money. But we were broke. I had to take my chances.

And I had another idea: we could sell my wristwatch, which was gold with a small diamond on either side of the face. Lucky thought this was a great idea. We knew that a pawnshop would be the place to go. With the hubcap experience fresh in my mind, I wanted to go in myself, but Lucky insisted that girls never went into pawnshops, that the proprietor would know I was a runaway and call the police. So he went to a pawnshop while I went to Bank of America.

My heart was galloping, my palms clammy, as I handed the withdrawal slip to the teller. She looked at me skeptically. "Why are you withdrawing so much money?"

"I'm on my way to Disneyland with my dad. He works for Bank of America. I saved the money just for this trip."

With my seventy-five dollars in my purse, I returned to the car and sat on the hood to wait for Lucky, who had the key.

"Well, I see you didn't get arrested," he yelled from half a block away.

When he got closer, I said, "You'd better be careful what you say, or we *will* get arrested." Then, eagerly, "How much did you get?"

"Twenty dollars."

"Twenty dollars! That was real gold and real diamonds!"

"When you pawn things, you never get what they're worth."

"You just don't know the value of things. How do you think we're going to live until we find jobs?"

"I told you my sister would help us. You think you're pretty goddamn smart, but you don't know everything," he snapped.

"I know that people will take advantage of you if they can." I paused to scrutinize the man I wanted to marry before screaming, "And you seem dumb enough to let them do it!"

So this was what adulthood was like: anger, frustration, uncertainty, fighting about money. We didn't speak again until we reached Los Angeles, where the sky, pearlescent gray with smog, reminded me of the sea that morning. In bumper-to-bumper traffic, we inched our way toward Newport Beach, where Lucky's sister, Gayle, lived with their mother.

"School'll be out when we get there," he said.

"Are you still mad at me?" I asked.

"I can't stay mad at you—you know I love you," he said, reaching out to pull me closer to him on the wide front seat.

"I'm sorry about what I said. I love you too."

Late in the afternoon we reached Newport Beach, where everyone wore sunglasses and shorts and had very tan legs. Lucky, who knew his way around because he'd lived there, suddenly swerved into a parking place. "I see Gayle!" he said, pointing to a girl with a dark ponytail in a grocery store parking lot. "Wait here."

He was out of the car and running toward her before I had a chance to ask why I should wait in the car instead of going with him. Then, almost as quickly, he was running back toward the car.

"My mother's in the store," he said. "We have to get out of here!"

"What did Gayle say?"

"She said we should go home."

"Can't she help us?"

"She'll be in a lot of trouble if she gets caught, but she's going to try. She's going to meet us tomorrow."

We checked into a motel that night, and it felt really luxurious to be in bed with Lucky. I tried to remember another time when I'd been completely comfortable making out, but all I could come up with was images of conduits, toolsheds, cars, and my cousin Jan's playhouse. So this was what it was like for grown-ups. Well, they certainly had it good. We kissed and caressed for a long time. I was wearing my bra and underpants; Lucky was wearing his shorts.

"I don't want to hurt you," he said. "I feel responsible."

"You're not hurting me."

"I could hurt you, but I'm not going to."

We slept through the hours when the other guests were packing up and driving off. When I finally forced myself out of my dreams of marriage and babies, the Oldsmobile was the only car left in the parking lot.

I went to the beach while Lucky met Gayle. It was a muggy, overcast day. Lying on John's blanket, I quickly fell asleep, despite the many hours of sleep I'd had the night before. A couple of hours later, when Lucky came to wake me, the whole left side of my body was bright red.

"I didn't know you could get sunburned when the sun isn't out," I said.

"There are a lot of things you don't know."

We went to a shopping mall, where I bought a tight blue cotton skirt, a plaid blouse, and iridescent blue flats to wear when I started looking for a job on Monday. It still wasn't clear whether Gayle would be able to help us. I hoped she'd find someone for us to stay with until we got our first paychecks.

That night Lucky and I went to Balboa Island. After having hamburgers and milkshakes for dinner, we saw *Never on Sunday*, which wasn't romantic enough for my taste. The next day, Sunday, we went to the Pike at Long Beach to ride the octopus and Cyclone Racer and chat with the man who was turning to stone. When we got back, Gayle gave us the bad news: she had no money to give us, and she couldn't find a place for us to stay.

Lucky said, "We're going home."

I protested. Having tasted freedom, I didn't want to give it up so quickly, although I realized that going home was the sensible thing to do.

We took the valley route because it was shorter than the coast route and we wanted to conserve gas. When we got to Bakersfield, I said, "I'm starving. Let's get something to eat."

"You'll have to steal it," Lucky said as he pulled into a supermarket parking lot.

We entered the store separately. I went to the fruit and vegetable section and put two red apples into a brown paper bag. Then I put a piece of cheddar cheese and a package of cookies into the bag and walked out of the store.

"What did you get?" I asked as Lucky started the motor.

He held up a package of hot dogs. He was smiling, pleased with himself.

"That's disgusting. Couldn't you have gotten anything better than that? We'll have to eat them cold."

"Beggars can't be choosers," he said.

By now I was eager to get home, not so much because I was homesick (although I was beginning to miss my father), but because I was sick of Lucky.

He drove fast through the Central Valley, past farms and oil fields. The land was flat and monotonous. When the windows were rolled up, the heat was stifling, even though it wasn't even summer yet; when they were down, the stench of oil and manure was nauseating. I was glad I lived near the coast. I didn't think I could ever get used to the heat and smell of the valley.

After sleeping in the car again, we got back to Oakland on Monday morning and surprised my father at Bank of America. He hugged me, then shook Lucky's hand, saying, "How good to see you." We were grubby and disheveled; I wondered if my dad's coworkers knew we had run away. Instead of calling my mother, he suggested that we surprise her too.

"Evelyn! Evelyn!" he hollered as we entered the house. "Some important people are here to see you."

"You should've called first," she yelled, sounding annoyed, from the dining room.

Lucky and I walked into the living room so that my mother, standing just beyond the dining room table, could see us. Suddenly she looked very happy.

"Dick, you shouldn't trick me like that," she said. "Where did you find them?"

"I didn't find them. They picked me up at the office."

She turned to me. "Where have you been?"

"Los Angeles."

"Why did you go there?"

"I needed a little vacation."

"This is no time to joke," she said. "Well, I'd better call the police to let them know you're back."

After making the call, she started screaming. "You're going to jail! The police are coming to take you to jail! You'll get what you deserve! You're a disgrace to the name of Lang! I hope you rot there!"

"Evelyn, Evelyn, calm down," my father pleaded, but she continued to yell until Officer Vasey, the Piedmont juvenile officer, and another cop arrived.

"I have to take you to Juvenile Hall," Vasey told Lucky and me.

"Why?" I asked.

"You've broken the law. You ran away, and a police report was made."

"But we came back."

"And you stole a car."

"But we brought it back."

"And you stole license plates."

"We'll give those back too."

"I still have to take you to Juvenile Hall."

My parents were standing side by side. My father was as tall and fair as my mother was small and dark. She barely reached his shoulder, even in heels. They'd always looked like such an odd couple! Now they both looked worried and tired. My mother had stopped yelling. I kissed them good-bye. Then the two cops handcuffed Lucky and me and led us to their car.

Juvie was a big ugly green building on a hill above 150th Avenue in San Leandro. A heavyset woman at the front desk of the girls' division pointed to a large book and told Officer Vasey to enter my name and the charge against me. He wrote, "Grand theft, petty theft, and runaway." The woman looked at it and said, "Juveniles are booked on only one charge. Which is the most important?"

"Runaway."

"Then cross the other things out."

I wondered if Officer Vasey had ever taken anyone to juvie before as the woman opened a cabinet in front of the desk and took out a frayed and faded blue cotton blouse and a similarly frayed and faded cotton skirt printed with little blue flowers. The skirt looked too big, the blouse too small. The woman said she had no other sizes. Then she asked for my purse, saying that I could keep one lipstick and one eyebrow pencil.

Another woman came to escort me to a bathroom. She gave me a comb, toothbrush, bar of soap, and bottle of shampoo and ordered me to strip. I felt degraded, but not at all nervous or worried. Satisfied that I wasn't smuggling any drugs or weapons into juvie (although she didn't say so, I supposed this was what she was looking for), she told me to shower and wash my hair. The water was lukewarm, and the shampoo smelled like rotten eggs. It was one of the fastest showers I'd ever taken. But I needn't have rushed. In my baggy skirt and tight blouse, with dripping wet hair and carrying my lipstick and eyebrow pencil, I was put into solitary confinement.

Top: Lucy and Lucky, July 1961
Bottom: Lucy and Dick on Lucy's fourteenth birthday, December 5, 1961

chapter 2

Boy Crazy

My cell at juvie was midway down a long corridor with tiled walls.
Just to the right of the doorway there was a small washbasin beside
a toilet with no lid. At least it had a seat! At the end of the room, on
the left side, a small table and plain wooden chair stood in front of a
barred window that looked out on a grassy hillside behind the building.
To the right of the window was a hard, narrow bed with a single gray
blanket, a flat pillow, and yellowed sheets. The room stunk of Lysol;
periodically I heard heavy doors banging shut.

I asked the warden for a pencil and paper. "They're forbidden."
I asked for something to read. "This isn't a library." I asked why I'd
been allowed to a keep a lipstick and eyebrow pencil, since there was
no mirror in the room. "This isn't a beauty parlor." Nevertheless, she
brought me a hand mirror and said not to tell anyone, because it was
against the rules. I would rather have had a book or a pencil and paper.

Lying on the bed, alternately looking at myself in the mirror and
counting the cracks in the ceiling, I heard girls screaming and crying
in nearby cells. Bored but not frightened, I was determined not to go
berserk. I had expected going to juvie would be an adventure, just as
running away had been. It had never occurred to me that juvie might
be boring. I thought about Lucky, who was somewhere in the boys' section of the building, and wondered if he was thinking about me. When
we ran away, I was surprised that he got on my nerves. Was it always
this way with a man you loved, or was he not the right one? I felt older
than my thirteen years.

I sensed there was something just beyond my consciousness that I needed to know about my life. If only I had a pencil and paper, I'd write down everything I could remember, especially the things I hadn't dared to put in my sixth grade autobiography, and maybe that would help me figure it out. I traced my memories, searching for the missing piece.

I remembered how, when I was a toddler, sometimes my mother would lie on the floor and cry. I'd kiss her and tell her everything was okay, but she just kept crying and crying. This worried me. When we went to see Aunt Ethel and Uncle Dick, my mother would yell at my father to drive faster: she said someone was chasing us. She even wanted him to go through red lights. I'd look back, but I could never figure out which car was chasing us.

One night I was awakened by my mother's crying. By now I knew how to climb out of my crib, so I got up and went to her. Sitting on the stairs, weeping, she told me she'd read in the newspaper that Auntie Ethel was dead. Daddy said it was just a bad dream and I should go back to bed.

Not long after that my mother went to the hospital. She'd had a nervous breakdown. I was two years old; she was thirty-eight. After the nervous breakdown I felt like I couldn't trust her to take care of me or even herself, and I always feared that she might have another one.

Someone slid my dinner through a slot at the bottom of the door: cold mashed potatoes, a cold, rubbery fried chicken leg, and some grayish-green canned peas. This was even worse than my mother's bland casseroles, but better than starvation, so I ate.

I thought about my parents' gambling: poker, bingo, horse races, Reno. My dad, who'd introduced my mom to gambling, took greater risks than she did, and she'd recently shown me the little black leather book in which he kept track of his daily winnings and losses at Golden Gate Fields and the card clubs, because she was concerned about the losses. I wished my parents would take up dancing or gardening—anything else! Why couldn't they be athletic or musical?

Gambling seemed like a horrible way to spend their time, especially since my mom was so worried about losing money.

My bed in juvie was hard. I would have liked another blanket and a better pillow. I folded the blanket in half lengthwise to make two layers and stuffed my skirt into the pillowcase. Thinking about the time my mother came back from Reno wearing a mink coat, I fell asleep.

The next day I alternated calisthenics with thinking about my childhood. There was nothing else to do except at mealtimes, when a tray of awful food was delivered to my room. When I finished eating, I'd shove the tray back through the slot at the bottom of the door.

My mother had only that one nervous breakdown, but she remained anxious and discontented, and she expressed it by yelling and nagging. "You're nothing but a bookworm," she'd say when I was reading. If I didn't answer, her pitch would rise: "You're ruining your eyes. Children need to play outside!" If the shades were up when I came home from school, she'd scream, "Pull those shades down! Any burglar on the street can look in at us." If the shades were down, she'd scream, "Put those shades up! It looks like a funeral parlor in here." I couldn't make any sense of it.

Yet she tried to please my dad, me, and others. She fixed Thanksgiving dinner every year for twelve to fourteen people and never even asked for help with the dishes. She never asked my dad or me for help with the day-to-day dishes or laundry either. And she was generous to a fault: throughout my childhood she'd loved to buy not only me, but also my friends, toys and clothes whenever we went shopping downtown.

I thought a lot about my mom at juvie, but I couldn't understand her unhappiness. Not until I was an adult would everything finally become clear: she'd lost her mother when she was seven and seen her father for the last time when she was twelve, and my father had gambled away her inheritance from her grandparents. My birth certificate gives his occupation as self-employed bookkeeper. I don't know if he ever actually kept any books. What I do know is that my mother inherited five houses and money from her grandparents, that she gave one house to her sister and sold three, and that when the money was gone and the house we lived in was heavily mortgaged, my dad finally got a real job, as a teller at the Bank of America. They'd been married for twelve years, and I was four years old.

Often one girl or another was crying or screaming in a nearby cell. Between dinner and bedtime it got particularly bad, with several girls screaming at once. The place sounded like a torture chamber, and in a moment of panic, I wondered if the girls really were being tortured. No, I assured myself, they were just going crazy because they wanted out of there.

On my third day at juvie, I was still in solitary confinement, and no pencil or paper had appeared. I was tired of cold oatmeal, cold mashed potatoes, and cold, dry meatloaf and hamburger patties. I'd have given anything for another rubbery chicken leg like the one I had the first day.

I hadn't figured out what I needed to know about my life, but I'd convinced myself that adults were no wiser than I was. The adults said it was wrong to steal. *Is it really wrong?* I asked myself. I decided it was wrong to steal from individuals but okay to steal from stores, because the store owners had more money than other people. The adults also said that sex outside of marriage was wrong. This, I decided, was ridiculous. Every animal on Earth does it. What could be more natural? I wished Lucky and I had made love when we ran away. Everyone was going to think we did, so I was going to get all of the notoriety and none of the pleasure. I wanted to have sex as soon as possible. Sex and marriage, in that order, would be my ticket to freedom. It was absurd, of course, but I could not escape my flawed logic.

My thoughts turned to my father's mother, Grandma Ada, whom I'd adored. She had a guitar and an orange cat named Oscar. Although she always wore pajamas and a robe, her closet was filled with long dresses, some beaded, others with puffy sleeves. As a toddler, I thought the dresses were beautiful and hoped I could wear them someday, but what I liked best about visiting Grandma was that she never scolded me. She'd just coo, tell me the names of things, cut out paper dolls, and bounce me on her knee. The last time I saw her, I was four. She asked me to pull a blanket over her and said, "I'm so lucky to have a sweet little granddaughter like you." A few days later my father told me she'd gone to heaven, and not long after that Grandpa Bill moved in with us.

Grandpa Bill died when I was ten, and I wore a yellow dress to the funeral. My mother urged me to go look at my grandfather, but I wanted to remember him sitting in his favorite spot, where he'd worn the upholstery thin on the red sofa in the living room, or reaching into his pockets for nickels and dimes to buy my artwork. "Why doesn't Lucille want to look at her grandfather?" Aunt Ethel asked Aunt Liz. "Maybe she's afraid," Aunt Liz said, "or maybe she's just too young to know what's going on." I thought, *They have no idea what I'm thinking and feeling.* It made me feel frightened and alone.

Now, at juvie, I was really and truly alone. By the morning of the fourth day, I was starting to wonder if they were ever going to let me out. I could understand what the girls in the other cells were screaming about, but I was determined to keep calm. I kept telling myself, *They can't keep me here much longer. I haven't committed a terrible crime.*

That day my lunch tray didn't arrive. Instead, an enormous lady warden (was there a size requirement for working there?) escorted me to a dining hall, where I ate my cold, dry hamburger patty and instant mashed potatoes with the other girls, all of whom were wearing ill-fitting cotton skirts and blouses. After lunch the warden took me to a communal bathroom and told me to put my lipstick and eyebrow pencil into a big rusty red box with everyone else's. I was surprised, because it was so unsanitary. Then she led me to an art class, where I started drawing a potted plant. Before I'd finished, she came back and said I was going to be released into my parents' custody to await my hearing.

•••

I had no concept of myself as a troubled teenager. I felt that I was normal and the rest of the world was screwed up, especially my aunts and uncles, my parents, and their friends, who included contractors, a carpenter, a barber, a car salesman, salesladies, housewives, and retired petty officers who'd served with my Uncle Dick in the Navy. All they liked to do when they got together was play bingo or poker and complain about taxes. This was not how I wanted to spend my time when I grew up. Worse, my Uncle Bob and Clyde, one of the petty officers, always raged about how the Democrats were ruining the country and the "niggers" and welfare mothers were bilking the system. I hated these racist and antipoor tirades. Although my mom and dad weren't the pontificators, they didn't raise objections either. It made me aspire to be a Democrat and a welfare mom. I wanted to be as different as possible from my family and my parents' friends, although I was fond of Pete, a retired machinist who came from Denmark, and Eddie, a lawyer with one hand crippled by childhood polio, both of whom seemed more open-minded than the others and sometimes offered a compassionate word for black people.

I never hesitated to express my own dissent, and my aunts and uncles would have liked to muzzle me. Aunt Liz and Uncle Bob didn't have any children and were strict adherents of the "should be seen and not heard" theory of child rearing, and I always infuriated Aunt Ethel and Uncle Dick by telling them they shouldn't force Jan to clean her plate, on which Uncle Dick heaped adult-sized portions. She weighed 150 pounds when she was eight years old and had to get her clothes at Lane Bryant, a store in San Francisco for oversized people.

Unfortunately, I couldn't tell the difference between my commendable insights, such as the injustice of racism and enforced obesity, and my naïve ideas, such as the ethicality of shoplifting and the desirability of teen sex and marriage. Maybe what I needed to figure out about my life was that I wasn't always right.

Part of the problem was that I wouldn't take my mother's word on anything because I felt that of the two of us, I was the more mature. My evidence included the fact that my mom and Aunt Ethel always took sides in my arguments with my cousin Jan, making our disputes their own.

On one occasion, when Jan was five and I was eight, we were eating at a card table in the living room. "My rose is bigger than yours," said Jan, pointing to the pink rose on her slice of chocolate cake.

I called my mother and pointed at Jan's cake. "Jan's rose is bigger than mine."

My mother took Jan's plate and exchanged it with mine, saying, "That's your piece." When Jan started to scream, Aunt Ethel jumped up from the dining room table and yelled at my mother that it was her fault I was a spoiled brat. Then she rushed to the living room and took the plate to give it back to Jan. As my mother tried to grab it from her, the card table went over. I wasn't sure if it was my mother or my aunt who pushed it, but I thought it was my mother. Jan and I stared at each other for a moment, then went to comfort our mothers, who'd started to cry.

I couldn't imagine anything like this happening in the homes of my friends. The next day I asked my mother, "Who pushed over the card table, you or Aunt Ethel?"

"I don't know what you're talking about."

"Yesterday, when Jan and I were fighting about the cake, one of you knocked over the card table."

"That never happened! You're a liar!" she screamed, drawing back her hand and striking me on the shoulder.

I knew she loved me. I loved her too, but I also hated her, especially when she lied, yelled, or hit me. I knew that many kids had it much worse than I did, that some were starving in India and Africa (I was frequently reminded of this), and others were beaten by their parents or locked in closets right here in the United States. No one beat or molested me (my mother often hit me, but not hard enough to cause physical injury), and we always had enough to eat. The problems in our house were no greater than those in many homes. Still, I couldn't forgive my mother for her yelling, spankings, and lies. I was unhappy and thought the love of a teenage boy and a baby of my own would solve everything.

•••

Soon after getting out of juvie, I heard about a party. To look pretty, I wore a rose-colored pleated skirt and a white angora sweater printed with pink roses. Perhaps I would meet a boy there who'd like to have a baby with me (also a wedding, of course). I was no longer sure that Lucky, whom I hadn't seen since getting out of juvie because he was on restriction again, was my true love. The party was at the Craigs' house, a couple of doors away from Eileen's, so I told my parents that I was going to see Eileen. Her mother, who was on to us, said Eileen couldn't go.

The house was already hopping with teenagers when I arrived. I sat on the sofa in the darkened living room and lit a cigarette. A gangly boy handed me a beer. Feeling ill at ease, I tapped my foot in time to "Alley Oop," hummed along with "I Love How You Love Me," and looked at the boys. Most of them wore pointed shoes and had long greasy hair slicked back on the sides and tumbling down their foreheads in "waterfalls." Perhaps because this kind of boy would evoke disapproval in adults, this was just the kind of boy I liked best.

A boy in a black shirt and white jeans asked me to dance. His face was very long, like a horse's. It was a fast dance, and he was a good dancer. Thinking people were watching us, I felt awkward. The alcohol hadn't hit me yet, but I started pretending I was high. This gave me an excuse: if I wasn't a good dancer, it was because I was drunk. Smiling at my partner, I exaggerated my movements.

More boys asked me to dance, which made me feel special. Between dances I kept drinking beer, and before long I was stumbling and slurring my speech—no need to pretend. Galen Craig, who was throwing the party with his sisters, Carrie and Diane, took me outside and told me I was drinking too much. He said I'd get sick, people would take advantage of me, I'd get in trouble with my parents, and I might end up back in juvie. I listened, then went back inside and continued to drink.

Someone put "Deserie" on the record player, and a pimply boy in grimy jeans asked me to dance. As soon as he put his arm around my waist, something didn't feel right. He was holding me too close. He started grinding his crotch against mine and trying to feel my right breast. I kept pushing his hand away. It felt more like arm wrestling than dancing. I thought sex was okay, and I wanted it as badly as he did—just not with him, and certainly not in a crowded room during our first dance!

As I resisted, he became rougher and more insistent. Before the song ended, I pushed him away and rushed to the kitchen. A handsome boy (the kind Eileen and I called boss, tough, or fine) I recognized from school grabbed me and started kissing me, then lifted my skirt and tried to put his hand into my pants. When I pulled away, another boy grabbed me and kissed me harshly. His breath was ninety proof and smoky. I was frightened, but a lanky boy put his arm around me, saying, "Leave her alone," and led me out of the room.

He took me to a bedroom upstairs and locked the door. We lay on a bunk bed and he said I was very beautiful and that a beautiful girl shouldn't drink so much, because guys figure she doesn't know what she's doing. I thought he was very beautiful too, with his black hair and green eyes. He said he was seventeen and went to Oakland Technical High School. We talked for a long time. Then he kissed me and said I could trust him.

Suddenly the music stopped downstairs, and a woman screamed, "Get out of here! Right now or I'll call the police!" The mother of the house had come home. Tom Ogden and I stayed in the bedroom, hoping to sneak out later, but she came upstairs and banged on the door. We opened it, and she screamed, "Whore!" as I fled past her, into the night.

Thoughts of seeing Tom again and making love with him sustained me. I told my friends I thought I was falling in love, and maybe I should break up with Lucky. They said to forget it. Tom was in love with a girl named Cindy, who'd broken up with him. He'd never been interested in anyone except Cindy, who was so gorgeous she made Brigitte Bardot look ordinary. I took their advice and started meeting Lucky at the skating rink again as soon as his father and stepmother allowed him to go.

•••

My grades at the end of seventh grade were not great, but I got an A in art. Returning my portfolio, my teacher said, "You have real talent. This is one of the best portfolios I've ever seen."

"You can keep it to show the students next year."

"Don't you want to give it to your mother?" She lifted her hand to her face to brush back a few stray hairs.

"No. She'd just throw it away." My mother had thrown away everything I did in elementary school except my sixth grade autobiography. She would have thrown that away too if Mrs. O'Gara hadn't written on it, "I know your mother will cherish this forever."

"Then why don't you keep it yourself?"

"I've tried that before. My mother would just find it and throw it away when I wasn't home." Although my father praised every sketch and scribble I produced as though it were a Picasso, I didn't ever want to take my creative work home again.

•••

Eileen and I shoplifted at grocery stores, taking whatever our mothers had asked us to buy and pocketing the money. Once, as we left the Safeway on Grand Avenue, the manager—a round-faced man with a shining pate and handlebar mustache—grabbed Eileen's sack of mayonnaise, cat food, and bread, saying, "Tuna would make a better sandwich." He sent us on our way, warning that next time he'd call the police.

Undeterred, we started taking cosmetics from Guy's Drugs. We quickly graduated to shoplifting clothing from Capwell's and Kahn's, the two big department stores in downtown Oakland. In the dressing rooms we stuffed clothes into our gargantuan purses or put them on underneath our school uniforms. Eileen told her mother that her new clothes were old things of mine, and I told my mother that my new clothes were old things of Eileen's. They believed this at first, although I was tall and lean, whereas Eileen was short and fighting a tendency to be apple-shaped like my mother. We often went on shoplifting sprees after school, stopping first at Guy's, then proceeding to the department stores. Both of us had a special passion for angora sweaters. I was doing it for the thrill. My mother would have bought me whatever I wanted.

We also stole books from the Piedmont High School library and books that students left on the steps during rallies and at lunchtime. I hid the big ones with color illustrations under my bed. My father found these and returned them, but he missed others in my closet and on my bookshelf.

Jan, almost eleven, was intrigued by my tales of shoplifting and said, "I want to do it too."

At Capwell's, while she talked to a salesgirl, I slipped a bracelet and a pair of slippers into my purse. At Payless, while I distracted the clerks, she slipped a bottle of red nail polish into her pocket. As we walked out of the store, a penguin-shaped lady security guard stopped us.

I waited outside the room where Jan was questioned. When the door opened, a stern-looking man with sunken cheeks ordered me to come in and open my purse. I argued that I hadn't done anything, but he said Jan had said I'd stolen things at Capwell's. What's more, my plump little cousin had said I made her take the nail polish.

On probation for a year for running away, every week I went to the juvenile hall at the corner of Eighth and Poplar in West Oakland, where the other delinquents and I sat in a line of hard chairs in a dingy corridor, waiting to enter the offices where we'd see our probation officers and tell them we were being good. After the shoplifting incident my probation officer, a plain, thirtyish woman with sandy hair pulled back from her face, told me that a teenager who broke probation twice had to go back to court to be sentenced to the California Youth Authority. Shoplifting, she explained, was my second violation. The first was getting drunk (my mother had told her about my coming home drunk from the party). "However, I won't be handling your case anymore," she added. "Your new probation officer is expecting a baby soon, so you won't hear from her for a few weeks. When she does contact you, it will be to give you a court date."

The California Youth Authority was the prison system for minors, but I wasn't frightened. I didn't believe I'd be sent there and locked up with teenage murderers, prostitutes, and drug dealers. The idea of going to prison for running away, shoplifting, and drinking beer seemed preposterous. I said, "The police didn't arrest me the night I was supposedly drunk. All you have is my mother's word. She could have been wrong."

"It's already part of your record."

"It's hearsay."

"You can tell that to the judge."

•••

When school started in the fall, I still hadn't heard from my new probation officer. I told my mother I hoped they'd lost my record and forgotten about me.

That fall I had more dates than a date tree. My boyfriends included Ronnie from San Leandro, whom I'd met roller-skating; Mike, who went to Bret Harte Junior High with Lucky's friend Steve, who was now my friend too; Bob, whom I'd met at a church dance and who went to Oakland Tech; and Ken, who was half Mohawk and also went to Oakland Tech. I'd met Ken in the spring when my friends Sandy and Joan and I followed him and his friend Tony to the Rose Garden one afternoon after we spotted them smoking outside Guy's Drugs on Grand Avenue.

Lucky had broken up with me in July because I kissed another boy at a party. I don't know why I did it. Maybe unconsciously I wanted to sabotage our romance because I was unsure of my feelings about him, maybe I wanted to test his feelings for me, maybe I thought the boy I kissed was the prince who would wake me into my real life, or maybe I wanted to be a junior femme fatale. All I can say for sure is that I was thirteen years old and feeling my hormones. I was obsessed with boys, but I didn't like their preoccupation with sex and virginity.

They were either trying to get into your pants or having a fit for fear that someone else would. I was preoccupied with sex and virginity too, but I didn't accept the nice girl/bad girl dichotomy, and I thought sex should be beautiful. The boys weren't on my wavelength.

My mother worried about what I was doing when I was out with the boys, and my father tried to lure me away from them by suggesting our own movie dates and weekend excursions to museums, Playland at the Beach, and the Santa Cruz Boardwalk. I remember one Saturday morning in particular, when he said, "Let's go to San Francisco today! We could go to the California Academy of Sciences and see the planetarium show." I hesitated, although I'd always loved the Academy and the planetarium. I'd been entranced by the dioramas of tundra and savannah, the alligators at Steinhart Aquarium, the planetarium's shimmering dome of stars, and the Foucault pendulum, knocking over its little pegs as the Earth turned. My dad and I had gone on frequent weekend outings throughout my childhood, and these were the source of some of my happiest memories, but now all the pegs were down, and my world had turned away from my father. When I didn't answer, he said, "We could ride the cable cars afterward and have dinner in Chinatown. Call Eileen. She might like to come too." I shook my head and said, "I can't. I promised Ronnie I'd meet him at the skating rink." My dad looked crushed. He wanted to be the beau he'd been during my childhood, but now nothing he offered could compete with the opportunity to hold hands with Ronnie during "couples only." I felt guilty, but I didn't relent.

My mother, too, tried to engage me in the activities we'd shared during my childhood, such as baking cookies, brownies, and cakes. Now, though, it seemed that any sweets I found time to bake with her got served to the boys who came to my house after school. When I was younger, Mom and I had also enjoyed having lunch downtown and shopping together afterward, but now these trips produced only frustration and disappointment for her, because for me the great draw of lunch at Capwell's or Kahn's had become the chance to flirt with the busboys, and I wasn't interested in shopping for anything except outfits to wear on my dates.

Why didn't my parents just put their foot down? I think they wanted me to be happy and didn't yet see where all of this was headed. Their worst fear was that the boys might try to pressure me into having sex. They had no idea that I wanted sex too and was hoping any day to meet my true love and give myself to him.

My mother was wrapped up in her own regrets. She wanted to travel, and she wanted a higher standard of living. My father not only lost all her money, but he was afraid of boats, trains, and planes, and they never got any farther than he was willing and able to drive. They made it as far as Vancouver to the north, Los Angeles to the south, and Reno to the east. What she had in mind was Europe, Hawaii, and Mexico.

My dad was a metabolic optimist who exuded childlike excitement over many things, including poker, fireworks, Santa Claus, merry-go-rounds, and the Peter Pan ride at Disneyland. Although he loved my mom and me, he didn't seem to notice that she was seriously unhappy (he didn't even appear to hear her when she yelled and complained) or that I was charging down a dangerous avenue. He thought we were a happy family. So what if I was overdoing it a bit with the boys?

•••

My house was an after-school hangout for boys from Oakland Tech and my crowd at Piedmont. Most days five or six boys came over, but one afternoon I counted eleven. Some of them went upstairs to play records, while the rest stayed downstairs to play cards. I set up two card tables—one for poker, the other for knuckles, a game in which the loser got his knuckles smashed with the deck of cards.

Bill Arthur was at the knuckles table. I'd met him at a party a couple of weeks earlier. Nineteen and out of school, he worked as a bicycle delivery boy for a blueprint company. He had acne and a longish nose, and his ears were a little too big. Nevertheless, I had a crush on him. Maybe it was because he was older and seemed more mature. High school was behind him, and he was part of the adult world I wanted so badly to enter myself.

During the knuckles game, I flirted with Bill. He got the message, and when the game ended, he whispered, "Are you doing anything Friday night?"

He arrived for our date in his Model A Ford, and as we drove down Grand Avenue, I felt like a princess with her prince in his fine carriage. I sat in front with Bill. His friend Vernon, who didn't have a date, sat in back. Over hamburgers at Kwik Way, a downscale drive-in near the Grand Lake Theater, Bill said he was Italian and told me about gondolas in Venice, vineyards in Tuscany, and St. Peter's Basilica in Rome. I was really swept away—he was so much more interesting than the guys who didn't have anything to say except where they went to school and what kind of beer they liked. Later I would learn that his older brother Jack had been stationed in Italy when he was in the army, and that not only was Bill not Italian, but Reno was the closest he'd ever been to Italy.

Bill asked me out again, and soon we were getting together several times a week. As I sat in my classes, while Mrs. L'Esperance talked about nouns and verbs or Mr. Swartzell droned on about Ohm's Law, all my thoughts were focused on Bill and how romantic and marvelous it would be to get married and have a baby with him. More immediately, I wanted to have sex with him, but I couldn't simply go to bed with him. When he tried to touch my breasts, I always pushed his hand away and firmly said no. My hope was that he'd keep trying, and that in a frenzy of passion, after my vain attempts to prevent it, we'd make love and he'd understand how much I loved him. However, he always stopped as soon as I said no.

•••

At school I hung out with the crowd that gathered every morning on the porch of the Piedmont Recreation Center, a.k.a. the Rec, a Tudor-style mansion with a swimming pool and tennis courts. We were the ones who smoked, swore, cut classes, wore our hair long, and would rather go to parties than football games on Friday nights. The porch where we met had a panoramic view of the San Francisco Bay Area.

There was an open deck we used when the weather was good, and a covered area overhung with wisteria where we gathered when it rained. If any of us ever noticed either the elegance of the setting or the irony of being bad there, we didn't mention it.

I became more and more alienated from the clean-cut kids who paid attention in school while I fantasized about Bill, read *True Confessions,* passed notes, and drew pictures of tombstones bearing the names of my teachers. I often had detention—for smoking in a restroom, wearing a nonregulation blouse, whispering in class, or breaking some other rule.

One morning two boys yelled "Whore!" as I entered the school building. In elementary school the boys had stuck out their tongues, thrown dirt clods, hollered "Lou the Seal!" and made seal noises when they saw me coming. The adults said it was because they liked me and didn't know how else to express it. Eileen always said she didn't know how I could stand it. When I heard "Whore!" I couldn't stand it anymore. It wasn't the fact that I hadn't had sex yet that made me mad: I was angry because I didn't think girls who did have sex should be called whores. I drew back my fist and slugged black-haired, oily-looking Conrad in the jaw. When he fell over backward against the wall, then slid to the floor beside a row of lockers, I was as surprised as he was. I turned toward crew-cut John, who was smaller than me, and drew back my fist again, but he turned and ran down the hallway. I chased him into a classroom and pushed him across a desk. He got up and pushed me, and I fell. Before I could get up, he grabbed my arms to hold me down. While I kicked and writhed, he yelled, "I got her down! I got her down!"

Mr. Ferry came to the doorway in his gray suit. He put his hands on his hips and yelled, "Okay, break it up!" Then he told me to come to his office.

"What happened?"

"Conrad and John called me a whore."

"They don't know what it means."

"They know damn well what it means."

"You invite those comments by wearing your hair too long and your skirt too short. You're asking for it."

"Bullshit."

"Watch your mouth and don't come back here for a week. You're suspended."

Neither Conrad nor John was suspended. If they were reprimanded, no one told me about it. I considered it a great travesty of justice, although I was happy I didn't have to go to school for a week.

My ex-boyfriend Woody, now a freshman at the California College of Arts and Crafts, sometimes stopped by my house. The week I was suspended, we went every day to Music City in Berkeley to buy 45 rpm records. My mother always said, "You're not supposed to go out when you're not in school. You'll get arrested!" but she didn't try to stop me. I loved Music City because they carried all the hits from the fifties, and I stocked up on the Drifters, the Platters, and Elvis Presley.

Bill came over almost every evening after dinner. Sometimes we went upstairs to play "Save the Last Dance for Me" and "Anyway You Want Me" over and over again and make out. Other times we drove to the Oakland hills to look at the view, drink Budweiser, and make out while listening to the latest hits on the radio.

When I returned to school, my mother, the snoop, found and read my seventh grade diary, in which I'd written daily about my love for Woody. Holding the diary up when I came home, she said, "What do you write stuff like this for?" I grabbed it from her. "That's none of your business." I was so mad that I tore out all the pages, crumpled them, and threw them into the wastebasket in the corner of my room.

The next day when I came home, Woody was sitting on my bed with the wastebasket beside him. One by one, he was smoothing out the crumpled pages, reading them, and placing them in a neat stack on my umbrella-girl quilt. I could have died! Thank God I wasn't keeping a similar diary about Bill.

"What are you reading that crap for?" I looked at him hard. His complexion was still as bad as it had been when he was in high school.

"I just wanted to see what girls throw away."

I was embarrassed not just because of the content of the diary, but also because I knew it had no literary merit. When I started the diary, I'd wanted to write something profound and compelling, like Anne Frank did, but I knew that my entries weren't even in the same literary league as greeting cards.

•••

Bill had a switchblade, and I wanted it. One night when we were parked on Skyline Boulevard, drinking beer and watching the lights of San Francisco and the Golden Gate Bridge sparkle in the distance, I said, "Let me see the knife." I pressed the brass button that made the blade pop out. "Can I keep it?"

"You don't need a knife, but I do."

"Why?"

"For protection." A lot of the boys I knew carried knives, and though they all said it was for protection, I'd never seen any of them use the knives for anything except cleaning their fingernails.

"A girl needs protection too."

"You could get hurt with it. I'll protect you."

"I'll give you anything if you give me the knife."

"Anything?"

I said yes. I hoped he'd want sex. Instead, he asked me to go steady.

I carried the knife everywhere and showed it off to my friends. It made me feel like a true rebel. I had no desire to fight with it. Just carrying it in my purse made me feel like I was no one to mess with, and that was enough.

Sometimes I went to Bill's house to be there when he got home from work. His brother Jack, Jack's wife Darlene, and their two kids hung out there too, and I spent a lot of time talking to Darlene, who was eighteen. I wanted to get married at sixteen, just as she had. Since I was almost fourteen now, I only had two more years to go.

For my birthday, December 5, Bill gave me a bracelet with a heart with "Laura" engraved on it. He'd bought it at a pawnshop and thought "Laura" was close enough. My father took it to a jeweler who inscribed "Lucy" over "Laura" so that it looked only a little messy. In mid-December I took Bill's picture in front of the Christmas tree at my house. On the back of it he wrote, "To Lucy, the sweetest girl that I have ever known. Love always, Bill." I'd never been happier.

•••

On Tuesday nights Bill dropped me off and picked me up at model-ing school in downtown Oakland. My four-volume textbook set, *The Nancy Taylor Course,* was printed on pink paper and filled with line drawings of women who looked like Betty Crocker putting on lipstick and combing their hair. My parents were willing to pay for this because they thought I had the makings of a high fashion model. Many parents think their daughter is exceptionally beautiful, but mine thought they'd created Helen of Troy.

My mother hoped I'd learn a more conservative approach to makeup and hairstyles. The instructor, who was short and buxom and didn't look like a model, did recommend that I use brown eyeliner and mascara rather than black, but after trying this once, I went back to black. She said I should keep my hair long, because I had a neck like a crane, and she never said anything about the way I ratted the top into a four-inch dome and glued it into place with Aqua Net. She must have known this was nonnegotiable.

On three sides the classroom had mirrors and counters like a beauty parlor. The students sat in chairs in front of the counters. A tall, aristocratic-looking black woman was the only student who looked like a model. For the rest of the group, mostly women in their twenties and thirties, it looked like self-improvement would be a more realistic goal. As for me, I did indeed aspire to be a model someday, but in the nearer future I just wanted to make myself more beautiful for Bill.

The instructor told us to shave our arms and thighs, not just our lower legs, and to use depilatory cream to remove any hair above our upper lips or elsewhere on our faces. I shaved my arms once, but this practice then went the way of the brown mascara. My instructor's pock-marked face put me in mortal fear of depilatory cream.

I was five-seven and weighed 114 pounds. The instructor said this was my ideal weight and that my hip and thigh measurements were also perfect. I'd always been afraid of getting fat, but now I became obsessively determined not to gain weight. When Bill and I had hamburgers at Kwik Way, I would eat half of the patty and none of the bun. At home my mother always urged me to eat more, reminding me that I was still growing.

●●●

The afternoon of Christmas Eve, my parents went to a party at the home of some friends. Bill and I stayed at my house, drinking beer and listening to records. When we started making out on my bed, I pretended to be higher than I really was, and when he took my breast in his hand, I didn't try to stop him. He pushed my black sheath up around my waist and tried to enter me.

"You're tight," he said, pulling away and putting his fingers inside me.

Everything he did was mildly painful. I kept thinking about how much I wanted a baby until I realized I was bleeding. "I have to go get a towel," I said.

When I came back, I spread the towel on the bed, then lay down and pulled my dress up again. I shut my eyes and tried to concentrate on names: *Aaron, Eric, Priscilla, Adela.*

Bill pressed his lean body against mine, whispering something. I wanted it to be "I love you," but he was saying, "Are you sure it's safe?"

Afterward he held me and said he loved me. To make myself cry, I bit my lip and pretended my father had died. Crying, I thought, would reassure Bill that I was a nice girl. Then I got up, changed my dress, and asked Bill to drop me off to join my parents. We stopped on the way to throw the bloody towel into a public trash can.

I was ecstatic for a couple of weeks. All I could think about was being pregnant and getting married to Bill. Every day I woke up hoping to be sick and put a tunic on for practice. My fantasy lasted well into January, even though Bill hadn't called me since Christmas. By mid-January, when my period came, everyone knew that Bill was now going with a girl named Nancy. I feared he thought badly of me for having sex with him, but my memory of the way he held me afterward and said "I love you" told me this wasn't so. Whatever the reason, though, he'd dropped me, and the only sensible thing to do now was to forget him. I cried a lot, without any need to bite my lip or think sad thoughts. When my mother was in a good mood, she reminded me, "There are plenty of fish in the sea." When she was in a bad mood, she interrupted my blubbering by screaming, "Shut up! Stop acting crazy!"

My fantasies of sex waned. My experience with the act itself had been mediocre, more of a small ordeal than the fulfillment of my romantic dreams. I did not think doing it was all it was cracked up to be. Still, I was glad that I'd done it. I'd proved to myself that I was in control of my own body, that neither society nor my parents could tell me what to do. My disappointment in the sex act did not diminish my desire for pregnancy and marriage, though, and I hoped that my future experiences with sex would be better.

Tom Ogden was the only other boy I could imagine being with. I told my friend Donna, who, like Darlene Arthur, was already married at eighteen and had two children, and she called Tom and hinted that I liked him. He asked me out, and I felt like the luckiest girl in the world. He was not only kind and gentle, but also better looking than Elvis or Fabian (at least I thought so). My bliss lasted for about two weeks—until someone told his former girlfriend Cindy that Tom had found someone else. She called him right away and invited him over for dinner, and that was the last I saw of him. It hurt, but not as much as Bill Arthur's leaving me. Still, I played records like "The Great Pretender" and "Only the Lonely" over and over again, while I cried.

At the Rec I began flirting with Mike, a boy who'd lived in New York and told stories about kids who actually fought with their knives. I thought he was cute, with his thick wavy hair and deep-set brown eyes, but the morning he tried to kiss me, I slapped his face. He was supposed to try again, but I guess he didn't know that. He just looked startled, then walked away to talk to the other boys. I tried to catch his eye the next day and the day after, but he started going steady with my friend Cia and never flirted with me again.

I didn't have a steady boyfriend, but a lot of boys still stopped by my house after school and even more called me. My mother kept saying I was boy crazy. Some of the boys who called and came by were infatuated with me and wanted to go steady, but what I really wanted was a husband, so I had to choose carefully. Getting married was neither an original idea nor a liberated one, but it was the only idea I had for getting away from my mother and catapulting myself into adulthood. None of the boys I knew was the right one.

In February I planned a party, hoping that the man I hadn't met yet, my future husband, would show up. I asked my parents to leave the house, but they said no. The compromise was that they would stay upstairs in my bedroom. I invited all my friends from the Rec and Oakland Tech, they invited theirs, and all the hoods from miles around showed up. The Mickens siblings across the street—Karen, Pat, Mike, and Sue—set up chairs behind their living room window to watch the action outside. My mother stayed upstairs as she promised, but my father came down to meet the guests, and the guys kept congratulating me on how cool he was.

Tom Ogden came with Cindy, and she certainly was as beautiful as everyone had warned. In fringed, green-and-white striped pants and a matching blouse, she looked like a model for *Seventeen* or *Mademoiselle*. She had olive skin, long brown hair, and large almond-shaped eyes. I liked her and started trying to emulate the slow, sexy way she spoke.

As I put Little Richard on full blast and stacked beer, brought by my guests, on the dining room table by the potato chips and Coca-Cola provided by my parents, I started hoping Bill Arthur might show up too—without Nan. When the doorbell rang again, however, it was the Piedmont Police. My father answered the door.

"What's going on here?" asked the officer, who looked surprised to see an adult.

"We just have a few friends over for the evening," said my dad, stepping onto the porch. My friend Pearl, sitting on a stack of six-packs in a brown paper bag just outside the front door, kept a straight face.

"How long are they going to be here?"

"Until eleven o'clock."

When the cops left, I turned to my dad. "Eleven o'clock! That's so early! Why couldn't you have said twelve or one?"

"I think we should let the neighbors get some sleep."

At eleven o'clock the party moved two blocks away, to the Craigs' house. My parents wouldn't let me go, which was just as well, because I had a headache and stomachache. I took Bufferin and Rolaids and stood outside to say good-bye to everyone. Bill hadn't come, nor had anyone else I'd like to marry. As I waved to my guests, I wondered what to do next to find a husband.

Top: Lucy with Steve Labate, 1962
Bottom: Mark and Lucy, 1962

chapter 3

Will I What?

On a Friday night in late February, I took a Greyhound bus from Oakland to Walnut Creek, about twenty miles away, to hang out at Al's Drive-In on North Main Street. I hoped someone I could fall in love with might drive through. It was colder than usual for the San Francisco Bay Area, and standing under one of the outdoor heaters, I shivered in my tight black-and-white plaid skirt, black sweater, and beige car coat, aptly named because it was so thin it was only suitable for wearing inside a car. There weren't as many kids at Al's as usual, but two cute boys, Chet and Mark, showed up as I sipped my Coke. I'd met them a couple of weeks earlier, when they passed through Al's in the back of a pickup truck.

Between drags from a Marlboro, I said, "I'm cold." I didn't expect the boys to do anything about it, but Chet took off his jacket and handed it to me.

Mark said, "Mine is warmer," and held it out to me too.

I felt the fabric of Chet's plaid wool jacket between my thumb and forefinger, then the fabric of Mark's, which was beige and made of a foamy synthetic material. I said, "I'll take both," and I put them on— first Chet's, then Mark's—over my own.

Chet Sandler had curly light brown hair and lashes so thick they made his eyes girlishly pretty. He didn't look like a hood, but then again, he didn't look square either, so I figured he was okay. Mark Day was tall and slender, with lively blue eyes and wavy dark brown hair that looked like it was held in place with axle grease. He had more of a bad-boy aura than Chet did, which I liked. He described his family, which included three brothers, a sister, and four stepbrothers and stepsisters. Having no brothers or sisters, I thought this sounded like paradise. His family lived in Pleasant Hill, but he'd dropped out of Pleasant Hill High School and, at sixteen, was working as an apprentice cabinetmaker with his father and living in Oakland with his grandmother.

I pointed out that none of us had a date that night. Chet was none too happy about it. "I need a woman," he said. "I really like to be engaged or going steady."

I turned to Mark. "How about you?"

"I'm never getting married; I'm a confirmed bachelor."

I took this as a challenge: consciously or unconsciously, he was daring me to try to win his heart.

•••

At school Mark was all I could think about. Suddenly, inexplicably, I felt like I was in love. I wanted to record my passion and yearning in exquisite poetry, but the verses I scrawled in my notebooks always came out as variations of "I love Mark Day/and always will in every way." Oh, to write a poem like "How Do I Love Thee?"! I was absent from classes even when I was sitting at my desk. My father, who was generally pretty easygoing and even fondly called the room where I kept my record player and had hung pictures of my friends "the rogue's gallery," got short tempered and started lecturing me about the importance of graduating from high school.

I stayed home from school as often as I could get away with it. My mother nagged, trying to make me go, but I ignored her. One morning my father said, "I'll take care of it," when I said I didn't feel well and wanted to stay home. He came upstairs to my room and, red faced and trembling, pulled my blue Princess phone from the wall and threw it on the floor. In the days before cell phones, this was serious. "That's the problem," he said. "You spend all your time talking on the phone instead of doing your schoolwork." I headed downstairs, but he grabbed my arm while I was still on the staircase, and with his other hand he spanked my behind, saying, "I should have done this a long time ago!" This is the only time I can remember his hitting me.

My mother said, "Don't worry. I'll have the phone reinstalled."

I looked at my dad. "The problem isn't the phone," I said. "It's that Piedmont Junior High isn't the right school for me. I want to live with Aunt Ethel and Uncle Dick and go to Bret Harte."

That night at dinner, pushing my succotash around on my plate, I said, "Please, please, please enroll me at Bret Harte. If you do, I promise to work hard and get good grades." I didn't mention that Mark and his grandmother lived not far from Aunt Ethel and Uncle Dick, who'd recently moved from Oakland's busy Fruitvale Avenue to a quiet neighborhood near High Street.

My dad said, "We'll have to talk to Aunt Ethel and Uncle Dick about it."

"Sheets are on sale at Capwell's. I'll have to get down there." My mom often seemed not to be paying attention when other people were talking.

My aunt and uncle agreed to let me stay with them during the week. On weekends I'd come home. I was ecstatic my last day at Piedmont. As I handed my books back to my teachers, I gave them the required form and said, "Sign here!" Mr. Moore, my history teacher, said, "I don't take orders from you. If you want me to sign it, you'll have to ask politely." My friends at the Rec congratulated me. Getting out of Piedmont was a real coup. I was leaving the uniform and all my detentions behind.

I told everyone at Bret Harte to call me Jamie, a name I picked because there was a hit song I liked about a girl named Jamie. I was instantly popular, which surprised me, because I hadn't been popular in elementary school, where a lot depended on your coordination in sports, or at Piedmont Junior High, where, I'd come to realize, a lot depended on how big your house was and what kind of car your father drove. One of the popular boys at Bret Harte asked me to go steady the first week. He said the name Jamie made him think of Henry James, so he was no dummy, but I turned him down. I didn't want anyone but Mark.

He hadn't called. I knew he wasn't going to, because boys who were interested always called right away, so I called him and said I'd left my lipstick in his jacket pocket: Max Factor's Pink Pastel. Holding the lipstick as we spoke, I described the case: "It's oval, black and gold, and has a little mirror inside." He went to check his jacket pockets, then came back to say he didn't have it. I asked him to search his car and house, because it must have fallen out, and said I'd call the next day to see if he'd found it.

I called every day to ask about the lipstick. Then he started calling me. Each day, after establishing that he hadn't found the lipstick, we turned to other subjects, like Top 40 music and what our mutual friends were doing—who was going with whom, who was flunking out of school. Then we read comic strips and astrology forecasts to each other and competed to see who could cut whom the lowest with remarks like "Is that your head or your neck blowing bubble gum?" and "When God passed out brains, you thought He said trains—and said you didn't want any." In a teen magazine I found an article entitled "101 Ways to Insult Your Boyfriend," and Mark and I soon knew all 101 insults by heart: "Your teeth are like stars: they come out at night," "The last time I saw a face like yours, Tarzan was feeding it bananas," and so on. One night Mark read me his grandmother's shopping list. When he came to BBQ sauce, I said, "That's a good name for you: BBQ." The next item was soap. He said, "That's not quite you, but almost. I'm going to call you Bubbles, Bubbles LaVerne." Bubbles LaVerne was a stripper. We talked every night for two weeks, and I kept hoping he'd say he wanted to see me. Finally he did, and we made plans to get together the following evening.

•••

Aunt Ethel and Uncle Dick had a small two-story white stucco house with a huge backyard. My cousin Jan wanted me to come outside while I waited for Mark, but I was afraid that the wind might blow and mess up my hair, which was ratted just so, so I stayed inside.

I kept checking my hair in the ornately framed oval mirror in the hallway behind the front door. Spotting an imperfection, I teased the top a little more, then sprayed it again with Aqua Net. I was standing right behind the door when the doorbell rang, but I waited a moment before opening it.

I thought Mark was the most handsome boy in the world. It made me a little breathless to look at him. He was Irish and Cherokee, with high cheekbones, eyes that sparkled like sapphires, and the greasiest brown hair imaginable. Maybe he'd put in extra grease that night because he wanted to look good for me. He was wearing the same beige jacket he'd loaned me at Al's Drive-In. He seemed a little nervous, but he was smiling as he took a small box from his pocket and handed it to me, saying, "You win."

I felt all tingly inside as I opened it and lifted out a Max Factor Pink Pastel lipstick in a golden oval case with a mirror. "Thank you."

"I couldn't get a black-and-gold one."

"It's okay." I felt guilty, also like I was going to faint.

"Do you want to go for a ride?" Are leaves green in summer?

I followed him to his old white Ford as Aunt Ethel hollered, "Come back in twenty minutes! You have to do your homework!"

•••

We continued to talk on the phone each day, but he didn't ask me out. It was perplexing. After school I often went to Steve Labate's house near the noisy intersection of 35th Avenue and MacArthur. Steve had an older sister, Sheryn, and a younger brother, David. I felt close to the whole family, including the parents, Betty and Babe, and I told all of them I was in love with Mark and didn't know what to do about it.

Steve had another sister, Susan, who was mentally slow but joyful and loving. She always hugged me and made a fuss when I came to visit. In seventh grade I'd spent a lot of time with her, discussing music, clothes, makeup, and boyfriends. I wasn't just being charitable; I genuinely liked her and was touched by the affection she showed me.

But Susan wasn't there now when I went to her house: she was dead. I'd found out when my mother gave me her obituary. At sixteen she'd died of a respiratory virus, and it made me realize that life was temporary and fragile. On top of wanting true love, to be an adult, and to get out of school and away from my mother, I now felt I'd better fulfill my romantic dreams as quickly as possible, because otherwise I might die without ever doing so.

And something else had happened: my mother, who never missed anything, gave me another newspaper clipping—one that said William Lyndon Arthur (my ex-boyfriend!), age nineteen, and Tabitha Nancy Blaine, age seventeen, both of Oakland, had taken out a marriage license. I wanted to get married too: I wanted to marry Mark. I didn't want to be left behind by Bill and Nan.

Steve's mother, Betty, a small, slender woman with silver hair, told me that if Mark didn't ask me out, the feelings I had for him would eventually pass and I'd meet someone else. Babe, who had a compact build and dark hair like Steve, told me just to give him more time. They both thought I was capable of being reasonable, because Mr. Swartzell, my math teacher at Piedmont, was a regular at the restaurant where Betty worked as a waitress and had told them I was very intelligent. Whenever they talked to me, they reminded me of what Mr. Swartzell had said, perhaps hoping that if they could convince me I was intelligent, I might start acting like it.

But I was obsessed with Mark. I asked Steve to call him to find out how he felt about me and try to get him to ask me out. Steve did call and reported back that Mark liked me but was afraid of being hurt. Steve was adamant, however, that he could do nothing to make Mark ask me out. He said, "I have some advice for you: forget the middleman."

"*I* can't tell him to ask me out, either," I moaned.

"Then ask *him* out."

I was terrified. I wanted to do it but didn't want to be rejected. I thought about it for days, trying to figure out what to say so he

couldn't say no. This would have to be no ordinary date. I wanted
it to be awful, *insulting*, even sacrilegious to say no. I finally braced
myself and dialed his number on my Princess phone on a Saturday
morning. When he answered, I asked him to go to church with me on
Easter. He said yes, and when we hung up, I jumped up and down
and spun around, then collapsed on my bed, laughing.

The Saturday night before Easter, I stayed up all night reading and
rereading a little book called *Love Poems and Love Letters for All the
Year* and swooning over poems like "The Passionate Shepherd to His
Love," "How Do I Love Thee?," "A Red, Red Rose," "So We'll Go
No More A-Roving," and "Love's Philosophy." I especially identified
with the following verses by Robert Herrick:

That age is best, which is the first,
     When youth and blood are warmer
But being spent, the worse, and worst
     Times still succeed the former.

Then be not coy, but use your time,
     And while you may, go marry:
For having lost but once your prime,
     You may forever tarry.

Mark arrived in casual beige pants and his beige jacket, the same
jacket he always wore—he'd had it on both times I saw him at Al's
Drive-In, and also the night he came to Aunt Ethel and Uncle Dick's
house. I wasn't surprised. I knew he wouldn't be wearing a suit,
because he'd told me he didn't own one, so I wasn't very dressed up
either. I had on one of my school outfits—a tight, rose-hued wool skirt
and matching sweater.

During the service I wanted to believe that God existed and
Jesus had risen from his tomb and climbed a golden stairway to
heaven, but my spiritual feelings were evoked more strongly by
the Easter lilies on the altar and the sunlight streaming through the
stained-glass windows than by the words of the minister. Still, I felt

peaceful and happy. Mark and I were sitting so close, I could feel the rhythm of his breathing, and the poems I'd read the night before kept echoing in my head.

•••

We became inseparable. Sometimes we went out in Mark's Ford, other times in his stepmother's '56 T-Bird. He said, "Bubbles, baby!" whenever he saw me, and I said, "BBQ!" and rushed into his arms. Then he'd pick me up and twirl me around, and when he put me down, we'd kiss and say how much we loved each other. Sometimes we held both hands, leaned back, and spun together. As the weather got warmer, instead of wool skirts I often wore cotton dresses with full skirts that lifted when I ran or spun, and I felt like I was dancing through my life in my billowing skirts like a woman in a movie. Neil Sedaka had a new hit, "Breaking Up Is Hard to Do," and Mark and I declared it our song.

Mark and Steve became best friends, and sometimes the three of us went to movies or cruising together. Other times we just sat around talking and drinking Olympia. Mark's self-confidence increased when he drank. After a couple of beers, he got animated and told jokes and stories. Sometimes he talked about the cabinet shop where he worked, and this always impressed me. He seemed so much more mature than boys who were still in school. Steve liked to tell jokes too, but sometimes the jokes the boys told were stupid, their only purpose to use forbidden words: "This is station FUCK broadcasting from Pussy Mountain. Here come the Kotex Kids now, singing, 'Oh, how it tickles my balls.' " I tired of hearing jokes like this one.

But I never tired of being with Mark. My obsession grew. Nothing was more important than being with him, holding his hand, spinning, kissing, making out passionately. His touch made my whole body quiver. I wanted to be even closer, for our two bodies to merge.

•••

All was not well at Aunt Ethel and Uncle Dick's house. I tied up their phone a lot, left my unrinsed breakfast dish with raisin bran hardening on it in the kitchen sink, stunk up their bathroom and entry hall with hair spray, and increased their gas bill by turning the heater on early every morning. Moreover, under my tutelage, Jan had been dieting. Uncle Dick, who had a heart condition and wanted to keep his only daughter fat enough to be disdained by boys and live off her bulk in the event of a nuclear war, said I had to go.

I was also in trouble at school. Miss Pond, my counselor, had called me into her office several times to say my hair was too high and I was wearing too much makeup. This seemed fishy because no one had mentioned my hair or makeup my first few weeks at Bret Harte, and neither had changed. Also, I had neither the highest hair nor the heaviest makeup at the school. Moreover, I'd been doing my schoolwork. I felt that I was being singled out and picked on, and I wondered if my mother or Mr. Ferry from Piedmont Junior High had called Miss Pond and Miss Hindmarsh, the vice principal, and asked them to keep an eye on me.

My last class was P.E., and I got permission not to participate when I had bronchitis. It was boring to sit and watch the other girls exercise, so one afternoon I just left. I didn't think Miss Pickette, the rickety, gray-haired P.E. teacher, would notice, but Miss Hindmarsh was looking out her office window as I walked away from the school. When she confronted me the next day, I argued that missing a half hour of a class in which I couldn't participate wasn't the same as cutting, but she disagreed.

On all three counts—truancy, hair, and makeup—I said I was not sorry and was not going to change. Miss Hindmarsh said I could think about it more at home and suspended me for the last two weeks of April for "truancy, willful disobedience, and defiance of authority."

•••

Aunt Ethel and Uncle Dick said I couldn't come back to their house when my suspension was over, so I asked my parents if I could stay with Mark and his grandmother, Danny, until the end of the school year. It seemed like a wild idea at first, but both Danny and my parents said okay.

Both of my parents accepted my romance with Mark. Perhaps they were relieved that I was now going out with just one boy instead of several. My mom's only reservation was, "I'd think you'd want someone with a better job."

The day before I was to move in with Mark, my father gave me a lecture while he was shaving. Standing in front of the bathroom mirror in his BVDs, he warned me that boys were hot-blooded and I should be on guard. I said, "Don't worry about that. I've already done it with Bill Arthur."

My father's face turned redder than it had the morning he pulled the phone out of the wall. He gripped the sides of the old-fashioned washbasin with the pipes showing underneath and growled through clenched teeth, "I never liked that guy, and now I like him even less." He didn't look at me as he spoke. I was sorry I'd told him. It was a terrible mistake, and I decided never to tell him about my sex life again.

•••

Danny's cottage had a kitchen, bathroom, bedroom, and living room. The whole house was decorated with copper pictures that Mark's father had tapped out with a hammer and nail when he was in prison for passing bad checks. I took over Danny's bedroom, and Mark and Danny slept in the living room. Danny babysat, crocheted, worked at the polls, kept a vegetable garden, and drank a lot of Coca-Cola. She was soft and round, with short, straight gray hair and a bad eye. She was also bighearted and funny, and I adored her.

The first night we were alone at the cottage, Mark and I made out on his narrow bed in the living room. When he put his hand on my breast, I pushed it away, but then he put his hand under my lavender angora sweater and undid my bra, and I didn't try to stop him.

I wanted to make love. I wanted it as badly as he did, but in 1962 girls were not supposed to want it, so I had to pretend he was seducing me. As he touched my bare breast, I could feel moisture forming between my legs. He pushed up my tight purple-and-lavender plaid skirt and reached into my pants, and I squeezed his hand between my legs. I was much more turned on than I'd been when I did it with Bill Arthur. I took off my skirt and he took off his pants and entered me. He was still wearing his red plaid Pendleton shirt, and I still had on my sweater. I didn't feel like a teenager who was being bad or a girl who was easy. I felt like a woman in love. I wanted to be with Mark for the rest of my life, to fix his dinners, bear his children, and make love with him every night. He withdrew before he came, but I didn't understand why. Secretly, I hoped I'd get pregnant.

He sat up. "You're not a virgin."

"I was raped."

"Did you call the police?"

"No, I was afraid." Lying made my face flush, but I knew Mark couldn't see it in the dark.

He put his pants back on, lit a cigarette, and opened the front door. As he stood in the doorway, staring at the lights in the distance across San Francisco Bay, I lay on the bed, just a few feet away, watching him. He was barefoot, in silhouette, his shirt not tucked in. A cool breeze drifted over me. Awash in feelings of love, I smiled to myself, wanting always to remember this moment, because I was so happy. Now that we'd made love, I felt fully connected to Mark. I also felt like an adult. I knew that boys sometimes used girls for sex, but I was sure Mark wasn't using me.

•••

Mark and I set his friend Marty up with Jan, who'd lost about thirty pounds. Marty had an acne-scarred face, but his voice was rich and resonant, and he sang like Elvis Presley. It gave me the shivers when he did "It's Now or Never." Marty was sixteen, Jan eleven. We told him Jan was fourteen, and to look at her, it was believable. Her period had started when she was ten, perhaps due to her excellent nutrition, and her breasts were bigger than mine.

Jan and I got the boys to play wedding with us. In the role of Mark's and my marriage counselor, Jan asked if we were sure we were ready for marriage. We said yes. Marty officiated, and both he and Jan signed as witnesses on the marriage certificate. I officiated for Jan and Marty, and Mark and I signed. Mark and I then made out on the sofa, while Jan and Marty snuggled in the overstuffed chair where my dad always sat to watch television. We were now honeymooners. I'd always found the sofa and matching chair ugly and old-fashioned, with their red brocade upholstery and tassels at the bottom. I wanted nicer furniture in my real honeymoon suite.

When the boys had to use the bathroom, they always said, "I'm going to see a man about a horse." Jan had heard Mark and Marty say this many times, so I was surprised when she jumped up during her honeymoon and followed Marty into the bathroom.

They came right back out and Marty said, "This broad is crazy! She won't let me use the john."

Mark and I looked at each other, baffled. I asked, "Why?" I thought maybe she considered this kind of intimacy okay now that they were married.

Marty said, "She wants to see the horse!"

Mark and I doubled over in laughter as Jan admitted that she was only eleven years old and liked horses.

•••

The evening of June 5, I rummaged through Danny's cottage, looking for paper to do my homework. Mark was outside working on his car. On the floor under his bed, I found a notebook of lined paper— exactly what I needed. I opened it. In the center of the first page, "I Love Lucy" was printed in large red-and-black wavy letters. The rest of the page was covered, with "Lucy" written over and over again in blue ink. Mark was embarrassed when I showed it to him, but he let me keep it.

The next evening we sat together on Danny's back porch, sipping Olympia and listening to my transistor radio while Danny watered the young bean and tomato plants in her garden. Occasionally she bent to pull a weed, her housedress fluttering around her ankles. I handed Mark a Certs breath mint, then popped one into my own mouth (we went through a couple of rolls of Certs every day to keep our breath sweet after smoking). When Danny went inside, Mark picked me up and twirled me around. That movie again! When he stopped, we kissed, standing and dizzy, before returning to the stoop.

From time to time I got up to dance, or just to step back and look at Mark. He was wearing Levi's, low on his hips, and a blue plaid Pendleton shirt. I admired his slouch and his thick brown hair, slicked back on the sides and falling in greasy waves across his forehead. A good catch. We'd been going steady since April.

We started talking about marriage, and I told him I hoped someday to be a good wife and to mother four children. "There Goes My Baby," already an oldie but goodie, wailed on the radio.

His blue eyes were intense and serious. "Well," he asked, "will you?"

"Will I what?"

"Marry me."

"Yes." I thought no couple had ever been more in love.

He said he'd fallen in love with me at first sight but was afraid to get involved because I had a reputation for "loving 'em and leaving 'em." I thought about Bill Arthur and Tom Ogden, both of whom had left me, but I didn't mention them, because this was no time to talk about other guys.

"I'll never leave you," I said.

•••

Uncle Dick had a heart attack. This was the second one, and the doctors said it didn't look good. I sat in the waiting room in an uncomfortable metal chair while my dad visited him at Oak Knoll Naval Hospital, a collection of low, wood-sided buildings nestled in the Oakland

Hills above the Warren Freeway. When my dad came back, his face was ashen, his eyes watery. He said Uncle Dick had rambled about his first wife, Mendel, and his Navy days, and didn't seem to know where he was in time or place.

The next morning my mother called me at Danny's to say a doctor had called Aunt Ethel in the middle of the night to tell her, "Your husband has expired." My mother continued, "It's your fault. You killed him by not behaving yourself when you lived there." She always said I was killing her with my behavior, so it wasn't too surprising to hear her say I'd killed my uncle. Still, it was hurtful. I was pretty sure that his death wasn't my fault but felt guilty anyhow, because at the very least, I'd done nothing to make him happy during the last few months of his life.

That night at Mark's and my favorite restaurant—the Cozy Corner, a little Mexican place on East 14th Street—I told him what my mother had said. He said he didn't think my uncle's death could possibly have been my fault, that maybe my mother had said that because she was in shock. I was about 99 percent sure it wasn't my fault, but that last 1 percent kept nagging me. My enchiladas, rice, and beans grew cold on my plate. Sounding like my mother, Mark kept saying, "You have to eat," but my stomach was in a tight knot and I couldn't swallow. We talked for a long time, but I couldn't completely dispel the fear that maybe my mother was right, even though my uncle had smoked two packs of Lucky Strikes a day and President Kennedy had recently set up an advisory committee on smoking and health because many people believed smoking caused heart disease and cancer.

I was sad that Uncle Dick had died, even though I hadn't gotten along with him, and I felt sorry for Aunt Ethel and Jan. I knew Uncle Dick had loved Jan deeply. He was the only man I'd ever seen changing diapers, and I could picture him working with Jan on her homework at the dining room table. She was his only child, born when he was past fifty, and he'd acted like helping her with her homework was the most interesting and important thing he'd ever get to do. He'd called her "pumpkin" and "dumpling" and walked her to and from school every day. I felt bad that he wouldn't be able to see her grow up, but I also thought that maybe she was better off without his strict discipline and distorted ideas.

I'd wanted him to listen to me and to like me, and I'd secretly hoped this might happen when I grew up. I wanted the other adults in my family to like me too. But I wanted them to accept me for who I was, not for acting like the person they wanted me to be.

Jan cried for days, and I was surprised by the intensity of her grief. I'd expected her reaction to her father's death to be a mixture of sorrow and relief, like mine. Clearly, I had no idea either how she felt about her father or what it's like to lose a parent.

As I emerged from my own initial shock and sorrow, my thoughts oscillated between memories of Uncle Dick and visions of marriage to Mark: now I'd never get to convince Uncle Dick that *gene* wasn't a dirty word; to be different, I wouldn't wear white at my wedding. My thoughts swung back and forth like a pendulum.

On a form that asked if I'd be returning to Bret Harte in the fall, I checked the "No" box. For the reason, I wrote that I was getting married. Not only Bill Arthur and Nan, but also Tom Ogden and Cindy had gotten married, and Cindy was expecting a baby. This was what life was all about!

•••

In July Mark pulled another gift from his jacket pocket: an engagement ring. It was white gold and had nine diamonds—one big one and eight small ones—and came with a matching wedding band that had nine more small diamonds. The diamonds in both rings were set in groups of three in little waves that flowed from left to right like slanted S's. I thought the rings were prettier than my mother's. As Mark put the engagement ring on my finger, I was certain I'd be in love with him for the rest of my life.

I showed it off that evening to my parents.

My dad said, "That's quite a ring for a girl your age to snag."

My mother said, "It will take him a long time to pay for it."

"You have to wait until you're sixteen," my dad added.

"If you don't let me get married, I'll run away or get pregnant."

"I don't understand what the rush is," he said.

Consciously, I was in a rush because I wanted to get away from my mother and to be an adult. I believed in the movie version of true love and thought I'd found it with Mark. I'd never fully trusted my mother, perhaps because she'd lied to me whenever convenient throughout my childhood (no, the doctor wouldn't give me a shot; no, she'd never had sex, never even heard of it, etc.). Maybe this contributed to my powerful need to love and trust a teenage boy instead.

Also, I didn't have much to do except hang out and make out. I had no involvement in music or sports and had not yet discovered my interest in academics. Since elementary school I'd thought I was destined to be a writer or artist because my father, grandfather, and teachers had always praised my creative work, but I didn't understand that one needs to study writing or art, or that marrying Mark might interfere with other goals.

"We'll think it over," my mother said.

Why did they put up with this at all? I think they had a hard time saying no to me, and they just didn't get it, the way most adults do, that getting married at fourteen, or even sixteen, is a very bad idea and likely to lead to great unhappiness later on. They had their own fantasies. My dad was a movie buff and my mom pored over the fan magazines. Maybe they thought I was taking after Jean Harlow and Marilyn Monroe, both of whom had first married at sixteen. If they did get it that teen marriage did not, in general, lead to fame and fortune, perhaps they thought the gods would make an exception for me.

A few days later when I saw Steve, he said, "I think you're a fool, even though your fiancé is my best friend." I thought I knew everything there was to know about love, but even Steve knew that I didn't.

•••

In August my dad, my mom, Aunt Ethel, Jan, and I drove to Seattle to see the World's Fair. Our first morning there I woke before dawn, nauseated and with a pain in my right side. My mother said I'd feel better after breakfast.

At the café just the scent of eggs made me feel like vomiting. My mother kept saying, "It's all in your head." That's what she always said when I was sick or hurt. When I broke my wrist at five, my parents didn't even take me for X-rays until the next day, after my mom's friend Phyllis urged them to do so. My mom just kept saying, "It won't hurt if you don't think about it."

"If you think you're sick, you'll be sick and you'll miss the fair," she now warned.

"Shut up!"

"You'll be sorry when I'm dead and gone!" she screamed as my father helped me up and put his arm around me to take me back to our room.

I headed to the john to throw up the few sips of water I'd been able to swallow, while my dad went to the motel office to ask for help. I felt like I was the one closest to being dead and gone.

A nurse staying at the motel said I had either a pelvic infection or appendicitis and should see a doctor immediately, so my dad took me to the emergency room of North Gate General Hospital, which was above a shopping mall near the motel. A doctor there felt my abdomen and ordered a blood test. When the result came back, he said my appendix was ready to burst. Before noon I was in the operating room with an IV line in my left arm and a nurse standing over me, saying, "Count backward from one hundred."

I woke up thinking that I wanted to marry Mark and have his baby before I died. I didn't think I was going to die from the appendectomy, but an unexpected illness or injury might kill me at any time. I also thought about my family. They were all at the fair, and I was jealous.

In the evening when my parents came to visit, my mom said they were leaving the following morning to visit friends in Vancouver. I begged her not to go, because I didn't want to be left alone in Seattle. "We'll just be gone one day," she promised.

At a junction outside Vancouver, a car skidded across a rain-slicked highway and slammed into my dad's Oldsmobile. No one was hurt, but the car was impounded in Canada, and my parents couldn't get back to Seattle for several days.

I shared my room with an eight-year-old girl who'd had a tonsillectomy. Her mother visited several times a day, and every time she arrived, it was all I could do to keep from crying, because no one was visiting me except the doctor.

I called Mark collect and wept while we talked. "I hate being alone here," I said. "I feel like my parents are never coming back."

The next day after lunch, a nurse came into my room and said, "You have visitors!" I thought my parents were finally back from Vancouver, but Mark and Steve entered, bleary-eyed and disheveled. They'd hitchhiked all night from Oakland.

Mark sat on the bed and hugged me. Furious that my parents had left me, he said, "I want to get married as soon as you're well."

I thought he was the one who really loved me. He'd hitchhiked hundreds of miles, whereas neither of my parents thought that visiting me in the hospital was important enough that they'd even take a bus from Vancouver, which wasn't all that far away. "We'll do it," I said, "no matter what my parents say."

••• ••• •••

Left: Mark and Lucy outside the First Methodist Church in Reno, Nevada, on their wedding day, September 8, 1962
Right: Lucy and Liana, 1964

chapter 4

Married at Fourteen

In her slip and corset, my mother was not a pretty sight. Even in the corset she was shaped like a potato. It had real bones in it, or at least she said it did. To my thinking, any amount of hunger was preferable to needing such a thing. Unpacking her suitcase, she picked up a floral-print cotton nightgown that I thought only a very old lady or very little girl should wear. Watching from the bedroom doorway, I said, "Mark and I want to get married next month."

"What about school?" Putting dirty clothes in one pile, clean ones in another, she didn't look at me.

It was mid-August. School would be starting soon. "I don't want to go back. It's boring."

"Your father wants you to wait until you're sixteen." She sniffed a blouse, then put it on the to-be-washed pile.

I studied the bedroom wallpaper; its pink roses on a green background had always looked old-fashioned to me. "If you don't let me get married, I'll run away again or get pregnant." I'd said this so many times it was sort of a mantra. "I'm not bluffing."

My mother turned to look at me. "You look awful with all that black stuff on your eyes. Mark may think you look pretty, but I don't."

"Will you sign for me?"

"I'm tired." Her voice was sharp, more angry than tired.

•••

Kennedy was president and the civil rights movement was underway. For many people it was a time of hope, opportunity, and change, but Mark and I had a vision for our lives that one might have expected of teenage apprentices and servants before the advent of universal education. The first week of September 1962, we applied for a marriage license at the Oakland courthouse. When I told the clerk the year I was born, she thought I'd made a mistake. I said, "It's not a mistake. I'm fourteen."

She put on her glasses. With a get-your-hand-out-of-the-cookie-jar look, she explained, "California law requires an age of sixteen for both partners. You'll have to see a judge to make a special request for your license."

The next day my parents and I entered the judge's wood-paneled chambers. I sat in a comfortable leather chair; the judge, stern and stocky, watched me from behind his desk. My dark blond hair, which reached past my shoulders, was ratted high on top. I wore a lavender sweater and a tight-fitting dress with little black flowers on a white background.

"Why do you want to get married?" he asked.

"Because I'm in love."

"That's quite admirable, but at your age it's insufficient. There have to be other circumstances. Are there any?"

I knew exactly what the other circumstances had to be. I wished I could say, "Yes! I'm pregnant!"—it wasn't that I hadn't tried—but I answered truthfully: "No."

"I'm sorry, but I can't let you get married."

"Can't you make an exception? Isn't it better to get married because you're in love than because you're pregnant?"

"I agree entirely, but it's also best to wait. In California there's a law that says it's illegal to marry at your age. It's a good law; it was made to protect people. I wish you the best of luck, and I hope someday you'll marry for love—when you're older."

The idea of getting married made me feel liberated—free of childhood and adolescence, free of social conventions. The rules that society placed on others did not apply to me. In my own mind I was different, someone who could imagine alternatives to dull customs, a force to be reckoned with. Of course, in reality, what I perceived as a great act of liberation was the opposite: a leap into adolescent marriage, a practice that had limited women's options for thousands of years and that my culture had wisely outlawed and now found objectionable.

My father, who was taking time off from his job, looked relieved. As we left the courthouse, he urged me once more to wait until I was sixteen. He didn't understand that to me, waiting until I was sixteen seemed no different from waiting forever. I wanted to get out of school *now,* I wanted to get away from my mother *now,* and I wanted to fulfill Mark's and my love immediately by having his baby.

•••

The following Friday Mark and I drove to Nevada with my mother in the backseat. It was late afternoon as we came down the east side of the Sierra in my father's Oldsmobile, and I could see the town of Minden in the distance, in the long shadows of the mountains. We were still far from Reno, where we planned to get a marriage license that afternoon and wed the following day. It was already so late I was afraid the marriage license bureau in Reno might be closed when we got there, so I said, "Let's get our license in Minden."

We gave our real ages to the gray-haired justice of the peace who both issued licenses and performed marriages. In Nevada, he told us, it was not only illegal to marry at my age but also at Mark's: the Silver State required the woman to be at least sixteen, the man eighteen. Mark was seventeen. The justice advised us to come back when we were older.

All the way from Minden to Reno, I worried that we wouldn't be able to get married after all. My mother kept saying she was sure we would be able to: all we had to do was lie about our ages. I didn't know what had changed her mind, but she was on my side now. Maybe she wanted to get rid of me. I couldn't stand to be around her for very long, and I thought the feeling was mutual. It made her nervous just to look at me. Then again, maybe she knew how important this was to me and just wanted to make me happy. My dad still didn't think my getting married was a great idea, but it was two against one, and he was going along with the plan—anything for his girls.

My mother had never been able to distinguish between real dangers and false ones. She hadn't let me take swimming lessons as a child because she was afraid I'd drown. Now she seemed as oblivious as I was to the likely consequences of dropping out of school after eighth grade and getting married. The truth was, she'd dropped out herself after tenth, although she always told people she was a high school graduate. My father, I think, saw the danger, but his childlike optimism enabled him to deny it. He was a happy-go-lucky sort who'd risk everything at the poker table because he truly believed he was going to win. My parents thought I was magical, and they seemed to believe that everything would turn out right for me no matter what. They were as naïve as I was, and indulgent on top of it.

In Reno we were joined by my father, my Aunt Ethel, and Mark's parents and stepparents. I needn't have worried about the marriage license bureau closing before we got there, because the wedding industry in Reno was second only to gambling, and marriage licenses were issued twenty-four hours a day.

About ten other couples were in line ahead of us. I felt lightheaded and my heart was tap dancing. When we reached the front, I said I was sixteen and Mark said he was eighteen. Both of our mothers were present to confirm this, and our license was issued as quickly as everyone else's. I think now that Mark's mother lied for us because she thought my parents were more affluent than they were (we lived in Piedmont, a town known for its mansions), and that our marriage would give him a financial advantage.

The next morning Mark's father and stepmother took him to rent a suit and get a haircut. I would have been happy to have him stand at the altar in Levi's, and I liked his long, greasy brown hair just the way it was, but I didn't say anything. Mark's mother, Ellen, said I would have bad luck if I didn't wear something old, something new, something borrowed, and something blue, and loaned me an antique cameo brooch to take care of the old and borrowed. I was wearing new white shoes and a pale blue brocade Chinese dress. Ellen also gave me a pink corsage. I didn't think either the brooch or the corsage looked good on my dress but wore them anyhow. I was in a rare mood for indulging the adults.

On September 8, three months before my fifteenth birthday and the week before I should have started ninth grade, the sky was a luminous blue as Mark and I entered the First Methodist Church in Reno. Our mothers asked the organist to play "I Love You Truly." I'd have picked "Love Me Tender," but I wanted our mothers to be happy. Standing at the altar, I found it hard not to giggle. Mark looked so skinny in his rented navy blue suit! When I knelt, I thought my tight-fitting dress would rip, but it held. I stood again, and Mark put the ring on my finger. I knew that many people would call me a fool, but I was incredibly happy. I thought ours was a unique and wondrous passion. Antony and Cleopatra, Elizabeth Barrett and Robert Browning, F. Scott Fitzgerald and Zelda, step aside! Mark was the prince and I was his princess, and our wedding would fulfill the promise of our extraordinary love.

Afterward we all went to Lake Tahoe for steak dinners at Harvey's Wagon Wheel. Other than me, the women at the table came in matched pairs: Ellen and Judy, Mark's mother and stepmother, were redheads with sarcastic senses of humor and the worldliness of women who worked outside the home; my mom and Aunt Ethel, badgering the waiter with endless complaints, were identical twins, just over five feet tall, who wore shortened size 14 dresses over their corsets and told and retold the joke about the woman who pulled a sugar cube from her brassiere, then asked her guests if they'd also like cream. Mark's stepfather, Pete, a large man with a square jaw, ordered drink after drink and stood up to toast Mark and me each time a new one arrived. Mark's dad, Tom, and mine, masticating their steaks, said they felt lucky. At first I thought they were referring to Mark's and my marriage, but as the conversation continued, I realized they were talking about blackjack.

•••

We had a four-day honeymoon at Tom and Judy's house in El Cerrito, just north of Berkeley, while the adults stayed at Tahoe to play keno, blackjack, and the slot machines. For dinner the first night, I served leftover macaroni and cheese I found in a CorningWare casserole dish in the refrigerator. I left it in the oven too long and it burned on the bottom. I didn't know how to get the black stuff off the dish, so I washed and dried it, then put it back in the cupboard with the last of the charred macaroni still stuck to the bottom.

I didn't want to be seen naked, and neither did Mark. I was embarrassed by my small breasts. I don't know what his problem was. If I wasn't wearing a nightgown or blouse when we made love, I put a pillow over my chest to cover my breasts. Mark always made me close my eyes while he pulled his pants up or down. Even so, we had sex four or five times a day. I'd rather have spent some of this time walking on the Berkeley Pier, playing Scrabble, or shopping for things for our apartment, but I wanted to make Mark happy.

He invited our friend Steve and Steve's friend Mike, one of my ex-boyfriends, to visit us. I wished we could have had our honeymoon far away from the Bay Area, because their arrival made it very unromantic. Each time Mark and I came out of the bedroom, Steve and Mike had dopey grins. It infuriated me, but I didn't want to say anything that might spoil my honeymoon even more. After they left, with Mark's invitation to return the next day, I said, "Why do you want them here? Are you bored with me?" Mark said, "I thought you'd want to see them. They're your friends too."

The next time I saw my mother, I told her that someday I wanted to write about getting married at fourteen, to let the world know that teen love is lasting and real. My mother, who'd been sitting on her bed, got up abruptly, saying, "Don't talk that way! You don't want to be a writer!"

I was surprised, because whenever I said anything remotely amusing, my father said I should write about it, but before I could ask her what was wrong with being a writer, her expression softened to a sly smile. "Did you like it?" she asked.

It took me a moment to figure out what "it" was, because she'd always refused to talk to me about sex. "Yes," I finally answered. I was surprised she didn't know we'd been doing it all summer. "I never did. Your father jumped on me like a mad bear. I wouldn't let him do it more than once a week."

Wondering if this was why it took my parents eight years to conceive me, I decided not to tell her about Steve and Mike. If she thought sex was never any good, how could she understand when something spoiled it? I'd never seen my parents hug, hold hands, or kiss, which had always disappointed me, because most of my friends' parents were physically affectionate. I didn't want a marriage with minimal physical contact. I saw my mother as a sort of Victorian relic—a nervous, overweight housewife who hated sex—and wanted to be different from her in every way.

•••

Mark's and my apartment was a second-floor flat in a Victorian building on 24th Street near downtown Oakland. We furnished it with family discards that included a brown sofa, the upholstery of which had been shredded by dogs, and a pearlescent gray Formica table with matching vinyl chairs.

I knew how to dust and vacuum, but I'd never cleaned a stove or toilet. I noticed after a month or so that the range top was getting crusted over with dried and burned food and the toilet bowl had an ugly gray ring, but I didn't think too much about it until Mark said, "Aren't you ever going to clean the kitchen and bathroom?"

Every morning Steve, Mike, and any of Mark's other friends who were cutting school came over for breakfast, after which I packed lunches—apples and ham or bologna sandwiches on Wonder Bread—for anywhere from three to six boys. As I washed their coffee cups and cereal dishes, Mark and his buddies left to play poker, hang out at Caspers Hot Dogs, or go motorcycling in the Oakland hills. I told

Mark he should either look for a job (the cabinet shop had laid him off) or take me with him. Mark, the boy chauvinist, said my place was in the home.

We were living on $267 from a $500 insurance policy that would have matured when I turned eighteen, but that my father cashed in early to sustain us until Mark found another job. I resented spending this money to feed Mark's friends, even if they were my friends too. Mark said I was selfish, but I worried about what would happen when the money ran out, and I wanted to make it last as long as possible.

One morning as Mark and his friends stood in the driveway below our kitchen window, preparing to leave, probably discussing where to go, my rage and disappointment began to surge. Heart drumming, I picked up the hammer I'd been using to hang pictures from the Blue Chip Redemption Center. I started to cry at the same time as I hurled it at Mark and his friends through the closed window. It narrowly missed Mike's head; I was momentarily sorry it hadn't killed anyone.

Mark came back into the flat. His blue eyes were cold and hard, and I knew he didn't want to hear my side. "I thought I'd married a woman; I never thought I'd married such a baby," he said.

"Your childishness evokes mine," I stated with dignity.

•••

On September 30 my parents held a reception for us at Leona Lodge, a hall in a wooded area near the Warren Freeway, which they'd rented from the Oakland Parks Department for five dollars. I wore a white party dress with a sequined bodice and full skirt; Mark wore his own new sports coat, a gift from my father. There were no flowers, no musicians, no napkins printed with our names. The caterers brought open-faced tuna and egg salad sandwiches; the champagne was served in little paper cups. The table with the food was against one wall in a huge room, otherwise empty except for metal folding chairs along the other three walls. Our thirty or so guests sat in the chairs and ate their sandwiches. I opened the presents: eleven towel sets and an ashtray. My mother had told everyone we needed towels to ensure that I wouldn't take any more of hers. This affair was supposed to last from one o'clock until five but was cut short at about three, when Mark got sick to his stomach and had to leave.

In October my parents took Mark and me to visit my father's cousin Deedee in Watsonville, a town inland between Santa Cruz and Monterey. Cousin Deedee, an austere-looking but kind-hearted woman with a tight gray bun, offered Mark and me the room of honor—her own bedroom—in her modest home. While we made love, deep in the center of Deedee's mattress, Mark asked, "Do you want a baby?" I said yes, and for the first time, he didn't withdraw.

The next morning I ate Deedee's waffles and scrambled eggs with great gusto: I no longer had to keep my weight at 114, because I knew I was pregnant. I thought I was going to single-handedly show the world that teen marriage and pregnancy were okay. Mark and I were the living proof that teen love was real, and soon we would be the best parents imaginable.

Within two weeks my breasts were a little fuller and slightly tender, and I needed more sleep than usual. Sometimes I felt a little queasy, but the queasiness went away as long as I kept nibbling crackers, cookies, or potato chips. I kept telling Mark that I was pregnant, but he wasn't sure whether to believe me.

•••

A counselor from Oakland Technical High came by to try to talk me into going back to school, but I thought I already knew everything I needed to know about the things one learns in school: I could read, I could write, I could do math. She might as well have asked a zebra to shed its stripes. One of the great draws of getting married had been to get out of going to school. I told her thanks, but I wasn't interested.

Still, I didn't have much to do during the long hours when most kids were at school. Sometimes I read paperback books from a little drugstore near our apartment. One, called *Children Who Kill*, gave a Freudian interpretation of each murder: the murder weapon always symbolized a penis. I was annoyed by these interpretations, especially when the killer was a girl.

If I didn't feel like reading after my housework was done, I went shoplifting, usually at Capwell's department store, which was just a few blocks away. One rainy day I put a gray wool skirt into my big black purse, brought it home, and took a good look at it. It wasn't a pretty skirt, and I didn't need a skirt. I realized that I had gained nothing by taking it. My thinking continued to the next logical step: I'd had things to lose by taking it. Although my probation officer hadn't been in touch with me for more than a year, technically I was still on probation for running away, and by shoplifting I was violating probation. If I was caught, I might be sent to the California Youth Authority, and my baby might be taken away. (I hadn't had a pregnancy test yet, but I was certain that I was pregnant.) Would I rather have my freedom and my baby or an ugly gray skirt? I was not yet certain that shoplifting was morally or ethically wrong but, regardless, convinced myself that it wasn't worth doing.

•••

Mark often went to the motorcycle hill climbs with Steve, Mike, and other friends, and he always came back with a big hug for me. Poison oak is abundant in the Oakland hills, and a few days after one of his outings, I broke out in a blistery rash over about 30 percent of my body. Mark got it too, but not as bad. We took antihistamine tablets and went through calamine lotion by the quart. As soon as we recovered, Mark went back to the hill climbs and gave me poison oak again. My enthusiasm for hugging him plummeted.

In November he started looking for a job in earnest. I'd missed my period, which helped convince him that I really was pregnant and he'd soon have a child to support. He was hired by a construction company, and we moved twenty miles inland to a massive pink stucco apartment complex in Concord to be closer to his job. By now I knew how to clean stoves and toilets, cook hamburger in 101 exciting ways, and set mousetraps. The most remarkable thing about our second apartment was that it had more mice than the first. We lived near a field and shared our living space with field mice. There were so many that mousetraps did not suffice, and we had to use poison. Dirty dishes had to be washed immediately, I discovered, unless I wanted to deal with a sinkful of mouse droppings. These mice were not at all stealthy or timid. They believed in safety in numbers: when I opened a kitchen cupboard, they leapt out like a team of tiny football players.

Mark's friend Chet, who was really proud of the "Blue Angle" tattoo on his arm until I pointed out the misspelling, and Chet's new wife, a slow-speaking woman with bleached blond hair, came to stay with us. As the four of us sat at the gray Formica table in the kitchen, Chet told us how he liked to rip his wife's pants off when he wanted sex. His tone was jovial, but it still sounded like rape to me.

"I think a man and woman should have sex only when both of them feel like it," I said, then turned to Mark. "What do you think?"

I expected him to agree with me, but he said, "I agree with Chet. A woman should always be ready for her husband."

I felt hurt and disgusted. The next time Mark and I made love, I remembered what he'd said and couldn't get turned on.

On December 5, my fifteenth birthday, Mark got sick at work and was taken to the hospital. While he underwent an emergency appendectomy, I got the result of my pregnancy test: positive. I told him in the recovery room as soon as he woke up. We were both jubilant.

Because Mark couldn't work the rest of December, we didn't have money for our January rent, so we moved in with my parents after Christmas. I was glad to be home. I wouldn't have to worry about the rent anymore, and I wouldn't have to deal with mice. I was happy as I arranged my stuffed animals on the headboard of Mark's and my bed in my old room.

The next day I went next door to see my mom's friend Phyllis. I'd always admired her because she was slender, had dazzling red hair, wore purplish lipstick, and smoked. I'd recently quit smoking because cigarettes started tasting peculiar and unpleasant. I also cut down on salt and stopped drinking alcohol. My obstetrician hadn't told me to do these things. I just thought they would be wise. We talked in the basement while Phyllis did her laundry. "Your mother told me all her problems would be over when you got married," she said, "but I told her that her problems were just beginning. I said, 'Evelyn, she'll be back home before you know it, and you won't have just one teenager to worry about, you'll have two teenagers and a baby.' "

"I'm going to take care of my baby myself," I said.

•••

Mark didn't go back to work at the construction company: he said they couldn't hold the job for him. When he was well, he started looking for another job, but I found one first. I sold Beauty Counselor Cosmetics and did much better than I had selling Avon products a few years earlier with my mother. "Yes," I told my customers, "these creams really will smooth out wrinkles." "Yes," I said, "I use them myself."

I saved my earnings to buy baby clothes and a crib with a matching chest of drawers. The most expensive baby furniture at Storkland, the crib and chest were white enamel with inlaid pink and blue pearlescent tiles. I also bought a bassinet with a lacy skirt, which I decorated with pink and blue satin bows. Mark said, "We're ready for the princess."

In my fourth or fifth month, Mark and I visited the Arthurs—my ex-boyfriend Bill, his wife Nan, and Bill's parents. I was sitting on the sofa, chatting about my pregnancy with Bill's mother, when Mark suddenly jabbed me and said, "You've got what it takes to get into the movies—seventy-five cents." Mortified, I tried to ignore him, but he baited me again: "When God passed out looks, you thought He said cooks—and said you didn't want any." I gave him a hard stare, hoping to shut him up, but he said, "Your eyes are like pools—cesspools."

"You're the man of my dreams—they're all nightmares," I said. At that moment I meant it. What had been a fun game on the phone a year earlier was now a colossal embarrassment. What kind of man would the Arthurs think I'd married? I wanted to gag him. Instead I tried to act nonchalant as he hurled the insults my way.

On the way home I said, "I'm really mad at you. Can't you act like a loving husband when we're visiting friends?"

"I was just having fun," he said. "I didn't know you couldn't take a joke."

•••

In my sixth month Mark and I visited his mother. The three of us sat at the bar between her kitchen and dining room. After a few drinks she started nagging Mark that he needed a haircut.

"I don't think he needs a haircut," I said.

"Don't interfere when I'm talking to my son!"

"He's my husband, and I can say what I want."

She took a swing at me, but Mark grabbed her arm. Then she jumped off the barstool. Mark was still holding her, but she kicked, screaming, "Let me at her!" I knew I should go to the car, but I didn't want Ellen to think I was afraid of her, so I tried to hit her, but one of Mark's brothers, Dean, dragged me away, while Ellen's kicks fell a few inches short of my stomach and she screamed, "I'll kill her! I'll kill her!"

Dean took me to the car. Mark came out a couple of minutes later with Ellen close behind, her auburn hair disheveled, her face contorted. Before we could drive away, she stuck her head in the window and hollered, "Don't ever bring that tramp here again!"

"You'll never see your grandchild, you rotten bitch!" I screamed. Mark rolled up the window to muffle her curses as we drove away. "She's crazy," I said.

"She's just had one too many. She'll be okay tomorrow."

I thought about my own mother and her relentless nagging and spankings while I was growing up, and I realized I could have had it much worse. I knew that Mark's stepfather was an alcoholic and that Mark had been kicked out of the house at fifteen for slugging him when he was drunk and beating up Ellen, but I never thought anyone in his family would ever challenge me to a fistfight. I felt a new kind of hurt and anger that included, but went beyond, my concern for the safety of my child. I was shocked that Mark didn't think Ellen's behavior was any big deal.

I told my friend Cindy my troubles while she gave her baby, Becky, a bottle in the living room of their apartment. Pacing in front of the sofa where Cindy was sitting, I said, "He gives me poison oak twice, he takes his sweet time to look for a job, he thinks I should drop my pants when he snaps his fingers, he just sits there insulting me when we visit friends, and now his mother tries to kick me in the stomach!"

Cindy, who was having problems in her own marriage, snuggled Becky closer and said, "We just have to face it, Lucy: men are no damn good—and the same is true of some women."

I didn't think Mark was no good, but I'd begun to suspect that ours was not the greatest love of all time.

•••

Back when Mark and I were dating, we went to a movie called *Liane, Jungle Goddess*. We were in the backseat at a drive-in and didn't actually "see" the movie, but I remembered and liked the name. It wasn't in my book of baby names, so I looked it up in the dictionary and found that *liana* and *liane* are variations of the name of a tropical vine. I told Mark I wanted to name a girl Liana Sherrine or Sherrina Liane. I got Sherrine from my mom's friend Trudy, who'd named her grandniece Sherene (Trudy said she was inspired by *chérie*; I'd never asked how she spelled Sherene). Neither Mark nor my mother liked the name Sherrina, but we reached agreement on Liana Sherrine.

Boys' names were more of a problem. When I said I wanted to name a boy Byron after the poet, both Mark and my mother flipped. Mark said everyone would tease him at school, it was a sissy name, and we might as well call him Sue.

I worried about names for a boy, read Dr. Spock from cover to cover, arranged and rearranged baby clothes in the pretty white enamel chest of drawers, and told my obstetrician, Dr. Maurice Howard, that if he had to make a choice between my life and the baby's, I wanted him to save the baby. Dr. Howard assured me that I wouldn't die in childbirth: he said he'd delivered hundreds of babies and hadn't lost a mother yet. He was a dignified, white-haired man, a grandfatherly sort who regularly reminded me to take my vitamin pills and said, "Don't worry about it," whenever I brought up the subject of anesthesia.

I was not too wrapped up in my pregnancy to notice that the civil rights movement was gaining momentum and attention. While I waited for my baby, *Life* magazine published several photo essays on the protests. Some of the pictures showed demonstrators being attacked by police dogs or sprayed with fire hoses. Even some conservative people were angry about it. I understood that the world was changing, and I hoped it would come out right.

My due date was July 21. On Monday, July 15, I saw Dr. Howard and again asked about anesthesia. He said, "I like to discuss anesthesia during the last appointment before the delivery."

"This *is* my last appointment before the delivery."

"First babies are generally late. I think you have another couple of weeks to go."

Three days later I woke up with a contraction. I got up and ate breakfast, all the while having contractions about ten minutes apart. After breakfast, when the contractions were five minutes apart, I called Dr. Howard, who told me, "You're in false labor. When I saw you a few days ago, you showed no sign of being ready to deliver."

By noon the contractions were one minute apart. I called Dr. Howard again. He said, "Okay, go to the hospital, but I still think this is going to be a false alarm."

A nurse in the maternity ward confirmed that my contractions were strong and regular and I'd started to dilate. Dr. Howard came to check on me in midafternoon but said, "First babies are slow. I'll come back tonight to see how you're doing."

"I think this baby will be here by then. It already hurts so much I feel like screaming."

"Go ahead. You won't be the first, the last, or the loudest—but it won't make the baby come any faster."

A nurse gave me an injection for the pain, but I sure couldn't tell it was doing anything. I screamed with every contraction for a couple of hours. The way Dr. Howard talked, I thought I'd be in pain like this all night, but at six thirty the nurse said I was ready to go to the delivery room. Dr. Howard was not at the hospital.

In the delivery room I cursed everyone I could possibly blame: Mark for getting me pregnant, my mother for failing to warn me about the pain, and Dr. Howard for postponing the anesthesia discussion. I still had no idea the birth was imminent.

With my first hard push my water bag splattered, and I let out a long, piercing shriek. The anesthesiologist, in his neat green smock, said, "Why don't you shut up?"

"Fuck you!" I screamed.

"Breathe deep," he said, clamping a gas mask over my face.

Ten minutes later, when I woke up, Dr. Howard was stitching me up. "You have a little girl," he said, then told the nurse to show me the baby. I thought the anesthesiologist was a jerk for telling me to shut up, then knocking me out just before Liana was born. He could have quieted me just by saying how close I was to delivery.

"She's lovely," I said, looking at my wrinkly pink daughter. "I'd like a cheeseburger and milkshake now." I had wakened ravenous into motherhood.

Dr. Howard laughed. "One cheeseburger and shake coming up. Your snack'll be ready when you get downstairs."

I waited almost an hour before asking what had become of my cheeseburger and milkshake. The recovery room nurse, who'd heard nothing about my snack, got me a tuna sandwich and a glass of milk. When I complained to Dr. Howard about it later, he said he'd thought I was kidding, that most women want simply to rest after having a baby.

Mark and I brought Liana Sherrine home at noontime on Sunday. She was a gorgeous baby with big eyes and a single blond curl on top of her perfect oval head. I'd dressed her in a white flannel outfit trimmed with yellow piping, and I carried her in a matching receiving blanket. Mark had to climb in a window, because my parents were at church and neither of us had remembered to bring a key.

Liana had screamed all the way home, so I nursed her as soon as Mark let us in. She fell asleep but woke again about three hours later. I fed her again, but this time she didn't go back to sleep; she stayed awake until well into the evening. I'd read that new babies slept most of the time between feedings, and after mine had been awake for about five hours, I began to worry that she might be afflicted with some kind of waking sickness, so I called the pediatrician, who said that all babies are different and assured me that mine would sleep as much as she needed to.

That night I found it hard to sleep myself, not because Liana was fussy, but because I was so concerned about her. I woke every half hour or so and looked in the bassinet, which was next to Mark's and my bed. Each time, reassured by the rhythm of her breathing, I snuggled against Mark, who didn't even wake when I got up for feedings, and drifted briefly back to sleep.

A fanatical mother, I weighed Liana before and after each nursing to make sure she was getting enough milk. I wouldn't leave her in anyone else's care, not even my mother's, and I changed not only her diapers but also her clothes and bassinet sheets several times a day. To keep her receiving blankets fluffy, I brushed them lovingly after each washing.

Having a baby had fulfilled my dreams. As I settled into the routine of feeding Liana, bathing her, and keeping her well attired, I had no fears or regrets. I was now an adult.

•••

Whenever Mike and Steve came over, Mark kissed me and grabbed my breasts in front of them. I finally said, "You're just showing off for them, and it disgusts me. If you don't stop, I'll never have sex with you again." Mark stopped, but I was so turned off I didn't feel much like having sex with him anyhow. Nevertheless, whenever he and his friends told me I should be a Playboy bunny or Playmate of the Month, I considered it a high compliment.

The evening of my sixteenth birthday, Mark said he was going to the Standard station—where he'd recently taken a job—to work on his car. I thought he was really planning a surprise party for me, so I asked if I could go with him. I was playing along. He said, "Sure, but there won't be much for you to do." I dressed up in tight white pants and a purple-checked peasant blouse from Frederick's of Hollywood. I even left Liana with my mother, because I expected that friends would meet us at the station and we'd go somewhere to celebrate. My surprise, however, was that I spent the whole evening sitting on a stool, watching Mark work on his '56 Chevy, with a cigarette dangling from his mouth.

My feelings for Mark had been gradually changing, and the birthday surprise didn't help. My marriage bore no resemblance to the fairy-tale romance I'd hoped for. In my fantasies, Mark had been cast as my prince and savior, but in truth he was just an eighteen-year-old boy who'd been handed an impossible role. When we kissed now, I felt repulsed. It was mainly because I felt let down emotionally, but the fact that he never brushed his teeth was also on my mind. Mark knew my feelings had changed, although I'd never said, "I don't love you anymore," or even, "I'm disappointed." I'd distanced myself from him, and he didn't understand why. He wrote a poem for me with the refrain, "Where has my Lucy gone?" I was touched by the poem, but it didn't rekindle my passion.

In January 1964, when Liana was six months old, Mark's stepmother took me for a ride. We left Liana with my mother and, as usual, I felt anxious and guilty about it. Judy and I had a long talk. She said it would be better for Liana and me, as well as for Mark, if I let my mother take care of Liana more often. I think Mark had talked to Judy and Tom about my pulling away from him, and the three of them had concluded it was because I was too wrapped up in motherhood. Although this wasn't the case, what Judy said made sense to me. She'd gone back to her job as a social worker when her baby, Jason, was two months old, and although at first it was hard for her to be away from him, she said she thought it was important for a woman to have a life of her own. I told her I didn't want to be a housewife all my life like my mother, that I wanted my life to have some greater impact, and I thought I'd be a writer or an artist. My father had always encouraged me. Just as he thought he could win the lottery, he thought I could become a best-selling author or famous artist. It seemed in no way contradictory to me that I'd dropped out of school at fourteen. I thought I'd simply start writing or painting someday.

Liana had been sleeping through the night since she was only three weeks old, but she was wide awake and into everything the rest of the time. She'd started crawling at five months and had already figured out how to get out of her playpen: pile all toys in one corner, climb on top of toys, and dive headfirst onto floor. I really had to keep an eye on her. I wanted more help from Mark, and this was one more sore spot. Since I'd stopped nursing, he'd been willing to do an occasional feeding, but there was no way he'd change diapers or watch Liana for a whole afternoon or evening. He'd bounce her on his knee, toss her in the air, and call her Princess, but when she pooped or he felt like tinkering with his car, he always handed her back to me.

•••

On a rainy Saturday afternoon in March, Mark, Steve, and I drove to Mark's grandmother's house in the Chevy. Steve kept reaching from the backseat to mess up my hair, which I'd spent an hour arranging just so. It was ratted on top to a height of four or five inches. In the back I'd pinned several artificial flowers and a bow; from this bouquet my hair descended to my waist.

I told Steve to stop, but he persisted. I sat on the edge of my seat and said I was serious, but he said, "I'm doing you a favor. It looks better down!" (A few years later I'd agree with him.) When he reached for my hair again, I bopped his chin with my hairbrush, but he wasn't fazed.

The battle continued after we got out of the car. Mark's grandmother wasn't at home, and as he fumbled for his key on the front porch, Steve kept trying to flatten my hair. Fighting back, I hit him on the shoulder with my umbrella, and Mark grabbed it from me. As we entered the house and went to the kitchen for Cokes, Steve was laughing but Mark was not. Mark had a wild look in his eyes. Before I could figure out what that meant, he drew back his fist and slugged me in the eye. I saw stars. Then everything went black and I fell on the floor in front of the refrigerator.

When I came to, the world was still black and I thought Mark had blinded me, but after a few minutes my vision returned. I said, "It was enough to grab the umbrella. You had no right to hit me." He was no longer my husband, but an unfamiliar being with heavy breath and narrow eyes.

"You got what you deserved," he said.

Afraid he might do it again, I didn't argue. I went to the bathroom to examine my puffy red cheek and blackening eye, and I felt a hatred as pure and strong as any emotion I had ever known.

••• ••• •••

Top: *Bob Hoffman on his motorcycle, 1964*
Bottom: *Lucy and Bob, 1965*

chapter 5

Angel on 24 East

At sixteen I filed for a divorce before a lot of girls my age had even been kissed. Mark, who'd been living with his grandmother, came to my parents' house after he was served. He rushed into my room, where I was lying on the bed, reading an article about the Beatles, who'd just completed their first US tour. His blue eyes had a fierce gleam, and his usually well-greased hair fell across his forehead in disarray. He grabbed my left arm and pulled on my wedding and engagement rings, saying I no longer had any right to wear them. I said I wouldn't wear them anymore but insisted they were mine and he had no right to take them. He squeezed and twisted my arm. I told him he was hurting me, and he said he'd hurt me more if I didn't give the rings back. I was scared, remembering when he gave me a shiner, but I didn't want to give in. He kept pulling on the rings. He pulled so hard I thought my finger would come off too. I looked at him, hoping for a softening of his anger, but he was breathing hard and looked mean.

He got the rings off and thrust them into his jacket pocket, then turned to leave. As he walked away, I picked up a glass from the nightstand and threw it at him, but I missed and it smashed against the wall in the hallway outside my room.

He came back in, grabbed my shoulders, and put his face up close to mine. His breath stunk of cigarettes and beer. He said, "I could take Liana away from you if I wanted to, and if you keep acting crazy, I will." I didn't say anything, hoping he'd go away if I didn't argue. It worked. He let go of me with a push and left again.

The judge awarded me sixty dollars per month in child support and eighty in alimony, but Mark didn't pay it. My friend Cindy told me how to apply for Aid to Families with Dependent Children. This meant spending long hours at the welfare office, but I did it so that Liana and I wouldn't be totally dependent on my parents.

The welfare office sent me to the district attorney's office to file charges against Mark for nonsupport. I took Liana with me in her stroller. A wiry baby with blond curls and large hazel eyes, she was now ten months old and had been walking for a month. I had never seen such a tiny person walking. She looked like an animated doll. While I worked on the papers for the district attorney, she climbed out of her stroller, ran down a hallway, and before I could catch her, ran into an open elevator. "That's my baby!" I screamed as the doors clamped shut. I waited in front of the elevator, hoping somebody would bring her back to me, and after a few minutes that seemed like light-years, a woman did. From then on, whenever I went out with Liana, I tried to get Cindy or my mother to come along to help watch her.

Cindy and I spent a lot of time together, sometimes with our babies, but we also started going out at night. Often we dressed alike. We both accented our large eyes with plenty of eye shadow and black eyeliner and ratted our long hair high on top and let it fall in a tail in the back. We bought several identical outfits at Frederick's of Hollywood and Montgomery Ward and, when we wore them, told everyone we were sisters. They believed it, although Cindy's eyes and hair were darker than mine, and her eyes were more almond shaped. I'd always thought she was prettier.

One of our matching outfits consisted of metallic gold stretch pants that fit like waist-to-ankle girdles, gold lamé peasant blouses with elastic necklines that we pulled down over our shoulders, golden necklaces, dangling golden earrings, and shiny gold slippers. Another outfit included tight-fitting beige jeans, black velvet boots, and converted maternity tops with black corduroy panels on the front and back and strips of beige and rust corduroy on each side. We took the tops in and belted them to make a snug fit. With this outfit we wore black and rust rose corsages made of velvet and satin to hide the bobby pins in the back of our hair. We also had waist-length imitation leopard-skin jackets that we wore with black or white stretch pants and imitation leopard-skin boots. My mother often paid for our clothes. Cindy and I talked about having identical leaping leopards tattooed on our thighs, but we never did it.

Sometimes we went dancing at the Penthouse, a teen nightclub in Hayward. One time, when we went there dressed in our beige jeans, corduroy tops, and black velvet boots, the woman at the door wouldn't let us in. She said our hair was too high, but we knew the real reason was that she thought we were prostitutes. We certainly could have been if we'd wanted to, but both of us believed in true love and thought that if we could just make ourselves beautiful enough, we would find it.

Barred from the Penthouse, we went to a closed gas station across the street, where we spent most of the evening talking to a girl in jeans and a black leather jacket. Her bleached blond hair was ratted into a Mohawk shape, and she rode her own motorcycle. She said we should be glad they wouldn't let us into the Penthouse, that the guys there were a bunch of squares who thought they were cool and the girls were all stuck up. She thought about the Penthouse the same way Cindy and I thought about proms, but she couldn't convince me that I was lucky to be at the gas station.

Cindy and I started going to Cicero's, another teen nightclub, and to a bar on East 14th Street in Oakland. The bartender, who never carded us, chatted with us about everything from civil rights to the Beatles as we drank one Tom Collins or Singapore Sling after another, sometimes compliments of the house. We met a lot of boys and men at Cicero's and the bar, but I didn't fall in love with any of them, and I never went out with anyone more than a couple of times.

One man I went out with was about thirty-five years old, tall and angular, with dark wavy hair and an inscrutable expression. As we drove down East 14th Street, he told me he'd murdered his wife. I looked down at my lacy purple dress and thought, *Great. I'm all dressed up for a murderer. Fit to kill.*

I said, "You can let me out here."

"Don't worry, I'd never hurt you. You're too sweet and pretty," he said, turning to look at me.

I studied his pockmarked face and hollow cheeks. Unable to bring myself to make eye contact with him, I asked, "How did you do it?" although I wasn't sure I wanted to know.

"I strangled her. She was no good."

"Did you go to jail?" I wondered what I was doing in this rattle-trap car with this awful-looking man, who was a murderer to boot.

"I went to a mental hospital. I was declared insane."

"I feel sick. I'd like to go home." I really did feel nauseated by my fear and revulsion.

"Don't you like me? I thought I should be honest. l don't want to hide nothing."

"Yes, I like you, but I'm going to vomit very soon. Please take me home."

After this experience I thought twice before accepting a date with anyone.

•••

Not long after my date with the man who murdered his wife, I was walking down Broadway, not heading anywhere in particular, when someone called to me from across the street. It was Bob Hoffman, on a Harley chopper in front of Oakland Technical High School. I knew he must have graduated by now, so I figured he'd stopped by to show off the bike, which had high handlebars and a lot of chrome. Two guys talking to him were looking it over like they were really impressed. I was already impressed myself, even though I hadn't even seen it up close yet. Bob was taller than the other guys; he seemed even taller than I remembered. I also noticed right away that he was wearing a black shirt and light-colored vest, which made him stand out. He waved, and I waved back, then ran across the street and hugged him.

He invited me to go for a ride, and I said sure. I was wearing one of my outfits from Frederick's of Hollywood, blue-and-white checked shorts and a matching bare-midriff blouse with a scoop neck and puffy sleeves. Bob looked at my bare legs and told me to be careful not to burn myself on the pipes. Then I climbed on and put my arms around him, and we took off with a wonderful roar.

I was exhilarated. Riding the Harley made me feel special, like I was someone really important, someone to watch. The Harley was more fun than the rides at the Santa Cruz Boardwalk or Playland at the Beach in San Francisco. It was so much fun that I forgot Bob's warning, and as I climbed off at Kirby's parking lot on Piedmont Avenue, where my friends hung out, my right calf touched one of the two pipes that rose like twin horns on the side of the bike. It was a multisensory experience: I could see, feel, hear, and smell my flesh sizzling. Our next stop was the hospital emergency room. The scar lasted twenty years.

I wanted to ride again, and Bob was glad to take me. He said I was the only girl he'd ever loved and explained that he'd abruptly stopped dating me three years earlier, when he was sixteen and I was thirteen, because his mother had forbidden him to see me after her friend Mrs. May, the Piedmont Junior High School librarian, told her I'd stolen library books. Bob said, "But now I'm nineteen, and I do what I want." What he wanted was to be with me. He even said that when he received Liana's birth announcement, he'd wished she were his baby.

A few days later, when Bob took me to his house, Mrs. Hoffman tried to be nice, but I could tell by the way she kept taking deep breaths that she wasn't happy to see me. My mom liked Bob, but she didn't like to see me on the motorcycle and was worried about what kind of friends he might have.

I wrote a poem about meeting Bob again and riding the motorcycle. The point of the poem was the irony of riding a Harley with someone I'd originally met at a church dance. My mother said she didn't like the part about the motorcycle. As far as I was concerned, if there was no motorcycle, there was no poem. I thought it must be a bad poem, so I threw it away. I didn't understand that my mother wouldn't like any poem with a motorcycle in it.

Bob and I started seeing each other almost every day. He took a lot of pride in the bike, but no more than I did. We both gloated over the chrome scoop and oil bag and the Bates tank, which was metallic midnight blue woven with intricate silvery designs, and we both liked the powerful roar.

He usually told me when he was going to pull a wheelie. He'd ask, "Are you ready?" and I'd brace myself and say yes, but once he caught me off guard. As the front of the bike suddenly came up, my feet flew over his shoulders and he grabbed them. I found out what the sissy bar behind me was for! People watching said my hair was dragging on the ground.

I was always ready to ride. In fact, I wanted to ride more often than Bob did, even though I had to squat on the buddy seat with my knees pressed to his sides, my feet at almost the same level as my buttocks. The summer of '64 I could sit this way for hours and even dance afterward. I loved the sense of freedom and the rush of the wind. When Bob wanted to go to a movie or a party in his black Impala, I'd say, "No, let's ride." Once he said, "Sometimes I think you like the motorcycle more than you like me." This wasn't true, but there was a bit of truth in it: I think Bob was infatuated with me and I was infatuated with the bike.

Sometimes we took Liana to Fairyland, where she could see Little Bo Peep, Humpty Dumpty, and Mary with her little lamb; other times we walked all the way around Lake Merritt, stopping to give her a ride on the seahorse swings. Bob liked it when people thought she was his. I knew he'd make a good father, because he never got bored on these outings. Even so, I wasn't tempted to have another baby. Just one was so much work! I often thought about Cindy, who was pregnant again. She got less help from her mom than I got from mine, and I didn't know how she was going to manage.

I called Bob Cream Puff. Our friends speculated a lot about this. In truth, it was a reference to his soft heart. He hated being called Cream Puff, but I loved to tease him, so he started calling me Grace Dingleberry. He also called me the Christmas Tree, because I wore so many ornaments: dangling earrings, chunky necklaces, and lots of bows and artificial flowers behind my dome of hair. This name was affectionate, whereas Grace Dingleberry was supposed to make me mad.

Bob was a lone rider. He briefly formed a club called the Oakland Outlaws, but he wasn't the type to belong to a club or gang. He was too independent to let his own will be secondary to that of a group. As a lone rider, he didn't always ride alone, though. He was friends with other loners, and sometimes four or five other bikers on chopped hogs rode with us. One was his best friend, Bob Jacoby, whose wife, Nina, was a gorgeous Chippewa girl. My Bob told everyone that Nina was his cousin. He called her Cous and always asked, "When are we going back to the reservation?" However, with his haunting blue eyes and wavy light brown hair, he looked about as Native American as James Dean. Another of the loners was a little guy called Tarzan, whose wife always wore a lot of perfume. Nina said she wore the perfume because she never took baths.

Bob, who worked at a bike shop, met a loner named Rocky there and invited him to ride with us. Rocky was very slender, with fine, straight brown hair. He was in his early twenties, but his face was drawn, which made him look older. His chopper had a plain brown tank and no chrome. I guessed he'd just recently started riding, because he hadn't done very much to the bike. The guys who rode put all their money into their bikes: they always wanted fancier tanks and handlebars and more chrome. At about the time Bob met Rocky, he traded his own bike in for one with more chrome. The new bike had a yellow Bates tank with black Greek crosses on either side. I didn't care for it; I liked the midnight blue one better.

Rocky, Jacoby and Nina, and two other loners—Dick and Roger—met Bob and me at Bob's garage on a Saturday evening, and we decided to head east, toward the town of Walnut Creek. Roger was having trouble with his bike, so he rode with Dick. As we sped down the freeway, Highway 24, I suddenly realized that a stranger was close beside us. The rider turned to face me, and for several seconds I stared at him through my black plastic, rhinestone-studded shades. He was riding a Harley Sportster, and his eyes, too, were concealed by dark glasses. I held Bob tighter as the Sportster rider accelerated and waved at us to pull to the side of the road. The winged skull of the Hells Angels was visible on the back of his cutoff denim jacket.

Bob and the other loners pulled up behind the Angel, and Bob went to talk to him. When he came back, he said, "There's a party tonight. We should follow Birdman if we want to go."

"Sounds like bad news. There could be trouble," said Jacoby, lowering his eyebrows, which made a box of lines appear in the middle of his high forehead. This was the voice of experience: Jacoby, in his late twenties, was the oldest guy in our group.

"You're right, we should keep the fuck away from the Angels," agreed Roger, who had curly blond hair and an elfish face, which now tightened into a grimace.

These guys might be afraid, but I'm not, I thought, then said, "I want to go to the party. I mean, what else is there to do?" I thought about Liana, who was home with my mother. Although I felt a twinge of guilt, I wanted to go to the party, to garner adventure and experience and be with people who knew how to be free. I pictured my parents: my father huddled over *Reader's Digest,* my mother watching *Queen for a Day* on TV. How different from them could I be? How far away could I get? I looked at Birdman, straddling his bike. *That far.*

"I don't want to go looking for trouble," said Bob.

"If there's trouble, we can always leave," I argued.

Bob looked at me doubtfully. "I think it's a bad idea, but if you really want to go to the party, I'll take you."

"I really want to go."

"Are you sure? We could do whatever else you want. How about going to the airport to watch the planes take off?"

"I'd rather go to the party." Watching the planes take off always filled me with yearning. I'd rather go somewhere myself than watch someone else's plane take off!

"Well, I guess the Christmas Tree and me are going to the party," he said.

No one said, "Count me out," so Bob waved to Birdman to let him know we were coming, the guys jumped on their kick-starters, and we rode off, following the Sportster toward Walnut Creek.

The party was in a small white house at the end of a long dirt driveway. By the time we arrived, motorcycles bumping over ruts, the moon was gleaming like a jack-o-lantern grin. Bikes were parked at the end of the driveway and on a scraggly patch of lawn. Birdman quickly dismounted and went inside. Bob and I entered next, followed by Roger, Dick, and Rocky. Jacoby and Nina straggled behind.

The living room was packed with bikers and their women—some standing, others sitting on the floor or slouched on the sofa and chairs. The dress code was denim and leather. Most of the men wore Hells Angels jackets, but members of other clubs were also present. Heavy veils of smoke, illuminated by the glow of a rooster-shaped TV lamp, curled around the people, who were making out or swigging wine or beer. I caught a couple scraps of conversation: "That broad took on fifty dudes in one night!" "I turned the motherfucker into cranberry sauce!"

The loners and I stood near the doorway for a moment, observing, taking it in. Then we moved to the dining room and stood around the table, on which there were several cases of beer, some jugs of Gallo burgundy, potato chips, Dixie cups, and a green glass punch bowl filled with a reddish liquid that looked like Hawaiian Punch but had the greasy shimmer of chicken soup. Several men, huddled importantly in the kitchen, were visible under the arm of a fat Angel blocking the kitchen door. A plastic crucifix hung on one wall. I began to ladle some punch for myself.

"Take beer, Dingleberry. You don't know what's in the punch," Bob whispered. I chugged my first cup of punch and started ladling my second. I felt proud and defiant, a formidable woman. No one could tell me what to do, even if the stuff did taste like varnish. Bob and the other loners helped themselves to beer.

After my third cup of punch, I started feeling rather sociable and began to mix with the crowd in the living room. I was wearing the tight beige jeans and corduroy top in which I'd been barred from the Penthouse. I walked up to strangers and introduced myself: "Hi, my name is Lucy, but some people call me the Christmas Tree. What's your name?" "Dogfight! What an interesting name! How did you

get that name?" I was the hostess, the First Lady at a party for dip-
lomats. It was important that I talk to everyone: "What club do you
belong to?" "The Road Rats! I've always wanted to meet a Road Rat!
Great party, isn't it?" Bob watched from the dining room, a beer can
clenched in his fist.

Birdman suddenly grabbed my arm and pulled me through a dark
hallway to a bedroom. *This is it*, I thought. *Now I'm going to be raped
by a Hells Angel. Maybe he'll change his mind when he feels my pad-
ded bra.*

He led me to the bed, but rape was not what he had in mind. After
kissing me a few times, without trying to feel me up, he sat up, lit a
cigarette, and said, "I want to talk to you."

"About what?"

"About being my woman, about joining the Angels. I want you to
be an Angelette."

I took a good look at him for the first time. Short and muscular
with dark curly hair, he wasn't bad looking. "I'm honored," I said,
"but I've heard you have to fuck everyone in the chapter."

"No," he insisted. "That ain't it. I want you to be my woman. You
wouldn't have to do nothing like that. Only our whores do that. They
ain't even really members. If you was my woman, no one would
touch you, and I would personally take care of anyone that tried. The
other guys would look out for you too. With the Angels you would
have *protection*. A woman like you needs protection. I can see that."

"I've always admired the Angels. People say bad things about
them, but I've always thought they were really straight."

"What do you mean, 'straight'?" He sounded puzzled, and maybe
a little annoyed.

"That they stand by their friends, they're people you can trust, and
when you join, they'll always be there for you."

"You're absolutely right!" His tone was enthusiastic again. "We're
having an initiation next Saturday in Richmond. Will you join?"

"I'll think about it." I wanted to see what a Hells Angels initiation
was really like (I'd heard that when a guy was initiated, everyone
in the chapter urinated on him). I was intrigued, but I wasn't sure I

wanted to join the club or give up Bob for Birdman. "I'll give you my phone number. Call me, and we'll talk about it more."

We began opening drawers, looking for a piece of paper and something to write with. I scrawled "Christmas Tree" and my phone number and address on the back of a layaway receipt for a twenty-five pound bowling ball. Birdman stuffed the paper into one of his jacket pockets, then handed me a white card with red lettering on it that said, "You Have Been Assisted by a Member of the Hells Angels, Vallejo, California."

Terrible crashing sounds came from the other end of the house. It sounded like someone was dropping refrigerators in the living room. Birdman said, "I'd better see what's going on. It might be Crazy. He always gets kinda rowdy when he's been drinking." A glimpse in the mirror revealed that my hair, which cascaded past my waist in the back, was still in a perfect dome on top (I used a whole can of Aqua Net every couple of days to keep it in place while riding). I admired myself for only a moment before Birdman and I rushed out of the bedroom in the direction of the commotion.

Everyone was fighting. The walls were splattered with liquid, and broken bottles were everywhere. A blow sent one man reeling toward the dining room table, one of the few pieces of furniture that remained standing. Even the women were fighting. This was war. In the center of the living room, a huge bald man lifted a chair high over his head, and people scattered as he smashed it on the floor.

Rocky called to me from across the room, "C'mon! We gotta get outta here!"

As I tried to reach the door, bodies fell and rolled around me. People emitted yowls and screams. I made it to the door, but as I stepped onto the porch, the big bald man lunged for me, knocking me over backward, and I fell off the porch and hit my head on the cement walkway below.

Dick and Roger were already on their bike, heading down the driveway. Jacoby was jumping on his kick-starter. More screams, yells, and crashing sounds came from inside the house. A window shattered; a frying pan landed on the lawn.

"Where were you?" Bob asked. "I was looking all over for you. I saw you running off through the trees."

"It wasn't me. I just came out of the house. Someone pushed me off the porch."

"Someone hit me over the head with a wine bottle," he said, rubbing his head. "We're lucky it didn't knock me out—and we're also lucky the bikes are still here."

I looked back at the house to see two men carrying out the sofa and loading it onto a pickup truck backed up near the porch. Another man came running down the stairs, waving a knife. Bob started the bike. I climbed on and we rode off, chased by the man with the knife.

"Are you happy?" Bob asked.

"No." I was scared, still unsure that we would escape without worse injuries.

Rocky, just ahead of us, was weaving all over the driveway, hitting ruts he could have avoided. Each time he hit one, I thought he'd fall. "He shouldn't be riding," said Bob. "He's ripped outta his mind."

As we rode down North Main Street toward the freeway, Rocky was still weaving and wobbling. We pulled up beside him, and Bob motioned him to the side of the road.

"You're losing control," Bob said. "I know where there's an all-night café near the freeway. Why don't you go there and wait. I'll go get the truck and drive you home."

"I'm okay, man. I know what I'm doin'." His speech was slurred, and he swayed from side to side as he straddled his bike.

"Look, I know I can't tell you what to do, but if I was you, I'd go to that café and get some coffee. If you don't want to wait, the Christmas Tree and me'll go with you and have some coffee too."

"I don't need no coffee. I've rode when I was drunker'n this before. Let's get going." He reached up to brush his hair from his eyes, then jumped on his kick-starter.

It was a clear night. Despite the roar of the bikes, I felt surrounded by a peculiar silence. It wasn't a peaceful silence like the silence of my house at night when Liana and my parents were sleeping, but a charged silence, like the silence after lightning strikes, when you're waiting for thunder. As we sped toward the freeway, I watched the constellations. The stars seemed to be spinning in a frenzied dance. I also watched Rocky, who was weaving more than ever. As we accelerated on the on-ramp, he picked up speed faster than Bob and I. He was heading directly toward the island that separated us from the freeway. Images flipped through my mind: I saw Liana curled like a seashell in her crib; I saw myself back in school, not passing notes but listening to the teacher for a change; I saw the owners of the little white house returning from vacation, finding everything gone or destroyed; I saw Bob holding Liana; I saw Rocky hit the island. The impact hurled him into the air, and he landed on the freeway thirty or forty feet from the island. It couldn't be real. It had to be just one more image in the sequence. I looked at the constellations again, then looked ahead. Rocky still lay there. I closed my eyes, then opened them again. Rocky still lay there. I tried to wake up, but I couldn't, because I was already awake.

Bob parked on the shoulder of the road. Jacoby turned around and came back. He knew what had happened because Nina had kept looking back out of fear for Rocky. Dick and Roger, who didn't know, continued toward Oakland.

"I'll call an ambulance," said Jacoby, and he and Nina disappeared the wrong way down the on-ramp.

Bob and I walked slowly over to Rocky. Everything was still. No cars were in sight, and the stars were no longer moving. Rocky lay on his back. His face was very white, and blood was streaming from his head onto the pavement.

Bob kept saying, "I should've knocked him out back there. I shouldn't've let him ride."

"Don't move him," I said.

"I don't need *no* advice from *you*. You aren't the only one who knows anything." Gently, he placed his fingers on Rocky's wrist. "I can still feel his pulse," he said, removing his jacket and placing it across Rocky's chest. "Give me your jacket," he added without looking at me. "Think of someone else for a change." I handed him my beige windbreaker, which he used to cover Rocky's legs. By now a large pool of blood had formed around his head.

We walked back to the bike, and I sat on the ground while Bob took out the two flares he always carried when he was riding. I wanted to say something, but I could only weep, shivering, watching him light the flares and walk away from me to place them on the road.

•••

I woke up feeling nauseous, my head throbbing. I wondered if what I was remembering had really happened. I felt the back of my head, where a painful lump had formed—evidence that I had indeed been knocked off the porch the night before. I remembered the ambulance arriving to take Rocky to the hospital, and following it as it drove away, but I couldn't remember anything after that. I had no recollection of being at the hospital, riding home, saying goodnight to Bob, or going to bed. Could I have been asleep on the bike? Did I have a concussion? Was I unconscious? Why didn't I fall off the bike? Maybe I was in shock. I'd heard that memory loss was a symptom of shock.

I took a bath and tried to relax, but my mother kept yelling at me that I should think of Liana and not stay out all night with undesirables. When I got out of the tub, I started reading Liana a story, but we were interrupted by my mother, who said angrily that a horrible-looking man was at the door.

It was Birdman, in his Hells Angels jacket. I invited him into the house, but he said he'd rather talk outside.

"Are you going to join?" he asked. He looked haggard, and I wondered if he'd slept at all the night before.

"No." I could feel the neighbors watching from their windows.

He didn't ask for an explanation and I didn't offer one. The truth was I'd had enough adventure and experience for a while, and I'd learned something about who I was, or, more precisely, who I wasn't: I wasn't an Angelette. I didn't ever again want to be caught in another melee like the one the night before.

Birdman didn't argue or try to make me change my mind. He just hugged me and said, "Good luck," then rode away.

I waited until afternoon to call Bob, because I didn't want to wake him. Rocky was alive, he said, but he was in a coma and would probably have brain damage. Bob was very angry with me, not for having wanted to go to the party, but for not staying close to him once we got there and for disappearing with Birdman. I told him I was never going to see Birdman or anyone else from the party again.

I felt terrible about Rocky and partly responsible. I didn't think the loners would have gone to the party if I hadn't been there, and I was beginning to realize that one person's influence (in this case, mine) could have significant consequences for other people's lives.

"It's my fault," I said. "I wanted to go to the party." I'd never felt so guilty.

"It's not your fault. We all decided to go to the party. It's my fault: I should've knocked him out before we got on the freeway. I knew he was too drunk to ride."

Bob and I couldn't reach agreement on who was more to blame. My mother yelled at me to get off the phone. She didn't know anything had changed.

Left: Lucy and Mark, 1965
Right: Liana, age two

chapter 6

Tetanus

So much had changed since I was thirteen: I'd married and was going through a divorce; I had a small child. Yet something big was still the same: I was still living with my mother, whom I loved and hated, who was baffled by me, who still yelled and nagged, and who was now acting as though she were Liana's mother as well as mine.

When I was a kid, I'd wanted her to be like Eileen's mother, who came from Nicaragua and spoke with a Spanish accent. Mrs. Capion wore makeup and high heels, worked out with the Jack LaLanne TV show every morning, and knew how to keep a secret. Eileen could even talk to her about sex. My own mother, short and apple shaped, never wore makeup or fashionable clothes (she had a large wardrobe of what Eileen and I called old lady dresses), and her short dark hair was permed into a 1940s style. At sixteen I was making progress in accepting her: I forgave her for being plump and unstylish. What I couldn't forgive, though, was her yelling and lying, how she'd denied for so long that she'd ever had sex, how she was so much more a talker than a listener that I could scarcely get out a couple of sentences before she'd interrupt and go off on a totally different subject, and how if I did manage to tell her anything personal, she'd blab it everywhere.

If I were ever going to move out of my parents' house, I figured I'd need a job, so not long after the biker party, I decided to look for one. I felt ready to move on with my life.

It was August and hot enough to fry a hamburger on the sidewalk, but I set out on foot in my black wool dress. It had a white leather, V-shaped panel in front, which I thought looked sophisticated. I

walked down Grand Avenue toward Lake Merritt, then turned left
on Mandana, which went first uphill, then down, and ended at the
Lakeshore Avenue business district. First I went to the Little Daisy,
where I liked to shop for clothes. I was sticky as a well-licked lollipop.
A saleswoman who knew me asked, "Aren't you hot in that?" They
had no openings either there or at my next stop, the Imperial Café,
where I'd had many a tuna sandwich with my mother. I'd thought
maybe I'd have an in at these places because they knew me, but it
was no dice. They seemed no more interested in talking with me
about a job than they would have been with a stranger.

I walked back to Grand Avenue and caught the number 12 bus
to downtown Oakland, where I inquired about jobs at Woolworth's,
Capwell's, and the International House of Pancakes. My eighth-
grade education and six months' experience selling Beauty Counselor
Cosmetics didn't impress anyone. I stayed at the House of Pancakes
long enough to down a plate of blueberry pancakes before heading over to the phone company. I thought maybe they'd hire me as
an operator. When I arrived at the personnel office, my tight wool
dress was clinging to me like a swimsuit, but that wasn't my biggest
problem. "We don't hire people without high school diplomas," the
receptionist said. She wouldn't even give me an application.

When I got back home, Steve Labate was waiting for me. He
was like a best girlfriend, often arriving unannounced, just as I had
arrived unannounced at his house after school in eighth grade to tell
him and his family how much I loved Mark. Sitting on the old red
tasseled sofa in front of the bay window in the living room, I said,
"You'd think I was applying to give people polio."

More than any other guy I knew, Steve liked to tease and tell
jokes. I thought he'd say, "I'll take some," then start limping around
the room, but instead his dark eyes grew serious and he said, "You
can do whatever you want, but if you don't get a high school diploma,
no one will let you do anything."

"Knowledge and ability should count for more than a piece of
paper." I still thought I knew pretty much everything that people
needed to know.

Steve wasn't much older than I was, but he knew I didn't. He looked exasperated, the way my mother did when I smoked. "Getting the piece of paper will prove you have knowledge and ability."

The next morning I went to enroll at Oakland Technical High School, where classes would be starting in a couple of weeks. When I told the secretary I'd been out of school for two years and didn't have any high school credits, she said, "You'd better talk to the principal."

A tall, businesslike man in a gray suit, he said, "We don't take girls with babies."

I hadn't expected a red carpet welcome, but I'd thought I could go back to school if I wanted to. I said, "I won't tell anyone."

"I can't let you take daytime classes, but you can enroll in evening school."

I signed up for math and English. My mother was not thrilled. This would put her on babysitting duty Monday through Thursday evenings, and she was worried about missing bingo.

Classes started the Tuesday after Labor Day. Each class met two nights a week: math on Tuesday and Thursday, English on Monday and Wednesday.

The math teacher, a soft-spoken black woman, gave me a test on which I missed two problems on addition and subtraction of fractions. She then gave me several drill sheets on fractions. I finished them without any errors, and she gave me several more.

In English the next night, the teacher gave me a workbook with exercises similar to ones I'd done in elementary school: fill in the blanks with *went* or *gone,* put checks by incomplete sentences, and so on.

On Thursday night, when the math teacher gave me still more drill sheets on addition and subtraction of fractions, I said, "How about multiplication and division?"

"Be patient. It's important to practice one thing at a time."

The following Monday I told the English teacher, "I don't want to do these workbook exercises. I'm not learning anything."

She had a lean face and sharp features. "Then what are you here for?"

I was angry and bored. By the third week nothing had changed: it looked like I'd be adding and subtracting fractions and finding the incomplete sentences for the rest of the year. On top of that, I'd learned it would take me eight years to get a high school diploma from Oakland Technical Evening School.

"Can't you give credits faster if someone does the work faster?" I asked the counselor. Her gray hair was frizzed into a permanent, and like the day school principal, she wore a gray suit. In my black stretch pants and imitation leopard boots and jacket, with my high hair and dangling earrings, I must have looked like a visitor from Mars.

"Credits are based on hours spent in the classroom. There are no exceptions."

I looked out the window, where a light rain had started to fall. Although I now really and truly wanted a high school diploma, I couldn't imagine sitting in such boring classes four nights a week for the next eight years, so I said, "I'm going to withdraw."

My mother was glad. She'd missed only two weeks of bingo, and in addition to her not having to take care of Liana every evening, we'd now have more time for dinner, not that either of us was a gourmet cook. I liked to bake, and occasionally I tried a recipe from my *Better Homes and Gardens* cookbook, but the day-to-day reality was that my mother and I served up a lot of hot dogs, hamburger patties, lamb chops, and TV dinners. For variety we ordered Paul's Plates, which my dad picked up at Paul's Grill on College Avenue. Paul made pretty good meat loaf with mashed potatoes, and his franks and beans beat the stuff in a can.

Sometimes we ordered from Chicken Delight, a place that delivered hot fried chicken dinners with french fries and coleslaw. The week after I dropped out of night school, I opened the door for the delivery boy to see Bill Arthur standing on the porch.

I invited him in. He said, "Okay, but I can't stay long. I have a lot more deliveries to make."

I sat on one end of the sofa, and he sat on the other in the spot where my grandfather had worn the upholstery thin. Still wanting to know why he'd stopped calling me after we made love on Christmas

Eve in 1961, I blurted out, "Why didn't you call me again?" as though it had happened two weeks before.

"I didn't want to end up in jail. You were only fourteen, but I was over eighteen." He still had a bad complexion. As I studied his pimples and oversized nose, I no longer found him handsome. "I couldn't have kept seeing you without having sex," he continued. "A man needs sex. I thought there was no way your parents would let you marry me, and I didn't want to hurt you or get myself into trouble. When I heard you'd married someone else, I felt like an idiot." He looked like he might cry. "Nan and I are divorced." I thought he was brokenhearted about losing her, but he added, "I loved you then, and I love you now. I'll marry you now if you'll take me back."

"I think we should get to know each other again before talking about marriage. Besides, my divorce isn't final." I told him about my awful experience at night school. "What I really want now is to find a job."

"Chicken Delight always needs girls to answer the phone and take orders. You should apply, but tell them you dropped out after tenth grade, not eighth."

Lying did indeed give me enough credibility in the job market to land a position as a phone girl at Chicken Delight. When the phone wasn't ringing, I stapled lids onto the chicken plates, and to each lid I stapled a napkin and a package of salt. I wasn't allowed to use the cash register or compute what the customers owed, because the owner reasoned that a dropout couldn't do math, even though I insisted that I could.

What I liked best was making pizza. I shaped the dough into a ball, flattened it a little with my hands, then put it several times through a device like the ringer of an old-fashioned washing machine. Next I swirled on a ladleful of canned tomato sauce, sprinkled mozzarella on top, and put the pizza into one of the two ovens. I felt better about myself now that I had a job, even though I was no better off financially, since my salary was deducted from my welfare check. I saw this job as a step on the road to independence. Someday, I thought, I would be able to leave home.

•••

On a luckless Saturday night, I went to a party with Lucky, who by
now had forgiven me for kissing another boy when I was thirteen.
We had become friends again, but not boyfriend and girlfriend.
About a dozen kids gathered to drink beer in the musty attic of our
host, whose parents were on vacation. When Peter, Paul and Mary
and the Rolling Stones started blasting from the record player, the
neighbors called the police, who followed the music to the attic, from
which there was no escape. When we heard heavy footsteps on the
stairs and saw the flashlights, Lucky turned to me. "Don't write a long
confession like you did when we ran away. I know you could write a
book any day, but don't do it for the cops."

I thought the cops would be easier on me if I cooperated, so I
wrote a long confession in which I admitted to having drunk one can
of beer, swore it was my first beer in years, and vowed never to drink
again until I turned twenty-one. The truth was that at parties I often
drank until I passed out. I drank at home too. It didn't take me long to
consume whatever alcohol was in the house. My mother raged at me,
particularly when I drank in the morning. "You're degenerate! You're
a bad influence on your own daughter!" she screamed. I knew she
was right, but that didn't stop me.

I also wrote that I had a job and a daughter to support, and I might
lose my job if I went to juvie. After I handed over my confession, a
pudgy, balding officer put me into a cramped holding cell furnished
with a single hard bench. A bare light bulb burned overhead. I cried,
worried I'd be sent to juvie. I was in the cell for several hours and
expected to be there all night, but my dad came to get me at about
four in the morning.

The next week a young, dark-haired probation officer dropped by
my house.

I said, "Going to that party last Saturday was a mistake. I'll never
do it again."

I thought this was what she'd come to hear, but she said, "I haven't heard about any party. Your file was lost during a move three years ago. We just found it again last week, and I'm happy to see that you're doing so well and keeping out of trouble."

"I was arrested last Saturday for drinking."

"That's only one offense in three years. I'm going to recommend that you be released from probation."

•••

During the months after Mark's and my separation, the attraction between us returned. No one else could make me feel the way he did. When he came to see Liana, I felt the old yearning.

In October he invited me for a cruise on San Francisco Bay. With a crush of tourists, we took a Red and White Fleet boat from Fisherman's Wharf on a Saturday afternoon. Neither of us had ever done this before, despite having lived in the Bay Area our whole lives. As we leaned against the railing, looking at the Golden Gate Bridge and the San Francisco skyline, he said, "I still love you, and I hope we'll get back together someday. I'm sorry I hit you. Steve told me I was a fool, and he was right. I know now that it's wrong to hit a woman. If you give me another chance, I'll never to do it again."

I believed him and said, "I forgive you." I didn't think I could ever love anyone else the way I loved him. We kissed as salt wind filled our hair and a fog bank stood like a tidal wave beyond the city, ready to roll over the hills. "I'm not ready to go back together," I said, "but I'll think about it."

Each time I saw Mark, we talked about getting back together and getting our own place, but I knew now that marriage to Mark was not my ticket to freedom. A decision to get back together would have to be based solely on my feelings about him. Although I still wanted to get away from my mother, this would not be part of the equation. I was still waffling when, on New Year's Eve, he was arrested for unpaid speeding tickets. This wasn't unusual: he got a lot of tickets, never paid them, and often got arrested. I could understand his liking to speed, but not his neglecting to pay the tickets. It seemed like he wanted to go to jail, and I didn't want to be with someone who was always in and out of jail for traffic tickets.

Early in 1965 I started dating Eddie, who had big muscles and a big smile and liked to wear expensive clothes. He was ambivalent about seeing me because his best friend had been in love with me since I was thirteen. One Friday night Eddie was supposed to pick me up after my shift at Chicken Delight, but when I got off work, he wasn't there. My supervisor, a large black man named Tom, invited me to have a rum and coke with him while I waited. We put our dimes into the Coke machine at the back of the store, and the bottles tumbled down. As we poured Coke and Puerto Rican rum into paper cups, he advised, "Don't make no more dates with him if he don't show. A man who stands a woman up be no damn good."

We finished our drinks, then poured seconds, then thirds. After we'd emptied the bottle, he went to the liquor store across the street to get another, and I called Lucky and his friend Merv to come get me. By the time they pulled up in front of Chicken Delight, Tom and I had finished a second pint of rum.

High as a helium balloon and very angry, I climbed into Merv's truck, which was gritty like Merv. Our first stop was Merv's house. I remember swaying as I talked to his mother, but I have no idea what I said to her. Walking back to the truck, I fell through the front gate.

Merv and Lucky helped me up and put me into the truck, and we drove to the Spartan apartment Lucky shared with his sister, Gayle, who was going with my buddy Steve. Sitting on the sofa, the only piece of furniture in the living room, I called everyone a Mark: Eddie was a Mark, Merv was a Mark, Lucky was a Mark, and even Steve was a Mark. All men were Marks, and they were all no good. That's all I remember.

I woke up alone, lying on the sofa in my pale blue stretch pants and sleeveless white ruffled blouse. It was late morning. I was nauseated and had a dry mouth and pounding headache. I took two aspirins, drank a lot of water, and ate a sweet roll. I had just enough money in my purse for bus fare home.

"Where do you go when you're out all night?" my mother demanded, none too pleasantly.

I didn't answer. I had a romantic image of myself as wild and flamboyant, and I had to do things to live up to that image. Also, I suppose, I still needed to defy my mother.

Liana ran to me, and I picked her up and took her to her room to play. My mother always took care of her when I went out. I wondered how I could ever make it on my own. I'd need to make not only enough money to support us, but also enough to pay for a babysitter when I was at work or wanted to go out. I wanted to be free of my mother, but I needed her. It was a dilemma.

A few nights later, when I saw Merv and Lucky again, Lucky said, "You passed out Friday after saying everyone was a Mark. I tried to find your pulse, but I couldn't feel it, so I put a mirror in front of your nose to make sure you were still breathing."

Riding around all night in Merv's truck, I drank beer and complained about Eddie and Mark. "Eddie is a Mark and Mark is a Mark, but the rest of you guys are okay," I said.

In the morning, after they dropped me off, I lit a cigarette and sat on my bed, trying to decide whether I should get some sleep now or wait until night. I decided to wait, so I changed my clothes, snuffed the cigarette out in the ashtray on my dresser, and went downstairs.

While I ate raisin bran and drank coffee, my mother yelled, "Why do you stay out all night? You're putting me in my grave!" Then she asked me to help her make brownies. While she sifted flour, I melted butter and unsweetened chocolate in a double boiler. As I stirred the dark mixture, inhaling the chocolaty vapors, I heard a scratching noise upstairs. It sounded like someone cutting a screen. Fearing that someone was trying to break into my room, I went back up.

My dresser was covered with flames. As I watched from the hallway, my hairspray can exploded with a loud bang and sparks showered onto the rug. The room was filling with smoke.

I ran back downstairs and told my mother that my dresser was on fire. We were in the hallway by the wall phone. She took the receiver off the hook and said, "I'm going to call your father!"

I grabbed it from her. "What do you expect him to do?"

She grabbed it back from me. "Let me call Phyllis!"

I wrenched the phone from her one more time and put it back on the hook. Then I grabbed both of her shoulders and pushed as hard as I could, so that she fell backward against the basement door. Crumpled on the floor, she looked pathetic—a plump little woman, already dressed up in the nylons and corset she always wore, even with housedresses. I felt bad about pushing her, but I feared the house would burn down before she got around to the only call that could prevent it. "Stay away from me!" I screamed, and she started to cry.

I dialed o (911 hadn't been invented yet) and asked for the Piedmont Fire Department. The spreading flames crackled louder and smoke billowed into the hallway as I gave our address, 81 Cambridge Way. When I hung up, I asked my mother to come outside with me, but she refused. "Then wait right by the front door," I said and went outside.

Smoke poured from the upstairs bedrooms as a large crowd of neighbors and passersby gathered on the sidewalk. Standing on the sloped lawn, a few feet above them, I yelled, "Don't you have anything better to do than watch someone's house burn?" My hair was still ratted and my eye shadow bright from the night before. I paced the lawn, screaming, "Go home to your own house! You have no business here! Get away!"

"Is the baby inside?" asked Mr. Meisner, who lived next door.

He probably asked because he would have gone inside to save her if necessary, but what I heard was morbid curiosity. "Are you crazy?" I screamed. "Would I be out here if my baby were in there?" In fact, she was with her other grandparents, Judy and Tom, who now lived across the bay in San Mateo.

A fireman arrived in a red car. "Where are the trucks?" I yelled.

"They're on their way. Don't worry. We'll take care of this."

Sirens wailed. The trucks were coming down Oakland Avenue.

My room was the only one in which anything burned, but because of the smoke, the whole interior of the house had to be repainted and everything had to be cleaned. I saw this as an opportunity to start over. I wanted my parents to remodel the kitchen and bathroom, get rid of everything in the house (all the reminders of my childhood, which I recalled as a time of my mother yelling at me, boys bullying me, and my aunts and uncles calling me the Queen of Sheba and a spoiled brat), and buy all new things. They agreed to remodel the kitchen, which was something my mother had wanted to do long before the fire, and get new living room furniture, as well as new carpets and drapes throughout the house.

My mother let me get rid of a lot of things but insisted on keeping her bone china, sterling flatware, and silver tea set. Easier for her to part with were my father's books, stamp collection, records, viewer that showed Sally Rand doing fan and bubble dances, and his childhood toys, including a Panama pile driver that both Liana and I had played with, a steam engine, and wooden puzzles. For two hundred dollars my mother and I sold the living room furniture, the rugs, the drapes, my mother's cedar chest, Liana's and my silver baby cups, my father's things, and most of the artwork in the house to Luella, a black woman who did housework for us.

In years to come, I would miss the Oriental rugs, the silver cups, my father's mementoes, and the cedar chest, which was filled with such irreplaceable things as old photos and handmade quilts, and wonder why my father didn't try to get at least some of the things back. Maybe it took him too long to realize how much was missing. I still don't fully understand why I wanted to jettison everything, but I do recall an ongoing desire to be a different person in a different house with a different life. I was slow to accept myself and think fondly of the life I shared with my parents. Also, maybe letting go of everything was symbolically linked to my desire to move out and let go of my mother.

I set to work on a new look for our home. I chose white paint for the living and dining rooms, which had always been pale green, white drapes with gold flecks to replace the old floral print ones, and gold wall-to-wall carpeting to replace the green living room rug and the Oriental rugs in the dining room and entry hall. I also selected white-and-gold plastic room dividers to separate the dining room and entry hall from the living room. They weren't needed, but I found them pretty. In the bathroom I insisted on installing a shelf unit with poles that ran from floor to ceiling, although the poles were too short and had to be supported by plastic cups turned upside down. Proving the fallibility of my taste beyond any doubt, I lobbied to get rid of all the wooden doors in the house and replace them with such devices as vinyl accordions from the Montgomery Ward catalog. My mother let me replace the upstairs doors and the one between the dining room and kitchen. I chose a folding wooden door with slats for Liana's room, a folding mirror door for my room, and vinyl accordions for our closets and the dining room.

In the living room we replaced the classic mahogany end tables and coffee table with modern walnut ones, and the old red sofa with tassels at the bottom with a long modern blue-and-gold striped one. I also wanted to get rid of the mahogany furniture in the dining room and the china figurines on the mantel, but my mother refused.

Maybe my parents' letting me be the interior decorator was like their letting me get married at fourteen. Maybe I was like a steamroller when I wanted something, and they stepped out of the way. Maybe they loved me so much that when my happiness was at stake, they wouldn't even let common sense get in the way. Or maybe they just gave me much more credibility than I deserved.

I got rid of most of my clothes, because they all smelled like smoke, even after being cleaned. Bob took the imitation leopard jacket, cut off the sleeves to make a vest, and wore it when riding his motorcycle.

I had my fresh start, more or less, but I still felt restless and unhappy. I was tired of stapling lids to chicken plates and even of making pizza. Taking phone orders for chicken dinners and pizza, I remembered Mr. Ferry's words from long ago, "If I had your mind... I'd be a doctor or a nuclear physicist." *What if he were right?* I asked myself. *What if I really could be a doctor or a nuclear physicist? Why am I wasting my life at Chicken Delight?*

My social worker, an owlish man in his late twenties or early thirties, said, "You should talk to the counselor at the Oakland Adult Day School. They might let you earn credits based on the amount of work you complete, rather than on hours. Even if they don't, by taking a full daytime course load, the worst case would be to finish high school in four years instead of eight."

The Oakland Adult Day School was housed in the old Chevy plant office building, a red brick structure on Foothill Boulevard in East Oakland. Maggie McCornack, the counselor, was a conservative-looking young woman with dull brown hair and glasses. She assured me I could earn credits as quickly as I could complete the work, but there was a catch. The semester had already started, and she didn't know what level I was working on. I'd have to enroll in the remedial program for the first semester. I argued that I wanted to take regular high school classes and try to catch up, but she said no.

The remedial students worked independently. The reading exercises were not just similar to ones I'd done in elementary school, they were identical. We read passages on cards color-coded to indicate reading level. Each passage was followed by several multiple-choice questions. By answering all the questions correctly on a few cards, you could advance to the next level. At Beach School we'd used these materials from second through sixth grade. Suzanne Crosby and I liked them so well that we asked Miss Baer if we could take some cards home the summer after second grade. When she said, "You certainly may not," but offered other reading material instead, it was hard not to cry. Now, a decade later, it was disheartening to see these cards again, but I tried to make the best of it in order to get into high school classes in the summer.

I wrote stories and book reports, demonstrated that I was at the highest reading level or beyond on the color-coded cards, and showed I could handle fractions, decimals, percents, and long division. The teacher said she didn't think I belonged in the remedial class and asked me to help her teach the other students. She divided the class in two, and we each worked with half of the students. Still, there was no promise that I could enroll in regular classes in the summer.

I'd been at the school for a few weeks when Mrs. McCornack motioned to me as I stood at the blackboard, explaining percents to the class. I put the chalk down and went to the doorway, where she was standing. She smiled. "I talked to Miss Pond, your counselor at Bret Harte. She said you could handle high school classes, so you can enroll in whatever courses you want this summer."

I was pleased to know I could start making progress toward my high school diploma but disappointed that the decision was based not on what I'd shown I could do, but on what someone had said. Still, I was thankful that Miss Pond remembered me.

•••

In the summer I enrolled in English and algebra. The six-week session offered a half year's credit for each course, but I wanted to complete a full year's work, which meant I had to study pretty much constantly, and that my mother had to take care of Liana most of the time. After school each day I sunbathed for half an hour, then studied, ate dinner, and studied again until it was time to go to bed. My mother kept nagging me, saying I was working too hard, but I tried to tune her out and keep working.

For the first three weeks, I kept on schedule, but then I started feeling anxious and tense. At the beginning of the fourth week, I thought I heard the doorbell when I was sunbathing, so I rushed to answer it. No one was there. I went out on the porch and looked up and down the street. No one in sight. As I came back inside, a sharp piece of metal protruding from the bottom of the screen door caught my heel.

I cleaned the wound and put a Band-Aid on it, but I couldn't stop thinking about it. Over the next couple of days, I found it harder and harder to study. I hadn't had a tetanus booster for many years, and I was worried I might get tetanus. I got the booster but kept worrying it was too late. Lying in bed on Friday night, I couldn't sleep for fear I had tetanus. I needed a doctor, and this couldn't wait until morning, because my muscles were already starting to twitch.

I woke my parents and asked my father to drive me to the emergency room at Highland Hospital. My jaw was stiffening, and I had muscle spasms in my arms and legs.

When the doctor, an intern, tapped my jaw, my lips twitched—a characteristic of tetanus. Still, he wasn't sure. "The wound appears to be healing normally," he said with a Southern drawl. "It's clean. There's no sign of infection. You might not have tetanus. If you do, the symptoms will get worse. We'll keep you here tonight and see what happens. If you need antitoxin, we'll give it to you." He paused, gazing at me awkwardly, like he wanted to say something more but wasn't sure he should. Finally he said, "You have a great tan."

The next morning my symptoms were no better or worse. Because I hadn't had a period for about a year, the doctors at Highland thought I had a hormonal imbalance, which could cause both the twitches and the missed periods. They referred me to the University of California Medical Center in San Francisco, and I went there instead of home.

The doctors at UCSF checked for everything from diabetes to a brain tumor. I gave blood after fasting and after drinking sugar solutions; I collected all my urine for 24 hours; I had brain scans. All of the tests came back negative. The doctors seemed most concerned about my missed periods, but I wanted to know what was making my muscles twitch.

After several days of tests, I went home without a diagnosis. The doctors thought perhaps I was physiologically out of whack because I'd had a baby so young, but I didn't buy it. In some cultures it's common for teenage girls to have babies. Biologically, pregnancy at fifteen is normal.

The young doctor from Highland Hospital stopped by my house without calling. He said, "I've been concerned about you and wanted to see how you're doing."

"The doctors at UCSF did a lot of tests but couldn't figure out what's wrong with me."

"I think you'll be okay." He smiled. "I'm from Nashville. I've only been in Oakland for two months. Do you know any good places to go dancing?"

"No."

"Do you have a boyfriend?"

"Yes," I lied. He'd told me he was twenty-six, and that was really ancient as far as I was concerned. Moreover, at about five-five, he was too short. I was now five-nine. God had given me a normal-sized woman's body attached to the legs and neck of a giraffe.

After he left, my mother said, "You're a nincompoop. I'd think you'd want to go out with a nice man like that," but I was still at the stage where I'd take a tall man over an intelligent one any day.

I'd dropped my classes. My twitching muscles were the focus of my life. In my medical book I looked for a disease that matched my symptoms. The previous year I'd impressed Dr. Presant by making a correct diagnosis when I had the measles. When I told him on the phone, he said, "You're too old for measles," but when he saw me, he said, "You have the measles." Now I wanted to figure out what was causing the muscle spasms.

I came across tetany, a disease in which the parathyroids, a collection of small endocrine glands embedded in the thyroid, don't secrete enough parathormone, a hormone involved in calcium metabolism. The result is muscle spasms.

Sitting on the examination table of an endocrinologist I found in the Yellow Pages, I said, "I think I have tetany." A friendly man with a casual manner, he nodded as I described my symptoms. Then he tapped my jaw, making my lips twitch, concurred with the diagnosis, and prescribed calcium.

I took the tablets for a few days, and the muscle twitching began to subside. Then, suddenly, it got worse again. A curtain rose in my brain. *I don't have tetany,* I realized, *just like I didn't have tetanus. This is a psychosomatic illness.*

I went to the endocrinologist again. "I don't think I have tetany," I said. "I think this is psychosomatic, but I want a blood test for parathormone to be sure."

"You don't need a blood test," he said, stroking his chin. "Just keep taking your calcium."

"I want the blood test."

It came back negative, and the muscle spasms went away almost immediately. Now I knew for sure what the problem was, because I'd read about it in a psychology book. "Underlying anxiety," the book said in the section on neuroses, "can be converted into a physical symptom." Great. I hated myself. I'd dropped out of school again and spent the last three weeks of my life in the grip of an imaginary illness. My algebra book was still on my desk, alongside *The Good Earth* and *Pride and Prejudice,* neither of which I'd read yet. I'd rather have been reading the books than obsessing about my health. How could I be a good mother to Liana? I was worse than my own mother. If I was such a mess at seventeen, I wondered what I'd be like at twenty-five.

Was my life worth anything? Maybe Liana would be better off without me. Lying in bed that night, unable to sleep, I considered all the things wrong with me: I couldn't make progress in school, I couldn't get a better job than Chicken Delight, my muscles twitched for no good reason, I enjoyed a glass of wine after breakfast. I was disgusted with myself.

Suicide would solve everything, but I didn't want to commit suicide in a messy or dramatic manner, such as shooting myself or jumping off the Golden Gate Bridge. Carbon monoxide would be simpler and cleaner, but my father was always home when the car was in the garage. Sleeping pills would be best. I knew where to get downers. I'd just go hide somewhere and take them. I hoped no one would ever find my body, because I couldn't bear the thought of my parents weeping at the funeral. It would be better if I just disappeared, so they'd hold out hope I was still alive. I knew I shouldn't be thinking like this and had to stop it.

I kept thinking about my childhood, knowing even then that the disappointments and embarrassments I'd experienced were small compared to the real trauma that some kids endure. Yet I fixated on my own indignities anyway, such as the ridiculous, frilly dresses my mother made me wear as a child when the other kids were in play clothes, and the lessons in manners that took place outside my home. The first time I had dinner with Karen and Patsy Mickens across the street, when I was perhaps five, they made fun of me for chewing with my mouth open and couldn't stop giggling when I sniffed a piece of bread. Mrs. Mickens said, "Don't make fun of Lucille. She just hasn't been taught her manners. All animals chew with their mouths open and smell their food. Haven't you ever watched a dog eat?" *Thanks Mom,* I thought, *for dressing me like a doll and letting me eat like a dog.*

I wanted to die, but I didn't really want to die. Nothing worth dying for had ever happened to me. I didn't know why I felt so unhappy, but I kept thinking about my mother. When I was little, she yelled at me and spanked me every day. She hit me if I accidentally spilled or broke something; she hit me if I made lemonade without permission; she hit me if I forgot to put on my slip. She never struck me hard enough to bruise or injure me, but her slaps kept me feeling angry and hurt. My mother stopped hitting me only when I was ten and started hitting her back.

Liana was asleep in her crib in the next room. I wanted to see her grow up, and I wanted to be a better mother than my own and thought I could be if I could just get my life in order. I wanted to graduate from high school and not have any more psychosomatic illnesses. Now my muscles were twitching again.

Feeling guilty for disliking my mother so much, I tried to think good thoughts about her, how she bought me a lot of presents and always let me know I was the most important person in the world to her. One day when I was small and sick and home from school, I was downstairs in my parents' bed and wanted to watch television. My mother carried my television down from my bedroom. Straining and panting as she put the TV on her cedar chest, she said, "I wouldn't do this for anyone but you."

I got up and put on stretch pants, a sweater, and boots. I'd just go out walking. Maybe someone would kidnap and murder me. Then I wouldn't have to do it myself. *Stop it!* I told myself. *Stop thinking like this. It's crazy. Besides, if I die, Liana will probably be brought up by my mother.*

I tiptoed down the stairs and past my parents' bedroom, headed toward the back door, then turned around and went back to my parents' room. As I stood over my dad, he opened his eyes. "What's wrong?" he asked hoarsely.

"Please take me to Highland Hospital. I need a psychiatrist." Highland had a psychiatric wing, and I knew that people who were freaking out went there at all hours of the night.

As we drove along the empty streets, my dad said, "I know what your problem is. It's that you're smarter than everyone else. It was your problem at Piedmont Junior High, and it's your problem now." I didn't agree with him, but I was grateful. He'd always had unbounded faith in me, and I didn't want to completely let him down.

A middle-aged woman in a dark blue dress sat at a small desk at the entrance to a long corridor. What a strange job, I thought, to sit at the end of a long corridor in the middle of the night, waiting for someone to come in and ask for a psychiatrist or be dragged in to see one unwillingly.

"I want to see a psychiatrist," I told her.

"Why?"

"Are you a psychiatrist?"

"No. I'm a psychiatric social worker, and I'll decide whether or not you need to see a psychiatrist."

"I hate myself. I've recently had psychosomatic tetanus, and I keep thinking about suicide."

We talked for a long time. Then she said, "I don't think you're suicidal, but you certainly need help." She gave me the name of a therapist at Herrick Hospital in Berkeley and told me to call her in the morning. Remembering my experience in seventh grade with the psychologist who talked about a spaceship and the psychiatrist who gave me prescriptions for pills used to control the criminally insane, I was skeptical. I thought maybe I didn't need a therapist or psychiatrist after all, but I agreed to make the call.

•••

The therapist and I sat on opposite sides of an uncluttered desk. The office was businesslike, like a doctor's office. I don't know why I remember this, but I was wearing red shoes and a white sheath with red polka dots. The therapist had short brown hair and gentle eyes. When she asked me to tell her about myself, everything poured out as she took notes on a yellow pad. I told her about my marriage and divorce, psychosomatic tetanus, fantasies about suicide, arguments with my mother, and desire for wine after breakfast when I was feeling low.

We met every week. The sessions were very different from those with the psychologist and psychiatrist in seventh grade, maybe because I was there by choice and she treated me like an adult. More and more, the sessions focused on my mother.

Most of my memories and thoughts of her were negative. I described how when I was little she thought it was cute to make me use words I couldn't pronounce properly or didn't understand. For example, she'd ask, "Are you a male or a female?" "I'm a male," I replied more than once. All of the adults laughed, but I cried, both because they were laughing at me and because I was wrong. "I got your goat!" my mother teased.

When I skinned a knee, my mother would spank me, scolding, "You've ruined your pants!" Scrubbing the wound with soap and water, she'd say, "Why did you do it? Don't you know you can get blood poisoning and die?" How I envied my friends, whose mothers said things like "I hope it doesn't hurt too much" and "Let me kiss it and make it well."

When I was little, I thought she was being purposefully mean to me. I know now, of course, that adults often tease children without knowing when they've crossed the boundary from fun to hurt feelings. I also know that sometimes my mother's anger was just an expression of her anxiety, such as her fear that I might get blood poisoning and die. Even at seventeen I knew that my complaints about her were small on the great scale of things. I had seen Mark's mother's drunkenness and physical violence. But although I knew that my mother had never done anything truly terrible to me, she had done many things that were hurtful and had always been very short on empathy, and I wasn't yet over it.

I told the therapist about my mother's visit to the hospital when I had my tonsils out at five: she kissed me and asked how I liked the hospital (it was boring) and how I felt (my throat was sore). I asked her to read me a story, but she said she didn't have time.

"Please stay."

She turned to leave and I grabbed her coat.

She said, "I'm only going to the bathroom."

"Then why are you taking your coat?"

"Here, you can keep my purse." She handed me her alligator clutch.

After a long time a nurse came and said, "You should take a nap."

"My mommy is coming back to read me a story."

"She won't be back until tomorrow."

"Yes she will. She left her purse," I held up the clutch.

"That's just an old purse she brought for you to play with," said the nurse, taking it from me and opening it so I could see there was nothing inside.

It had been so long since these things happened that I felt guilty bringing them up, but the therapist looked sympathetic. "That must have hurt," she said after I related each incident.

It came down to trust. I couldn't fully trust my mother. I know now that the experts say trust is an important element of mother-child bonding, and when it isn't there, the kid is in for a rough ride. As a child and adolescent, I knew only that it hurt deeply when my mother teased me, failed to comfort me, or lied.

"Maybe I should talk about what bothers me now," I said. We were about a month into my therapy. "I think my mother is competing with me to be a mother to Liana, and Liana is starting to favor her, because Grandma always gives her what she wants when she cries. She treated me the same way, and look how that turned out! I argue with her that we shouldn't reward bad behavior, but she just keeps doing the same thing."

I thought the anxiety that kept me up at night and made my muscles twitch was due to the pressure of having tried to complete a year's work in English and math in six weeks, but the therapist said, "If you hadn't been living with your mother, I think you would either have stuck to your schedule or slowed your pace while staying in school. You need to be independent. Your problems most likely will get worse as long as you live at home."

It didn't take long to find a studio apartment near Foothill Boulevard in Oakland. The rent was fifty-four dollars a month, which I could afford with my welfare check. My father said, "You don't need to move. You'll always have a home here." My mother said, "You're wasting your money, and it's dangerous to live alone. Please don't go." It was August 1965. Liana was two years old; I was seventeen. I was both fearful and exhilarated. It had never occurred to me that I could do this without a husband, an education, or a job, but I moved out, and I knew, as much as anyone can ever know, that I was never going back.

••• ••• •••

SHAPELY AND STUDIOUS—Mrs. Lucy E. Day receives the congratulations of Carl B. Munck, president of the Oakland Board of Education on being nominated for a scholarship by the California State Scholarship and Loan Commission. Although she never attended a regular high school, Mrs. Day received nothing but A's and B's in Adult Day and Evening School and will receive her diploma June 16.

Left: Mark and Lucy with Liana on the day of their second wedding, Oakland, California, November 6, 1965
Right: Clipping from the Oakland Times, *April 5, 1967*

chapter 7

What I Want

I Want Mark

My new apartment, on the second floor of a gray stucco building, had a living room, dining room, and kitchen. The living room had a large closet with a revolving door to which a bed was attached. My green sofa, coffee table, and brown chair were all borrowed from Aunt Ethel, who'd moved in with my parents when I moved out. Before pulling the bed down each night, I had to move the chair and coffee table out of the way. Liana slept in the dining room, which was separated from the living room by frosted glass doors.

My cousin Jan, fifteen and pregnant, was now engaged to a boy named Carlos. He was short, with curly hair and a bad eye. He said she could put his name on the birth certificate and seemed proud to be at her side as her stomach grew rounder.

Jan and Carlos visited me almost every day. We played Scrabble, Monopoly, and Clue. I liked Scrabble best, but Carlos didn't think it was such a great game, perhaps because English was his second language and I always won. Mark, who visited more often than he had at my parents' house, was the only person who gave me any real competition. He was addicted to crossword puzzles and had memorized tons of strange words.

He was dating a nightclub dancer. Steve Labate, who must have felt conflicted but tried to be a friend to both of us, reported that she had long dark hair and large breasts and was in love with him. I'd started thinking seriously about going back to him, and jealousy made it seem urgent. I knew now that arguments and disappointments were part of all marriages, so I no longer expected fairy-tale bliss. He'd apologized for hitting me, which was by far the worst thing he'd done. The other stuff I chalked up to his having been a kid.

Sitting close beside me on Aunt Ethel's sofa, Mark said, "I want to get back together, but I want you to promise you won't go back to school."

I looked at him, asking myself if I wanted to spend the rest of my life with him. He was more handsome than ever, with his irresistible blue eyes and dark wavy hair. His high cheekbones were well defined, and he looked more like a man now than a boy. At this moment my love for him was the most important thing in the world. I hadn't enrolled in school for the fall semester. I said, "I won't go back." I really did want to go back in the spring, but I didn't want to argue about it now. I thought I could change his mind later.

I'd fulfilled my goal of getting away from my mother, but even with frequent visits from Jan, Carlos, and Mark, I was lonely. It was strange to go to bed at night and wake up in the morning with no one around except my small daughter, who frequently asked when we were going to see Daddy or Grandma.

"I want a simple life," Mark said. "A little house with a white picket fence around it, another child—a boy—and you to be there when I come home from work."

I thought of Liana, who understood that he was her father and was always happy when he was around. I said, "I want to be together again as a family." I knew I wanted more. I wanted a high school diploma, maybe even a college degree, and I wanted a good job someday, but this was not the time to talk about it.

He took my old engagement ring out of his pocket and put it on my finger. The wedding ring was lost. He said that the night he took the rings from me, he went to a park to drink with his buddies, and after a few beers he took the rings out and threw them as far as he could. Steve went looking for them with a flashlight, but he found only the engagement ring.

•••

On November 6, 1965, five months after our divorce was final, Mark and I got married again at the Laurel Methodist Church in Oakland. I wore a tight pink sleeveless party dress with a low neck; Mark wore a beige shirt with a dark tie, dark slacks, and no jacket. About a dozen guests joined us in the small sanctuary for the ceremony. The best man and matron of honor were our friends Aldo and Cathi Benassi, who were also Liana's godparents.

I felt both happy and a little embarrassed. I thought I loved Mark and that Liana needed him, but I wondered how much of my desire to marry him again had come from a fear of losing him to the dancer, and how much had come from the loneliness I'd felt since leaving my parents' house. We weren't a perfect match. He wanted to be the boss, but I didn't want to be bossed, and I feared this would lead to trouble.

Steve kept chuckling during the ceremony. I thought he was laughing at Mark and me for getting married again. Afterward I asked, "What's so funny?"

"Look at Mark's back."

Mark turned around. His T-shirt, which showed through his shirt, said "Olympia, Breakfast of Champions."

My new wedding ring was a plain white gold band. Mark purposely bought it a size too small so that I couldn't take it off.

We went to my parents' house for champagne, cake, and hors d'oeuvres, after which Aldo, Cathi, Mark, and I went to dinner at the MacArthur/Broadway Shopping Center, a grungy mall across the street from Mosswood Park in Oakland. Eating my chow mein at the Hamlet—a cafeteria with Chinese, Japanese, Mexican, Italian, and hofbrau sections—I looked at the children playing tag in the aisles, the napkins and food on the floor, and the fat people shoveling pasta into their mouths. This was not the wedding dinner of my dreams. I also looked at my new husband. He was handsome and intelligent, and he was the father of my child. He was also a high school dropout who drank too much and had never held a job for more than a year or so. I felt detached, like I was observing my life rather than living it. I'd also felt that way as a child when my mother was yelling.

Mark said, "A penny for your thoughts."

I wondered how soon I dared tell him that I wanted to go back to school. "They're worth more than that," I teased.

Mark moved into my apartment. A few days later, in the mail at his grandmother's house, he received a draft notice. I was worried when he showed it to me, although I knew that married men with children weren't drafted. I said, "Take our marriage license and Liana's birth certificate to the draft board." He said, "Okay."

Steve went with him. A couple of hours later, I heard his car pull up and went to the door to wait. "What happened?" I called out as Mark and Steve climbed the stairs.

Mark didn't answer until he reached the top. "I don't want to lie to you," he said. "I showed them the marriage license and birth certificate, but I also gave them a letter asking them to draft me anyhow. I said I wanted to go to Vietnam."

I was too shocked even to say, "Are you crazy?" I couldn't understand why anyone would want to go to Vietnam, and I felt hurt and betrayed that he would rather risk his life fighting in a jungle than be with Liana and me.

Steve said, "I told him he was crazy, but he wouldn't listen to me." Steve, who was now a Navy medic and had been to Vietnam, knew what he was talking about.

I looked at Mark for what seemed like a long time, then asked, "Why did you do it?"

"Because I want to serve my country."

I knew the truth was that he wanted to find himself, that he had a yearning even he couldn't name. I knew this because I had a yearning too, and as I looked into his eyes, I could see that his yearning was not so different from mine, but that he would act on it differently. I also knew that just as he had defied me, I would defy him to do whatever I felt I had to do, and that going back to school was high on the list.

The draft board canceled Mark's call-up, and we didn't talk about it again. In December we moved into a rear cottage on Lincoln Avenue in Oakland, below the Mormon Temple. It had a little more space than the apartment: in addition to a living room, dining room, and kitchen, it had a bedroom for us and a sleeping porch for Liana. The landlord, who lived in the house in front, called it his "old Kentucky home." Jan had married Carlos and taken Aunt Ethel's furniture back, so we furnished our living room with an old green rug, a white vinyl bench from my bedroom at my parents' house, and pink and white floor pillows.

Mark went to work as a maintenance man on the graveyard shift at General Foods, where he mopped the floor and cleaned the Jell-O machines. The day's first Jell-O run was always rejected, as were damaged packages. Mark brought the reject Jell-O home for us to eat.

I played games with Liana, read to her, and taught her the names of things. Mark liked to chase her, tickle her, throw her into the air, twirl her around, and give her rides on his shoulders. She was a talkative, outgoing child who wanted Mark's or my attention at all times. When he was out or sleeping and I wanted some time to myself, I would put her over the fence into the backyard next door, where she played with her friends Teddy and Elizabeth, or send her to the cottage on the other side of us, where a girl her age named Wendy lived. I was glad she'd already learned to make friends, but I wished she also knew how to play alone.

If I left her alone, even briefly, she got into trouble: she'd turned on all the burners on the stove, emptied many a drawer, and put her toys into the toilet. I spanked her hands if what she'd done was dangerous, or talked to her if it was simply messy. But she was clever and adventuresome and always thought of some new and awful thing to do, like "painting" the walls with Jell-O, scribbling in my books, or putting Ajax in her hair and telling me she was an old lady. Once when I was taking a bath, she emptied all the perfume bottles and lotions on my dresser into the center of my bed, and after my bath I found her splashing in the goo.

•••

I Want a High School Diploma

In January, when I told Mark I wanted to go back to school, he said, "You don't need to."

"I want to get a job."

"A woman's place is in the home. I'll take care of you."

I wanted to work, but not at a place like Chicken Delight: I wanted an interesting job with good pay. I didn't think I could count on Mark to always support me. Besides, going back to school would be a lot more interesting than sitting around the cottage, and it would help me answer Liana's questions, like "Why is the sky blue?" and "What makes the picture on the TV?" The only drawback was that Mark didn't want me to do it. I asked myself again and again whether it was the right thing to do. The answer kept coming back yes. My father had always thought I was smart, and so had Mr. Ferry and my teachers in elementary school and junior high. Now, more than anything, I hoped they were right and wanted to put it to the test.

In February I reenrolled at the Oakland Adult Day School. It was the spring semester of what should have been my senior year in high school, but I had only one high school credit: a half unit in algebra and a half unit in English from the previous summer. I enrolled in algebra, English, and typing at the Oakland Adult Day School, and a correspondence course in French through the University of California's High School Extension.

Mark said, "I feel betrayed. Before we got married, you said you wouldn't go back."

"I felt betrayed when you wanted to be drafted."

"That has nothing to do with this. Besides, I didn't go."

That night at dinner, looking at me across our gray Formica table, he stabbed at his hamburger patty, strawberry Jell-O, and peas. "You lied."

"I'm sorry."

I shouldn't have lied, but lying had been expedient. I'd wanted to have Mark and go back to school too. This was still what I wanted, and I hoped that once the semester got underway, he'd change his mind.

As I captured my last few peas on my fork, a thought began to form. It took shape as I chewed. After swallowing, I said, "I think there are emotional forces stronger than love, just as there are physical ones stronger than gravity."

Mark banged his fist on the table, knocking over his beer. "I think you're insane."

●●●

After dinner, when I took my books out, I'd ask Mark to watch Liana before he left for work, but instead of reading to her in another room or playing with her quietly, he'd start a raucous game. He chased her around and around the dining room table, where I was studying, and yelled, "I'm going to get you! I'm going to get you!" I always felt like he was talking to me.

He stopped coming home on weekends. After he left for work on Thursday night, I wouldn't see him again until Sunday. Not having him around didn't bother me. I found it easier to study. The problem was that not much was left of his paycheck when he finally came home.

He started refusing to watch Liana. When I asked him to read to her so that I could study, he yelled, "You're a bad mother and a bad wife. Instead of studying, you should watch Liana yourself. Then you should put her to bed and have sex with me!"

One night when I opened my algebra book at the dining room table, he started pacing. "Why do you study so much?" He'd already had several cans of beer, and his voice was slurred.

"I want to be a scientist." I still wanted to be a writer too. No one had told me these were both full-time jobs.

"That's ridiculous! Women aren't scientists."

"Madame Curie was a scientist." I'd read the biography written by her daughter Eve, and making discoveries sounded like a wonderful way to spend one's time. Also, I wanted to understand things at the deepest level. For example, I already knew that DNA was the genetic material that determined people's traits, and I wanted to understand exactly how it did this.

"You're crazy! You're nothing but a crazy woman!" His face twisted into a scowl. "I'm going to have you committed to Napa and take Liana away."

There was no point in arguing. Mark knew as well as I did that the state mental hospital in Napa had not been built to house young women who wanted to be scientists.

Am I going to keep taking this? I asked myself. *Not unless I truly am crazy.*

On a Saturday morning toward the end of March, I picked up some boxes at Safeway, then went back home and packed Mark's belongings: records, crossword puzzle books, tools, clothes. I put the boxes on the front porch and bolted the doors.

When I got up on Sunday morning, they were gone. I was glad Mark had taken them quietly, without yelling or trying to break down the door. Liana was still asleep. I sat on the bench in the living room and cried.

A few days later he came to see me, and we sat on the living room floor to talk.

"I don't want to get divorced again," he said. "It's too embarrassing."

"Tell your friends I was frigid and selfish. Say *you* left *me*."

"I'll miss Liana."

"She can spend weekends with you."

"It would be too painful. I don't want to see her unless I can be with her every day."

"Won't it be more painful not to see her at all?"

He lit a cigarette, took a deep drag, and exhaled. "You just don't get it."

"It's because you don't make any sense."

"I don't want to get divorced."

I thought about his not coming home on weekends, his drinking, and the endless arguments about my going to school. "I can't live with you."

"I won't pay child support." His breath stunk of beer.

"You won't have to. I'll get welfare." I should never have married him again. It had been a stupid mistake. He was immature and also threatened by the idea of my getting ahead of him. I thought he should go back to school too and had told him so, but he wasn't into it. He had his General Equivalency Diploma and was satisfied with that, but I knew he was capable of more.

•••

I Want My Independence

I had my wedding ring cut off at a jewelry store. My second marriage had lasted less than five months. When I told my mother, she recited her mantra—"I hope you get a man with money next time"—but a man who'd graduated from college was higher on my list.

The semester went by quickly. I earned credit for a year's work of English, a half year of algebra, and a half year of geometry. I also completed first semester French by correspondence and started writing poetry, not for assignments, but just because I felt like it. Typing was my worst subject: I was one word per minute short of an A.

In June I attended the graduation ceremony of what should have been my class at Piedmont High School. It was held in front of the school, which looked like a Spanish villa. You needed a ticket to sit on one of the white folding chairs on the lawn. Lacking one, I stood on the sidewalk, behind the proud parents and squirming siblings of the graduates. When Rhoda Basil received a prize in literature, I remembered how Mr. Clarke had raved about her essays and mine in seventh grade. How I wished I'd been there to give her some competition in high school! Watching the students, many of whom I'd known since kindergarten, receive their diplomas, I felt happy for them and terrible for myself. Hoping no one would notice, I cried.

During the summer I completed a half year each of history and geometry at the Adult Day School, as well as a correspondence course on the slide rule, and I started second semester correspondence courses in history and French. I was collecting high school credits with all the zeal I'd once devoted to collecting records and Revlon lipsticks. School was now fun, much more fun than hanging out. I wish I could bottle this attitude and sell it to parents everywhere, but I had to experience welfare, motherhood, a dull job, and a bad marriage to get there. Not a formula to pass around! I hoped to start college in the fall of the following year.

Mark came to visit again at the cottage. This time we sat on the plastic, turquoise-flowered chairs of my new white Formica dinette set, which I'd charged at a store downtown. "I've changed my mind about your going to school," he said. "It's okay if you graduate from high school and work as a waitress, but I don't want you going to college. That's the bottom line."

"I don't want to be a waitress," I said. In the spring I'd tried out to be a waitress at Herman's Koffee Kup on MacArthur Boulevard, but had not been hired because the manager didn't think I moved fast enough. "Besides, I'm no good at it."

"This is your last chance."

I now wanted to be a writer and a scientist as badly as I'd once wanted to get married and have a baby. "I'm passing it by."

•••

I Want to Be Treated Fairly

A local oil company had just started hiring girls as gas station attendants, and after summer school ended, I applied. After running a background check, a woman in the personnel office said, "You have three thousand dollars in credit card bills that have gone to collection agencies. We can't hire you."

"There must be another Lucy Day."

"Do you know Mark Day?"

I knew I was in trouble. Mark had recently gone through bankruptcy. Until now, I thought I'd been cleared too, but Mark had not put my name on the papers, so I was now responsible for his debts. After filing for bankruptcy, I was hired. I went through training with a wiry young man with fine blond hair and a triangular face. In the office at the training station, two burly men gave us each a black binder containing price lists for oil, lubricants, and other products, and told us to memorize everything. We would be tested, they said, and would have to score 70 percent or better to pass.

When the trainers went outside, the other trainee said, "Man, I don't think I can handle this. I never did too good in school."

"After you read each page, close your eyes and ask yourself questions about it."

When we turned in our tests, he said, "I'll be surprised if I pass."

The trainers told us that he scored 98 and I scored 72. I thought they'd switched our scores, so I asked to see my test. They said no.

They sent me to the pump blocks with a wad of bills in my pocket and a coin holder attached to my belt. At the end of the day, they said, "You're eleven dollars short." I knew they were lying and pocketing the money, but I didn't confront them.

I had to work at the training station for a week. Each day when my shift ended, the trainers said I was four or seven or ten dollars short, and that unless I learned to count, I'd be fired at the end of the week. The day before my deadline for learning to count, I went to the administrative office and reported them. The same woman who told me about my debts said, "Those two men are among our most loyal employees. I can't believe they would steal." Nevertheless, I didn't come up short the next day.

I was assigned to a station on MacArthur Boulevard. My mother took care of Liana. The guys gave me tips on how to cheat the customers: give lower-grade oil but charge the higher-grade price, and count wrong when you're making change. I tried these tricks a few times but stopped because I felt so guilty.

•••

I Want to Be Thin

I was eighteen years old but still kept my weight below 114 pounds, my modeling school weight at age thirteen. Sometimes I restricted myself to 250 calories per day. When my body screamed loud enough for food, I binged.

The more I tried to restrict my food intake, the more I thought about food. It all came to a head the day I decided to bake chocolate chip cookies after my shift at the station. The recipe was for four dozen, but I planned to eat just two cookies. After eating a couple of wads of dough, I told myself I'd eaten my allotment raw and wouldn't have any cookies after they were baked. But I had an urge to eat a little more dough. I dipped a teaspoon into the bowl and lifted it to my mouth. Just one more. I dipped the teaspoon into the bowl again, and then again. Each time, I told myself this would be my last bite, but in the end I scraped the bowl clean.

The pain was so intense I thought the dough must be expanding inside me, and that I was going to explode. I watched in horror as my stomach swelled. I called my mother, who was watching Liana. "I'm sick, Mom. I can't pick up Liana this afternoon. Can she spend the night with you? I'll go to the doctor tomorrow if I'm not better." I didn't dare tell her what I'd done.

All night I writhed in pain. In the morning I called in sick at the station and made an appointment to see Dr. Charles Greenwood, the pediatrician who now cared for both Liana and me. I felt better, although the cookie dough was now trampling through my intestines like a herd of wild horses. I didn't want this to happen again. With Dr. Greenwood, I planned to discuss dieting and my periods, which had been absent for two years.

He was about seventy years old, with thin white hair and a gentle, lined face. I said, "I've been trying to stick to 250 calories per day, but I broke my diet yesterday and got sick by eating a whole bowl of chocolate chip cookie dough."

"That's starvation! Two-hundred-and-fifty calories a day isn't enough for survival. You need twelve hundred calories a day just to maintain the functions of your body."

"The only thing that doesn't seem to be functioning is my periods. I haven't had one for two years."

"Of course not. The reproductive function is the first to go: nature doesn't want women to get pregnant during times of famine. But you'll also destroy all your organs, including your heart and brain."

He didn't say "anorexia." It would be years before I learned this word, but he really scared me. I didn't want to be fat, but the thought of destroying my heart and brain was worse. Throughout my teenage years, I had tried to avoid gaining weight, and I had succeeded. That day at Dr. Greenwood's office, I weighed 111 pounds. Now it was time to stop and ask myself, *Why am I doing this?* I was no longer in therapy, but therapy had taught me to examine my current feelings and behavior in the context of my entire life.

It was obvious that, in part, I was rebelling against my mother, who'd been nagging all my life, "You're too thin. You have to eat more!" I was also proving that I was different from my dad, who weighed more than 250 pounds for many years and was solid fat. Even when he was trying to get down to 200 because his doctors had told him his life depended on it, he'd put a mountain of food on his plate, finish it, and go for seconds. When we went to Saturday matinees when I was small, he bought Cokes, popcorn, ice cream bonbons, M&Ms, Jujubes, Mounds bars, Mountain bars, and Hershey bars. Afterward, we went to Fenton's Ice Creamery on Piedmont Avenue, where I'd have a black and tan or hot fudge sundae and he'd have a banana split. At the time, I thought he was indulging me with these feasts of sweets. Now I realized that he'd been indulging himself, and I was keeping him company.

My extreme dieting had been about self-control, something that neither of my parents exhibited much of, and it wasn't just about food. My father was a gambler, my mother a compulsive shopper who had several closets filled with dresses she'd worn only once or twice and would buy sheets just because they were on sale, even though she already owned enough for a hotel. My father had once used up an expensive box of fireworks before dark on the Fourth of July, despite my pleas—"Daddy, you're supposed to wait!"—and both of my parents always opened their Christmas presents as soon as they received them. Even as a small child, I refused to open mine early and begged them to save some of their own gifts to open with me on Christmas Eve. I finally hit on the idea of not giving them their gifts from me until Christmas.

They were the yes-parents of children's dreams. They indulged themselves, and they indulged me. I appreciated their indulgence, but it wasn't as much fun as most kids would think. They let a lot of things get out of control, including me. They let me get married before other girls my age were even allowed to date, and in the end it hadn't been much fun at all. After leaving Dr. Greenwood's office, I decided that I didn't need to starve myself to prove I was different from them, and I headed to Kwik Way to pick up a hamburger and french fries for lunch.

•••

I Want to Go to College

In the fall I quit my job, which like the one at Chicken Delight, had furthered my motivation to do well in school. I could hardly wait to hit the books! I enrolled in biology, physics, and third-semester French by correspondence, and in general science, algebra II, and English at the Adult Day School. My mother continued to babysit Liana. I felt bad about this, because I'd left home partly because I didn't want Liana to be confused by conflicting messages from my mother and me, but I had very little money and no other free babysitting.

I registered to take the Scholastic Aptitude Test and applied to Stanford, the University of California at Los Angeles, and San Francisco State College. Because the Adult Day School wasn't accredited, my SAT scores would be crucial to my getting into college. Aunt Liz and Uncle Bob advised me to take shorthand and advanced typing in case I didn't make it, but I didn't have time. I could have used another typing course; it was still my worst subject.

I ran into Woody, my first love, at the Grand Prix, a nightclub near Lake Merritt, where he was now bartending. He was gangly as ever, but his complexion had improved a lot, just as I had known it would when I first saw him at the skating rink when I was twelve. We started going out, but I didn't have much time for romance, because my SAT date in December was drawing near. I'd bought an SAT study guide with practice tests and vocabulary lists and was working my way through it, page by page.

On a Friday night in early December when I was studying, Steve dropped by to surprise me. He was just back from another tour of duty in Vietnam. I started to put my books away, but he said, "Don't let me stop you. Girl, don't let *anything* get in your way." For old time's sake, he mussed my hair, which was no longer ratted on top, then left, promising to come back after the test.

The night before the SAT, Mark called to say, "Good luck. I hope you make it. I know I've been a fool, and I hope I can make it up to you someday." This meant a lot to me. He was still a kid, but like me, he was maturing.

I took the test on a Saturday morning at Oakland Technical High School, where the principal had once turned me away because I had a baby. I had worked hard to prepare for this and was hopeful at the start, but there were many questions I couldn't answer. The real test was harder than the practice ones, and I felt more and more worried as the minutes ticked by. Whenever the thought *I can't do this* entered my mind, I countered it with an image of myself pumping gas or stapling a lid to a chicken plate. *I have to do this,* I told myself. *The alternatives stink.* If I couldn't answer a question, I took a deep breath and moved on to the next one.

Afterward I felt dreadful. There were so many things I didn't know! How could anyone miss so much and still get into college? I walked from my cottage, near MacArthur Boulevard, to the Mormon

Temple at the top of Lincoln Avenue. Looking at the view—low houses near Fruitvale Avenue, San Francisco Bay and the bridges in the distance—I wondered what I'd do if I didn't get into college.

Someone tapped me on the shoulder. When I turned, Woody put his arms around me, and I started to cry.

"How did you find me?"

"It wasn't hard. I know you pretty well. Now tell me what's wrong."

"I blew it."

"You don't know that. No one can answer everything on the SAT."

"What will I do if I don't get into college?" I looked away from him. It was a clear, windy afternoon, but there were no sailboats on the bay.

"I'll take you to Hollywood, and you'll become a movie star."

We both laughed. I knew it was much harder to become a movie star than to get into college. My most likely alternative would be to attend a community college and apply to transfer in two years.

•••

Mark called early Christmas morning to tell me that Steve's car had skidded off an embankment the night before.

"Is he okay?"

"No. He was thrown through the windshield and killed instantly."

"It must just be a rumor," I said, but Mark said it was no rumor, that he'd talked to Steve's brother Dave, who was in the car behind him. "I think it's a mistake," I said, even as I started to weep. Steve was one of my best friends, and I couldn't imagine never seeing him again.

I wore pink and purple to the funeral, because Steve had always said he didn't like me in black. I felt bad because I'd kept studying the night he came by. I wished I could turn back the clock and be with him that one last time. Mark said, "Steve loved you, and he knew you loved him. He wanted you to keep studying. In fact, he convinced me that I shouldn't try to stop you from going to college. He said I should be proud of you."

Steve didn't have to die. He was speeding, tempting fate. It was ironic that he was the one to die, because of all my teenage friends, he was in many ways the most mature. He understood the value of an education, the wrongness of domestic violence, and the terrible reality of war. He was witty and warm and a loyal friend. Decades later I can still weep for him. He should not have died at nineteen.

•••

I Want a Boyfriend

I was still dating Woody. He was a born storyteller. The tale of a traffic ticket was like a James Bond movie: there was a helicopter, a submarine, and a VW bug careening across a beach, trying to catch him. He was entertaining at a party, but wearisome when I wanted to talk about what was real.

When I complained that my correspondence course in physics was difficult, he asked to borrow my textbook. The next morning he brought it back and said, "I read the whole thing last night. It's actually quite simple."

"What's the difference between a scalar and a vector?" I quizzed him.

"I didn't memorize every detail."

"You didn't even read the first page!"

Woody had introduced me to apricot wine and french-fried artichoke hearts, shown me Cannery Row in Monterey and North Beach in San Francisco, and been supportive when I was studying for the SAT. He was a talented artist whose sketches and paintings looked as good to me as those in museums, but I wanted a boyfriend for whom lying was more difficult than breathing, so I started going out with Jerry, who had fine brown hair and a funny little mustache. Like me, he was a student at the Adult Day School.

Jerry and I got along pretty well at first, but when he told me he'd figured out how to turn a vacuum cleaner into a perpetual motion machine and was going to patent it, I got a sinking feeling in my stomach. I looked at the drawing. I hadn't even finished first semester physics, but I could see that friction would eventually cause the machine to stop.

"It won't work," I said. We were sitting at my dining room table.

"It will too." His little mustache twitched.

"Friction will make it slow down and stop."

"You don't know what you're talking about!"

When a physicist consulted by the patent attorney said the same thing I had, I knew I was dating a nut. The fact that he knew nothing about physics was not the turnoff. It was his cluelessness. How could he think he could break the law of conservation of energy? Or that he could invent such a machine without knowing what the law of conservation of energy is?

Each time Jerry came over, he brought boxes: toiletries, books, clothes. He said, "I need to store a few things here." After the perpetual motion machine bombed, I said, "Please take your things home." He said, "We're living together now. I consider us married." I knew it wasn't going to be easy to dump him.

About a week later, while he was at work, I rented two U-Haul trailers, and Woody and Tom Ogden, who was now divorced from Cindy, helped me move into an apartment on the other side of town. I gave Liana the bedroom and put my own bed and dresser in the living room, along with my bookshelves and the white bench.

•••

I Want Help with My Daughter

Liana was now three years old. In addition to worrying about conflicting messages, I feared that my mother was yelling at her and spanking her a lot, just as she had me, so I enrolled her at St. Vincent's Day Home, a child care center for low-income families.

Liana threw tantrums when she didn't get what she wanted. If a tantrum took place in a store, I'd drag her out, kicking and screaming, but if a tantrum took place at home, particularly when I was trying to study, I'd give her anything to keep her quiet. So much for rewarding good behavior!

She had clothes, food, toys, and a roof over her head. Every evening I spent a couple of hours reading to her and playing with her. I thought I was doing okay, although I knew she wanted more time with me. My schoolwork and boyfriends took up a lot, and Liana was always struggling to get more attention.

Our apartment had a fenced backyard with a patio where she could ride her tricycle. One Saturday morning she went outside to play while I studied. I warned her to stay in the yard, but when I called her to lunch, there was no answer. I went out back to look for her. She was gone.

Now I knew how my mother must have felt when I went on my "famous walks" as a toddler. There is no greater fear. I was about to call the police when the phone rang.

"Are you Lucy Day?" a woman asked.

"Yes."

"Your daughter is in my backyard."

She'd seen Liana playing with her own children and known she didn't live in the neighborhood. Liana gave her my name and phone number. The house was about a mile away, on the other side of the freeway and busy MacArthur Boulevard.

When I picked her up, Liana said, "I wasn't lost. I knew how to get home."

"That's not the point. I have confidence in you, but I don't have confidence in everyone else. In the first place, you could get hit by a car. You're not very tall, you know. In the second place, you could be kidnapped." Her blond curls reached her shoulders now, and with her large hazel eyes she looked like a miniature beauty queen. It terrified me to think of some sick person grabbing her. "Almost any grown-up could run faster than you."

"I wanted someone to play with. I know our phone number. I can't get lost."

"It's not enough for you to be able to call me. I need to know where you are too." I felt like I was arguing with a teenager.

Although I didn't want to rely on my mother again, I thought Liana would be happier, and therefore safer, at my parents' house because there were other kids nearby for her to play with. Also, I expected that my dad would take her to zoos, parks, museums, and movies on weekends, as he had me.

I dialed my parents' number, and my mom answered. "Can I bring Liana over on weekends when I need to study?"

"Yes. When do you want to start?"

"Today."

•••

I Want to Go to Berkeley

I transferred my application from UCLA to UC Berkeley, because I feared that I couldn't make it through college without my parents nearby to help with Liana. Every day I looked in the mailbox, hoping for a letter. My SAT scores arrived first. Though far from perfect 800s, they were high enough to qualify for a State Scholarship and admission to Cal without a high school diploma. In February a notification of admission came from San Francisco State, followed shortly by a rejection from Stanford. I didn't care, because Berkeley was where I really wanted to go. I could hardly think about anything else.

When the envelope finally arrived, I stared at it, wishing for magical powers. If only I could chant over it or sprinkle some herbs to make the news good! I took a deep breath and tore it open. It said I was accepted at Berkeley with full financial aid, and I jumped up and down and whooped. Liana, who was sitting on the floor scribbling in a coloring book, looked puzzled, so I picked her up, twirled her around, and said, "Mommy's going to college!" Then I called my mother.

I was briefly a local celebrity. My claim to fame was that I was Oakland's first adult school graduate to win a State Scholarship. The headlines said, "She Dropped Out, Then Back," "Didn't Attend High School; Wins Honors," and "Mother Gets 16 A's." It was both exhilarating and embarrassing. I received congratulatory letters from the Alameda County Superintendent of Schools, state legislators, and the president of the University of California. I felt good about what I'd done and enjoyed the attention. At the same time, I thought I was getting more attention than I deserved. I'd earned a high school diploma, won a State Scholarship, and been accepted by the University of California at Berkeley. It was similar to what hundreds of thousands of teenagers do every year without such fanfare. Imagine having your high school grades printed in the newspapers. It was surreal.

Mr. Ferry, still stuck dealing with kids like me at Piedmont Junior High, and the science teachers at Piedmont High School had let me borrow equipment for my correspondence courses in physics and biology. When I returned the last of the microscope slides, the biology teacher said, "I cut your picture out of the newspaper and put it on the bulletin board, and I told the students all about you."

"What did you say?"

"That you were the best student we ever had."

My grades at Piedmont Junior High had been mediocre. Maybe he meant that I'd made the greatest comeback of any student he'd ever known or was acknowledging my ability to apply myself. I'd finished high school in three semesters and two summer sessions and would be starting college just one year late.

I was happy to have a good reputation at Piedmont at last, but I was disappointed in myself for not graduating there. In the months and years to come, I would dream about being back there in my black pleated skirt and white blouse, taking a test I must pass in order to graduate. Something would always go wrong: my pen wouldn't write or I'd studied the wrong books or was there on the wrong day, in the wrong class. I'd wake up, knowing I couldn't go back, that I could get my Ph.D. but would never graduate from Piedmont High School.

The first time I saw my mother after getting my acceptance from Cal, she said, "You're the light of my life." I'd always wanted her to accept me for who I was. I think she did (though not without screaming), in that she always loved me unconditionally no matter what I did or how I behaved. Now it suddenly came to me that the bigger problem was that I had to accept her for who she was. She might not have been my first choice at the mommy market, but she was the only mother I had, and she loved me intensely. She could not help being who she was, and there was nothing to be gained by continuing to resent her. I put my arms around her and said, "I love you." She said, "I know you do."

My father was excited that I would be going to college, but he wasn't surprised. He'd never doubted my ability, so my acceptance from Cal came as confirmation of what he already knew. He considered this, as well as my future accomplishments, his and my mother's achievements too. He thought I was who I was not in spite of the way they raised me, but because of the way they raised me. Certainly their belief in me, especially his, gave me the confidence to set goals and pursue them.

•••

I Want to Be a Good Mother

Tom Ogden was courting me. I was still dazzled by his black hair and green eyes, just as I had been at thirteen. He was out of shape, his body a little softer and fuller than it had been when he was in high school, but I still thought he was one of the most handsome men I'd ever seen. He was no cheapskate, either. On one date he rented a plane and pilot and took me on a flight over the Bay Area. On another he took me to dinner at a restaurant where we could pick out our own steaks from a case near the entrance. At twelve dollars apiece, this was the most expensive meal I'd ever eaten. Tom could afford these luxuries because he worked on the assembly line at the Chevy plant in Fremont.

We drove to Nevada to visit my cousin Jan, who now lived in Reno with a Puerto Rican guy named Tony, who would become her second husband. One of Jan's friends, a tall, pale young woman named Rosemary, was giving away puppies, and I took one for Liana, who would soon be four. It was a squirmy little dog with short blond hair. I didn't name it, because I wanted to let Liana help select a name.

We got back to Oakland on a Sunday night. On Monday morning I dropped Liana and the puppy off at my mother's house. Liana was excited to be spending the day with the puppy, which we still hadn't named, instead of going to St. Vincent's.

When she saw the dog, my mother screamed, "That dog's not coming in the house. What in the hell do you want a dog for?"

In the afternoon, when I returned, the little white dog was sprawled on my mother's front porch with raspy breath and glazed eyes. Its legs were splayed at odd angles; blood trickled from the corners of its mouth.

The sight of the broken little body devastated me. "What happened?" I asked my mother.

Standing on the porch, she screamed, "You never should've brought the dog back from Reno. Liana is too young to have a dog. You should've known better than to get a dog." She was wearing nylons, a paisley print dress, and green beads. You'd think she was going out to dinner, but my dad was probably picking up Paul's Plates.

I asked again what had happened, and she told me the story: Liana had repeatedly lifted the puppy and thrown it down on the sidewalk. A passing motorist had stopped and rung the doorbell to tell my mother, and my mother had told Liana not to do it anymore. The motorist left but came back a few minutes later to tell my mother he'd seen Liana do it again. I was dumbfounded, because Liana had always been such a gentle, loving child.

My mother's voice rose in pitch. "Liana wouldn't mind me!" she raged.

"Why didn't you bring the puppy inside or ask the man to take it to a vet?"

"He was a stranger. You should've known better than to get a dog!" she repeated at full volume.

Liana, wearing a pink dress smeared with dirt, reached down to pet the puppy's head. "Don't touch that dog," my mother yelled. I was as mad at my mom as I had ever been. Full acceptance was still a ways off.

What had happened was incomprehensible to me. Throughout my childhood I'd wanted a puppy or kitten, but whenever I brought home a pet, my mother gave it away. It was one of the few areas where she wouldn't let me have my way. I thought I'd given Liana a marvelous gift. I started screaming too, as I whipped Liana's behind. "That's how it feels when somebody hurts you! If you ever do anything like this again, I'll put you in a foster home!"

"You can't give away your flesh and blood," my mother roared. "I'll take her. You can't give away your flesh and blood over a damn dog!"

Of course, I didn't really want to give Liana away. I just wanted to make her feel horrible, to share my pain. I was more angry with my mother than with Liana, but I unleashed my fury on Liana, although she really was too young to blame.

"Why did you hurt the puppy?" I asked her.

"It kept running away. I was trying to stop it. I didn't know it hurt."

I took the puppy to a vet, but it was too late. It had internal injuries and couldn't be saved. Tom and I cried all night. Liana cried too. She wanted the puppy and didn't understand why we couldn't bring it back home.

For the first time since Liana's birth, I admitted to myself that maybe I'd been too young to be a mother, maybe I couldn't handle this after all. I'd failed to teach her the basic fact that all animals feel pain and can die, and I wondered how else I'd failed. I'd always thought my mother was awful at parenting, and now I wondered if I were any better.

In later years, recalling the dog incident, Liana would hold me responsible. I knew about my mother's nervousness, emotional volatility, and dislike of animals. It was irrational for me to leave a dog and a small child with her. That is the argument, and it has merit. However, perhaps due to my own immaturity, I did not foresee the danger.

•••

I Want Integrity

During the summer before I entered Cal, an electronics company hired me as a lab technician, but my boss wouldn't let me work in the lab, because he didn't want me to be exposed to the cyanide fumes given off by a plating reaction. Instead he had me sit at a table in the corner of his office, reading literature about the company and listening to him complain about his wife.

As I walked to the bus stop one day after work, a man pulled up in a white Cadillac and offered me a ride. I was wearing golden hoop earrings and a sleek-fitting sleeveless dress printed with a tangle of ferns, vines, and brilliant flowers (like my mother, I liked to dress up even when I had no place special to go). At first I said, "No thanks," but he said he was the president of the company where I worked, showed me his driver's license, and told me he knew who I was. "Lucy, you don't need to be afraid." I got in. He was a big, muscular man with very short hair. Confident and smiling, he started telling me how good he was at tennis. He wanted to know if I played. I didn't. When we got to my apartment, he said, "I'd like to come in."

Sitting at my kitchen table, he said, "I married my high school sweetheart. I was captain of the football team and she was homecoming queen. I'll never divorce her, but I also need a mistress. I've had several. The most recent one broke up with me and now I'm looking for a new one." It sounded like he was shopping for a car or dog.

"I've visited every continent on Earth," he said, "but I've never met anyone more woman than you." I wasn't sure what he meant, but I knew he wasn't talking about my breasts, because except when I was pregnant, I've never had any.

"If you'll be my mistress, I'll pay for a nanny for Liana, buy you any car you want, and take you on vacations to Europe."

"I don't know you."

He leaned forward and ran his hand down my arm. "We can change that."

I wasn't attracted to him, and I didn't want to be a mistress, but because he offered to teach me computer programming and was president of the company where I worked, I agreed to meet him again.

He took me out for abalone dinners at a little Japanese restaurant in Berkeley. We always went back to my apartment afterward, but we never got around to the programming lessons. Mostly, he tried to make out and talked about all the things he'd do for me if I were his mistress.

The last time he came over, he pulled out his wallet, flipped through a stack of hundred-dollar bills, and said, "Do you need any money?"

I saw myself in a red cocktail dress, in a much bigger apartment with white carpeting, modern furniture, and a view of San Francisco Bay. A Mercedes whizzed through my head. I was at the wheel. He was beside me. I said no.

"I don't believe you." He handed me a hundred-dollar bill. "Take it—no strings attached."

Better judgment jumped off the bridge. I took the bill, used it to buy two dresses, and refused to see him again.

When my final paycheck came up a hundred dollars short, I complained to the payroll supervisor. "The president said he gave you a loan," she explained.

"He gave me a gift."

"You'll have to talk to him about it."

I went to his office. His secretary checked with him, then let me in. He sat behind an imposing mahogany desk. "Have a seat."

I sank into an overstuffed black leather chair beside a potted palm tree about five feet tall. "You never said that hundred dollars was a loan."

"You shouldn't expect something for nothing."

"You said, 'No strings attached.'"

"There are no strings. You're not even being charged interest."

Although I needed the paycheck for bills, by the next day I felt better about it, glad I hadn't taken any money from him after all. That same day a couple of friends gave me an opportunity to fill the gap in my budget. All I had to do was take part in a check-cashing scam. My friends had printed a stack of bogus checks. Someone had to forge a signature, and they offered me a hundred dollars to do it. I knew this was wrong, but I needed the money.

We sat in stained white patio chairs at a small round white metal table in the backyard of my apartment building to discuss it. Al said, "If we get caught, we'll never tell who signed."

"Why don't you or Troy sign?"

"Because if we get caught, it'll go better if the signature doesn't match our handwriting."

"What will you say if the district attorney says, 'Who signed these checks?'"

"We'll say we don't know."

My rent was due, my bank account was nearly empty, and my financial aid from Berkeley would not begin until the following month. Although my brain and stomach both said, *Don't do this,* I took Al's ballpoint pen and signed.

Guilty and *afraid* are not strong enough words to describe how I felt after they left with the signed checks. *Conscience-stricken* and *terrified* are more accurate. I felt sorry for the victims and hoped they'd be able to prove their innocence. I feared losing Liana, my freedom, and my scholarships, and I feared having Liana lose me. I wanted to be there to take care of her when she was sick, read to her at night, and share each day with her as she grew. Moreover, I didn't want to let my parents down after all they'd been through with me, now that their hopes were so high.

Writing a name on those checks had been stupid, maybe the stupidest thing I had ever done. All night I tossed, waking again and again to find I had not been pushed off a cliff and no one was chasing me with a gun. My friends were delighted with the scam, but I was not. I was no longer the kid who enjoyed illegal adventures. I wanted to do meaningful work in the world and be someone Liana could look up to. The first rays of morning light striped the ceiling over my bed with shadows, reminding me of prison bars. I didn't want to go to jail. I wanted to go to Berkeley and study physics, biology, and English. In not too many years, I would stay up all night calculating the allowed energies and wave functions of subatomic particles, study variations in the branchial crowns and thoracic collars of sabellid fan worms, and write about reverie and reality in the poetry of John Keats. My life as a crook was over.

••• ••• •••

Part 2

Left: Lucy in her junior year at Cal, 1970
Right: Lucy with Liana and Uncle Bob at her graduation from Cal, June 11, 1971

chapter 8

Coming of Age at Berkeley

It was a warm afternoon in late winter 1971, my senior year at Berkeley. I was at the kitchen table in my apartment in University Village, reading a stack of research papers for my physicochemical biology class. I lived in one of the old buildings, which were built as temporary housing for dockyard workers during World War II. Thinking about microtubules, I looked up at the huge hanging sculpture of a sperm penetrating an egg that I'd created with copper wire, glass fishing floats, and my Campfire Girl honor beads. At that moment Gil knocked. I knew it was him before I got up. We saw each other a lot, and I guess you could say he was my boyfriend.

"I've got something good," he said excitedly when I opened the door. "Orange Phoenix!"

"What's Orange Phoenix?" We headed toward my mattress in the living room, a more comfortable place to sit. I owned a bed, but it was stored at my mother's house because it was more fashionable to sleep on a mattress on the floor. Liana, now seven years old, slept in the bedroom. Right now she was playing with her friends in the eucalyptus grove across the street. I often sent her there when I wanted to study. Sometimes I felt guilty about studying rather than spending more time with her, but I figured that my getting an education would benefit both of us.

I'd put more effort into decorating this apartment than my previous ones. The living room walls held Indian bedspreads, mirror cloths, my charcoal drawings of friends and animals, and a poster of Tolkien's

Middle Earth. A curtain of fuchsia-colored beads hung between the living room and kitchen.

"Orange Phoenix is the finest mescaline anywhere," Gil proclaimed, taking two orange capsules out of a foil wrapper and showing them to me in his palm. "Truly great stuff. Wanna drop it on Saturday?"

I'd met him the previous fall when I enrolled in Introduction to Dramatic Literature. For my first project I'd selected a scene from *Oedipus Rex.* I'd be Jocasta. I scanned my classmates, looking for someone into whose arms I would like to throw myself while saying, "Oh, Oedipus, Oedipus...." I settled on a soft-featured young man with curly auburn hair that brushed his shoulders. I sat beside him and asked, "Would you be Oedipus for me?" Gil said yes.

He was a dramatic arts major and an archetypal flower child who believed in peace, love, and smoking pot as often as possible. I looked like I belonged with him. My hair, still past my waist, had long since come down for good. I wore moccasins, bell-bottom pants, and peasant blouses to school, long dresses and fringed shawls on special occasions. I'd stopped shaving my legs and underarms and no longer wore a brassiere. I was embarrassed when a blouse or sweater revealed my nipples, but instead of putting on a bra, I draped my hair over my breasts.

Yet I had never taken a psychedelic drug. I'd had plenty of opportunities, but in those days everyone knew someone who'd had a bad trip, and the newspapers carried stories about people who'd been killed by jumping out of a window or off a roof during an acid trip, thinking they could fly. I didn't want to test my wings.

"I don't want a bad trip." I didn't want to miss out altogether on the psychedelic experience, but I was wary.

"People don't have bad trips on mescaline. This stuff is really pure. You won't have a bad trip."

I was a good student, majoring in biological sciences with a specialization in cell and molecular biology, and I didn't want to mess up now. I had applications in to several universities for graduate school, but although I hadn't yet received my official acceptance letter, I hoped and expected to stay at Berkeley and join Wilbur Quay's research group to study age-dependent changes in the levels of brain enzymes and neurotransmitters in mice. In the spring I would be doing my senior honors thesis in his lab.

Since high school I'd wanted to be a writer and a scientist. Emily Dickinson and Madame Curie were my heroines. I'd decided to major in science because I thought it would be easier to make a living as a scientist than as a poet. I hadn't found much time to write during my undergraduate years, but during my senior year my muse woke up. I'd written a lot of poems and submitted some to poetry contests for Berkeley students. As a science major who'd taken three literature classes in college, I knew I was at a disadvantage, but I was hoping for a prize nevertheless (I would receive an honorable mention).

Except for smoking marijuana at parties and rock concerts, I'd pretty much avoided the Berkeley drug scene. My approach to drugs had taken shape at the beginning of my freshman year when, shopping for textbooks for my first quarter classes, I ran into Lucky on Telegraph Avenue. It had been six years since we ran away together. He was wearing blue jeans and a black leather jacket. His boyish cuteness had turned rugged, and he appeared older than his twenty years. He was very excited and showed me a wad of bills, explaining he'd just made a big deal in L.A. I hoped he meant a movie deal but feared he meant a drug deal. I didn't ask. I just congratulated him and hurried on my way.

"Are you sure no one has ever had a bad trip on mescaline?" I asked Gil.

"Well, maybe if it's contaminated with PCP or something, but you won't have a bad trip on this stuff. I can guarantee you that."

"Have you tried it?"

"Yes."

"Okay, let's do it on Saturday. Liana will be with my mom." I was twenty-three years old and had been a single parent for most of the last eight years. My mom did what she could to help, which included babysitting Liana on weekends so that I could study and date.

•••

Gil came back to my place Friday night. I poured two glasses of red wine and put Jim Morrison on the stereo. Gil wanted to make out, but I begged off, saying, "Not now. I've got a lot of stuff on my mind." My attraction to him was waning.

Lately my romantic hopes were focused on John, a graduate student in chemistry who had been one of my teaching assistants in organic the preceding year. He was slender and muscular, with long fine blond hair and a habit of quacking when he thought something was ridiculous. His friends called him Duck. He was taking physico-chemical biology too, and we always sat together during the lectures.

•••

Before starting college, I almost went back to Liana's father to try to make a go of it for the third time. She and I visited him in Carson City, Nevada, where he was working as a bartender and living in a trailer on his mother's property, lovingly known as the Funny Farm. Ellen and her new husband, a gentle man with a round face and large belly, had a small house powered by a generator. When Liana and I arrived, a few chickens were scratching the dirt outside the house, and an old brown mare was grazing in a field of dry grass near Mark's trailer, which was nestled in a patch of weeds.

Liana greeted her father with a hug and kiss, then shook her finger, saying, "Daddy, don't ever run away again!" Mark and I laughed, but in years to come her words would seem more sad than funny.

He was tan and more muscular than he'd been in the city. I could say I was still attracted to him, but calling it "attraction" is an understatement. His pull defied logic and dissolved caution. As I lay beside him in the trailer, breathing in his musky scents, our past arguments no longer meant anything.

My attempts at physical intimacy with other men had been various blends of awkwardness and embarrassment, but Mark and I had been lovers off and on for five years now, and it felt right. After making love, we talked about getting back together.

"I want you to come live on the Funny Farm," he said, "and go to the University of Nevada instead of UC." He said he was proud of me for getting into college and felt like a fool for ever having objected to my going to school.

"It isn't that easy," I explained. "I haven't been admitted to the University of Nevada, and I don't have scholarships there." I wanted him to come live with me in the Bay Area. We were still married. It wasn't too late to begin again.

By the time I got back to Oakland, however, going back to Mark no longer struck me as a great idea. I wondered what had come over me that I had even considered it. I remembered all the fights we'd had, and I feared that if we got back together, there would be many more.

I kept my old engagement ring in my wallet, which I carried with my books in a rectangular basket, open on top, with lavender plastic flowers on the front. My mother was quick to warn me that my wallet would be stolen if I continued to carry it around in the basket, and one day in November it was. When I called to tell her, she already knew more about it than I did: the person who took my wallet had thrown it into the men's toilet at a gas station near campus. The gas station attendant gave it to the Berkeley Police, and an officer called her.

She'd been worrying that whoever threw the wallet into the toilet had kidnapped me, and she was furious. "I told you to leave the ring at home and not to carry your wallet in that damn basket," she yelled. Then she hung up.

The ring had been the most valuable thing I owned. I felt terrible about losing it, but my friends said that unconsciously I must have wanted to lose it. It was an omen that Mark and I would never get back together.

•••

On Saturday morning Gil and I woke to the sound of neighbor children playing outdoors. I got up, put on my bell-bottom jeans and a lavender blouse, tied my macramé belt (I'd made it myself) around my waist, and made chocolate Instant Breakfast and toast for both of us. I thought about John and Mark and my college romances that hadn't worked out. Why did I care? It seemed like a lot of my peers just wanted to go out and have a good time. God, I was serious! Maybe the mescaline would help me loosen up.

Gil took the Orange Phoenix out of the refrigerator and said, "Are you ready?"

I said yes, but I was both excited and scared. I thought any illegal drug might turn out to be something different from what it was supposed to be, and that one or both of us might have a bad trip despite Gil's reassurances. Still, I put one of the orange capsules on my tongue and washed it down with the last of my Instant Breakfast.

We decided to take our trip in Golden Gate Park in San Francisco. As we drove across the Bay Bridge, the mescaline found its way to my brain. The beams and supports of the cantilever section formed intricate geometric patterns, a lattice of thousands of Xs shot through with multicolored beams of light. The great cables between the towers of the suspension span were upside-down rainbows; the towers themselves, reaching up to the throbbing clouds, were dazzling monuments with diamond-shaped windows through which poured the glittering sky. Everything was in motion, as though all matter were alive. Marveling at things I'd always taken for granted, I was glad that Gil was behind the wheel. I was in no shape to drive.

"How are you feeling?" Gil's question seemed silly and clinical.

I laughed. "Great! Do I look sick?"

"No, you look gorgeous." He reached out and took my hand. It was like an electric shock, and I pulled my hand away. I wasn't in love with him, and in my altered state of consciousness, I couldn't bear his touch.

•••

My first serious boyfriend in college had been Geoff. I met him at the beginning of my sophomore year at a reception for Alumni Scholars.

Also a sophomore, he had azure eyes that made it easy to overlook his slightly crooked nose. I had on a very short green dress with white fishnet nylons and white boots. With his neatly cut hair, tan slacks, sport shirt, and blue sweater, Geoff looked like a fraternity boy, which he was.

His parents lived in Europe. His mother, an artist, lived in Amsterdam; his father, though American, worked for the French government and lived in Paris. Geoff read the society pages to find out what his family and their friends were doing.

We heaped caviar on crackers, which we ate with champagne. When we made love, our bones knocked together because we were both so thin. He always scolded me for eating bread with both butter and cheese, saying this was not only unhealthy but also low-class. After we'd been dating for about six weeks, he wrote to tell his parents he was going to marry me. His mother promptly called to say she was coming to Berkeley the following week. Geoff was elated: he looked forward to seeing her and introducing us.

Five days later Mom was in town. She took us to lunch with Granny Bea at Granny Bea's country club, where the tablecloths were very white, the waiters had excellent posture, and everyone recommended the Caesar salad. I'd never had Caesar salad, but I ordered it anyhow. I didn't like it, and I guess my expression said it all.

"Don't you like the salad?" Geoff asked.

"It's delicious, except for the anchovies," I said, trying not to gag.

As Mom and Granny Bea's gazes lifted momentarily and simultaneously skyward, I knew I'd said something egregious. "Anchovies are what *define* a Caesar salad," Geoff explained.

Before returning to Amsterdam, Geoff's mother told both him and his father that our romance "would die a natural death."

In this world where women were called Bea, Geoff took me to dinner at a mansion in Pacific Heights, the home of another Bea, whose daughter he had previously dated. Bea's servants carried in the soup in a silver tureen and the bœuf bourguignon, potatoes, and peas in silver bowls.

Bea asked me my goals, then my Zodiac sign. When I said, "Sagittarius," she asked, "Aren't they the ones who aim high and fall low?"

"I don't know what you're talking about."

Raising her hand toward the chandelier in the motion of a rising arrow, she repeated, "They aim high." She took another breath, then lowered her hand toward the floor. "And they fall low."

I wondered why she wished me ill. Shrugging my shoulders, I said, "I've never heard of that."

My own mother was more eager for the wedding to take place than I was. Every time she saw Geoff, she asked, "When are you going to marry Lucy?" I wanted to wait until we finished college. Geoff said that was fine, but he insisted that I file for divorce immediately, so I went to the Legal Aid Society of Alameda County and got the process under way for thirty-five dollars by typing the papers myself.

I spent my twenty-first birthday, December 5, 1968, studying for my final in linear algebra. I hoped my knowledge of vector spaces and linear mappings compensated for my ignorance about Caesar salad and cheese.

I wanted my romance with Geoff to last forever, but his mother turned out to know more about people than I did. Troubles sprouted soon after she left. He moped around and said he didn't think I loved him when I was absorbed in my studies, and he talked too much about how wonderful his family was. These were not insoluble problems. He drank too much, but so did I. He was eighteen and I was twenty-one, and perhaps this was the only problem that mattered. Although he'd introduced me to caviar and taken me inside a county club and a mansion, he was a kid, and my infatuation waned. We lasted until March.

•••

Gil and I parked near the Conservatory of Flowers. The building was white and gleaming, with a central dome that made me think of the Taj Mahal. It was a radiant palace, its milky glass panes iridescent and, like everything else, pulsing as though breathing. The surrounding grounds were studded with palm trees and adorned with beds of shimmering red and yellow flowers.

"We can go inside later if you want," Gil said. "First I want to show you something." He led me down a path lined with tree ferns that formed a magical forest. I was on a different planet. Nothing was static. It was as though I could see the molecular structure of everything, the airiness of atoms, the vibrations of electrons, the photons whizzing about.

Again Gil reached for my hand, and again I pulled it away. I wanted to be left alone to enjoy the fantastical images around me. I could have spent hours just looking at a tree.

We passed a young woman with a baby in a carrier on her back, and great waves of love washed over me as I thought of my own little girl. I loved her more, I knew, than I'd ever loved anyone.

•••

The summer after my freshman year, shortly before Liana's fifth birthday, we moved to University Village, Berkeley's housing for married students. I enrolled her at the Albany Children's Center, which was two blocks from our apartment. When she came home each afternoon, I could hear her half a block away, singing "Mary Had a Little Lamb" or "I'm a Little Teapot."

She also became very loud whenever I opened a book. When I suggested that she go outside to ride her tricycle in the courtyard, she went out, tossed back her blond curls, and rode around the courtyard yelling and singing at the top of her lungs. The second time this happened, the irate students in the surrounding buildings came pounding on my door to complain.

I didn't own a television, but I started thinking seriously that I should. Maybe if Liana could watch television, she'd let me study. At the beginning of my sophomore year, I went to the financial aid office to see if my award could be increased by one hundred and fifty dollars so that I could buy a TV. I met with a counselor—a tall man, casually dressed in a plaid short-sleeved shirt. "I hope you're being facetious," he said when I asked for money for a television. "A television is not a bona fide educational need."

"Yes it is. My five-year-old daughter won't leave me alone when I need to study. I won't be able to pass math and chemistry if she keeps it up, but I think if we had a television, I could get my work done and she'd be happy."

"I see your point," he said, "but I can't change your award, then write in your file 'needed a television.'" He examined my budget. "You haven't requested much for medical expenses. Most people's medical expenses are higher, especially if they have a child. Don't you think you'll need more?"

I almost said, "No, I have Medi-Cal," but I stopped myself and nodded instead. "You're right. I underestimated my medical expenses by at least a hundred and fifty dollars."

Now in second grade, Liana had recently told me she didn't want to go to the Albany Children's Center anymore. She said a teacher there gave her a piece of paper to draw on, and when she finished her picture, she turned the paper over to draw on the other side. The teacher said she couldn't do that and took the paper away. Liana then asked if she could have another piece of paper. The teacher said no. I said I'd talk to the teacher, but Liana said she wasn't going back, no matter what. I told her this would mean she'd be alone every afternoon until I got home from school, and if she cried for me (as she'd already done on two occasions), the head resident would take her to the police station. She said she understood this and wouldn't cry.

So she ran free in the Village in the afternoon. Some of her friends had stay-at-home moms whose husbands were students. When I told them that Liana wasn't going to the Children's Center anymore, they said she was always welcome at their homes. Still, I worried more than I had when she was at the Children's Center.

I knew I was too permissive, but for the most part Liana seemed happy. She was unusually strong willed and independent, but she seemed otherwise to be a completely normal child. She had a lot of friends, and children were always coming and going at our apartment. She seemed so happy most of the time that it was hard to admit I might be doing anything terribly wrong. She was a good student, and her teachers and the other parents in the Village always raved about what a sweet child she was and what a pleasure it was to have her around.

The preceding Christmas, Gil and I had gotten parts in a play at the Montclair Community Church, where his parents were members. My part was to recite a few lines from Lewis Carroll's "Jabberwocky." At rehearsals Liana took part in the children's group scenes, which included a game of ring-around-the-rosy, and she wanted very much to be in the Christmas Eve performance. However, Mark's father and stepmother had invited her to spend Christmas with them, and they wanted to pick her up the afternoon of Christmas Eve. If Liana took part in the play, I'd have to drive her to San Mateo (a two-hour round trip) on Christmas Day. Gil begged me to let her be in the play. He even had the minister talk to me about it, but still I said no.

•••

As we came out of the fern forest into a meadow, Gil asked, "What are you thinking?"

The grass was deeply layered, forming vibrating patterns. "Liana should have been in the play." I felt guilty, but at the same time, the world was so beautiful that I thought no mistake could be irredeemable. I would be a better mother, I decided, from now on.

•••

After Geoff and I broke up, I still didn't know what to expect from a man, even though I'd been married twice and had a six-year-old child. My vision of true love was still based on the movies, where people fell in love at first sight and battled outside obstacles, not ones stemming from their interactions with and preconceptions about each other. I wanted to fall in love, get married, and live happily ever after, and I fully expected to find a man who had no little habits that annoyed me, never said anything hurtful, was always happy with the frequency of sex and amount of time together that I wanted, was never jealous of or competitive with me, and always did his share of the housework joyfully, without my ever having to remind him.

I called Joe, whom I'd dated briefly the previous year. He was enthusiastic about getting together when I told him I had quit smoking. He was tall and dark, the fairy-tale prince type, wearing not shining armor but faded blue jeans. He was smart too. He'd figured out all by himself that most of the great scientists, writers, and artists of western civilization were male not because women were inherently dumber or less creative than men, but because society had made it hard for them to do anything but tend to household chores and have babies, and had failed to recognize and record their achievements.

Good prince that he was, he enjoyed cooking and did things to food I never would have thought of, like cooking pork chops in beer. He said he'd learned these tricks from his father.

Unlike many of the students I knew at Berkeley, Joe didn't shun material possessions. He wanted to be rich. His family came from Texas, where they'd owned an oil well. When he was in kindergarten, he was chauffeured to school in a limousine. But the well went dry, and his family came to California. Joe dreamed of regaining everything they'd lost and more. His idea of a house was eight bedrooms, six bathrooms, a ballroom, a guesthouse, and servants' quarters. Remembering the grand houses I'd walked by on my way to Piedmont Junior High, I was happy to fantasize with him about such details as a mahogany banister on the grand staircase, tennis courts, an Olympic-sized pool, original Monets, and red-and-gold brocade wallpaper in the dining room.

Group marriages, shacking up, and gay partnerships were all okay by me; the lifestyles of consenting adults were nobody's business but their own. I still wanted a monogamous, heterosexual marriage for myself though, and as Joe made plans to move in with me, I spread the word that we were engaged. In fact, he hadn't actually proposed: I'd told him I wanted to get married, and he'd said okay.

Joe thought Liana should eat dinner with us. Geoff had also criticized me for this, but I thought children should be allowed to eat what they wanted, when they wanted, so I always bought plenty of the foods Liana liked (American cheese, hot dogs, tuna, fruit yogurt, and carrots) and let her fix her own dinner and eat it whenever she pleased. At Joe's urging, however, I now tried to get her to eat with us. She responded by sitting rigidly with her legs straight out under the table, kicking the table, and screaming until I sent her to her room. This happened twice. I couldn't stand the screaming at dinnertime, so we went back to our old ways.

Early in the fall quarter of my junior year, Mark called to tell Liana she had a baby brother. He hardly ever called, never visited, and didn't support her. (We would hear from him only two more times before she turned twelve.) The call raised her hopes that he'd call again or come see her. It didn't do me any good, either: I was jealous, not because he'd had a child with another woman, but because I wanted another child myself.

Bill and Peggy, the parents of Liana's friend Robin, invited Joe and me to a party at their apartment, which was across the street from ours. Joe spent a lot of time dancing with a woman with bleached blond hair teased into a bubble. She was wearing a bare-midriff outfit that exposed a wrinkled stomach. Peggy told me she was twenty-eight years old, had made the outfit herself, and was a high school history teacher, married with two children.

A couple of weeks later, the teacher and her husband invited Joe and me to a party at their house, and Joe spent more time dancing with the hostess than with me. Her husband asked me to dance and I accepted to be polite, but with his ultrashort hair and muscular build, he looked like a Marine sergeant, and I was not attracted to him.

During the following weeks Joe became distant and declined to discuss marriage. When I found the history teacher's address book on my dresser, he confessed that he'd been making love with her when I was at my organic chemistry laboratory on Tuesday and Thursday afternoons. He said he wasn't in love with her, that it was strictly a sexual thing. I believed this and didn't break up with him. In the absence of fidelity, I valued openness and honesty. If my boyfriend had another lover, I would always want to know.

I started thinking that perhaps monogamy was unnatural. Maybe the craving for different partners was programmed into our genes. Whenever the subject came up, I said, "Monogamy is unnatural. It's an artificial social construct that conflicts with the normal human sex drive." I stopped expounding this theory when I realized that men regarded it as an invitation to bed.

Joe sometimes seemed to enjoy hurting people's feelings. It bothered me when he did it to me, but it outraged me when he did it to the children, Liana and Robin. Once they came running inside, saying, "There's a butterfly by the parking lot! There's a butterfly! Come see it!" He said, "I don't want to see your old butterfly." They were crestfallen. Talking to him about these incidents only made him do it more.

On a cold March afternoon, exactly a year after Geoff and I had broken up, Joe was standing in the living room, in front of the heater, when someone knocked on the door. I opened it, and Robin ran past me. "I made this for you," she said, handing Joe a drawing she'd done at school.

"I don't want that thing." He flicked it away like a piece of moldy bread.

Robin started to cry, Joe laughed, and I said, "We're through." Forty years later, I doubt that Joe had an irredeemably cruel heart. Perhaps he was just letting me know he wasn't ready to get married.

•••

Gil and I walked through groves and gardens, stopping periodically to examine a flower beating like a heart, a vibrating pinecone, or a lake in which spectacular murals appeared and disappeared. The world was rich and vibrant, an ever-changing tapestry. I felt lucky to be alive and part of it.

I stood in a meadow, looking at a panorama of trees: redwoods, oaks, cypresses, pines, and eucalyptuses of many shades, not only green. The eucalyptuses had yellow and gray bark, as though painted, and silvery leaves. All of the trees were dappled with swirling bits of red and blue. Above them, clouds formed whirling patterns. The colors, textures, and motions of the trees and clouds enthralled me. It was like being inside a van Gogh painting, and I wondered if this was how the world had always looked to him.

I was ecstatic. Previously, the closest I'd ever come to this feeling was when I was walking across the Berkeley campus—so beautiful, with its groves and rolling lawns, its pink and white rhododendrons, its majestic buildings, and Strawberry Creek running through the middle. I was thrilled to be there after having been a dropout, teen mother, and phone girl at Chicken Delight.

Gil kept trying to hold hands and look at each other, but I wasn't interested in the textures of his skin or the colors of his eyes. I didn't want to say, "Don't touch me," but I hoped he would figure it out.

"What do you think?" he asked as we walked past a stand of redwoods.

"About what?"

"About the mescaline."

I looked at the trees. The needles were various shades of green, lighter at the tips of branches. Sunlight played on them, forming glittery designs and erupting in little showers of light, as though each branch were tipped with a sparkler. The trunks rippled like multicolored water—red, purple, brown, blue, green. Knots on the trunks turned into roses that bloomed as I watched. I knew that Gil was hoping that sharing all of this would bring us closer together and maybe even change my outlook on life. Instead it was having the exact opposite effect. I felt more estranged from him and more certain of who I was. "I think it's marvelous, but I wouldn't want to be in this state all the time."

"Why not?"

"The world couldn't function if everyone were in this state all the time."

"Why not?" he persisted.

Despite the great beauty around me and the pleasure of seeing everything in a new way, I hadn't lost sight of the fact that I also deeply enjoyed solving differential equations, conjugating French verbs, and analyzing poems, and I knew I would never be able to do these things on a psychedelic drug. "You couldn't get any work done," I said. "For example, I couldn't write a paper or solve a chemistry problem." I looked at the clouds. They were sparkling and undulating. I'd never realized how truly gorgeous clouds are. I loved seeing this, but at the same time I realized that I loved my normal state of consciousness more.

"What difference does it make?" His skin was a mass of amoeboid red and purple blotches, his nose large, bulbous, and throbbing.

"The real world is important to some people."

"This is the real world."

I turned away from him to enjoy the trees.

•••

During my sophomore year I learned that I was not a political radical. That spring, 1969, a group of students, hippies, and community activists took over a plot of land owned by the university. They planted grass, vegetables, and flowers, and named their creation People's Park. The university erected a fence around the site, police and National Guardsmen were called in to defend it, and a police officer shot and killed a twenty-five-year-old student named James Rector.

I stayed away. People's Park was not worth dying for. To me, the university didn't represent oppression, tyranny, or the military-industrial complex: it meant opportunity, freedom, and knowledge. The day after Rector's death, when I saw a crowd of about three thousand people swarming on Sproul Plaza, I headed toward the lower plaza to go home, but all the exits on the south side of campus were blocked by chains of National Guardsmen holding bayonets. When I went up to one and said, "Excuse me, may I please pass?" the young soldier pointed his bayonet at me.

There was no place to go but back up to Sproul Plaza. A helicopter buzzed overhead. I pushed my way through the crowd near Sather Gate and ran toward Dwinelle Hall, hoping the north or west gate of campus would be open. As I crossed the bridge over Strawberry

Creek, the helicopter swooped low, crop dusting the protesters with tear gas. Now it was hard to run, because I was choking on sharp splinters of air, my eyes bathed in onion juice. Coughing and trying to catch my breath, I entered Dwinelle Hall and splashed my eyes with water from a drinking fountain, but it didn't help. I sat on the floor in a hallway and waited to recover enough to go home.

At Berkeley in those days, protests came as regularly as finals. They were part of the cycle of campus life and especially plentiful in the spring. At first I didn't take part in the antiwar protests, but as the war in Southeast Asia escalated, I decided to join a march. It started at the west gate of campus. I noticed right away that many of the protesters were armed with bricks. As we passed the Life Sciences Building, they threw the bricks at the windows, and I felt queasy and dismayed. They also set trash cans on fire, shouting, "Burn it down! Burn it down!" I didn't think burning down the university was going to help anyone. It didn't even make a rational point. So I walked away, back to the small trials of my own life.

•••

I stopped to examine a leaf. It was large as an elephant ear and as scaly as the skin of a lizard, with exquisite, multicolored diamond designs on a green background. It reminded me of Indian beadwork, and I wanted to remember it. I might not ever take mescaline again, and I wouldn't get to see this leaf again even if I did.

Gil said, "Look at that," pointing to a red car parked by the side of the road. I suppose he saw something magnificent there, but I didn't want to be interrupted.

We reached the buffalo herd just beyond Spreckels Lake. They were stunning horned and bearded creatures with elegant brown-orange coats on their backs and darker fur on their bellies. As I watched, their coats changed to red and yellow, and they grew to the size of dinosaurs, then shrunk to the size of cows.

I could have watched the buffalo forever, but it was getting late and we were hungry, so we walked back to the car. When we reached the Conservatory of Flowers, I realized that the pyrotechnics were waning. The building was still lovely, but no longer otherworldly. We agreed to get pizza in Berkeley and headed for the bridge.

•••

As I drove to my mother's house the following day to pick up Liana, I was back inside my everyday mind, but things were different. I had broken up with Gil and decided to make my move with John on Monday after our physicochemical biology lecture.

If he still didn't ask me out, I would say I was having a party on Friday and he was invited. If he said he'd come, I would invite Tim, Gil, Bill and Peggy, and Vera, who'd gotten the part I'd wanted in the Dramatic Art Department's production of *Danton's Death*. I would also invite the members of Prince Bakaradi, a rock band whose bass guitarist I'd met in organic chemistry, and I would tell everyone to bring their friends. I'd get beer, Coca-Cola, potato chips, crackers, cheese, and a couple of jugs of Chianti and put the Who and the Stones and the Beatles on the stereo. John would show up without a date, and we would sit on the mattress to talk, at first about the physicochemical biology lectures, but then he would ask if I had a boyfriend. When I said no, he would ask me to dance.

When I entered my mom and dad's house, Liana rushed into my arms and hugged me as though I'd been in New York for six months. The feelings of intense love I'd felt the previous day when I saw the woman and baby washed over me again, and I held Liana closer.

My mom came into the room, and when I let go of Liana, she opened her arms and hugged me too, saying, "I love you too, Lucy. You're my best friend." More waves of love broke over me. I remembered how as a teenager I'd resented her so strongly that I lived to defy her and was obsessed by all the ways she'd hurt me when I was a child. I couldn't even get going in high school until I moved out of her home. Somewhere along the line, I now realized, it had stopped mattering that she'd snuck out of the house, leaving me with babysitters, and yelled at me when I skinned my knees. I had forgiven everything: the yelling, the spankings, and the lies. I accepted that she wasn't perfect. Why should she be? Nobody else was. She did my laundry, babysat Liana for free, and listened intently to blow-by-blow accounts of my failed romances. Maybe she was my best friend too. The thought made me laugh.

Top: Lucy and Ben's wedding, June 23, 1974
Bottom: Lucy and Tamarind, 1977

chapter 9

Polynesian Spectacular

The woman at the tours and tickets desk said, "The Polynesian Spectacular at the hotel across the street is the best show in the islands. Best fire dancer in the world." Yolanda and I paid our ten dollars apiece. We were in Hawaii! Which meant no husbands, no babies, no diapers. For a whole week. Through swarms of Japanese tourists slung with Nikons and Minoltas, we pushed our way to the street. Our skirts billowed slightly as we walked. It was 1975, a nice warm January night.

We'd both given birth to a second child the previous summer—a girl for me, a boy for Yolanda. I'd met her seventeen years earlier, the day she was introduced as the new girl in my third grade class. Like my parents, we made an odd couple. I towered over her, had long, straight, light brown hair, and wore little makeup. She wore her dark brown hair in a semibouffant style, freshly permed and frosted with a pale shade of blond, and didn't even go to the beach without mascara, eye shadow, blush, and bright pink lipstick. In Honolulu the waiters had been addressing me almost exclusively, offering me the wine for approval and giving me the checks. We giggled about it, but I could tell she wasn't altogether pleased. Married since she was eighteen, she was looking for adventure. I was ready to resume work on my doctorate in science and math education after this getaway. My father was taking care of my baby while my husband, Ben, a substitute teacher, was at work. We'd been together for three years and unhappily married for one. I needed to get perspective.

•••

Ben and I met on April Fool's Day in 1972, when my friend Paul, a graduate student in biophysics at Berkeley and fellow teaching assistant in Biology 1, had a party to celebrate selling his house. His real estate agent was a friend who'd just gotten her real estate license; the buyers were sex therapists who lived across the street. The real estate agent was a member of the Berkeley Poets Cooperative, and all the members of the co-op, as well as Paul's friends and the sex therapists and their clients, were invited to the party.

I wore a purple velvet headband, purple corduroy bell-bottom pants, a full-sleeved white blouse, and a black velvet Pakistani vest trimmed with silver cord and embroidered with red, blue, and purple birds and flowers. Tiny silver bells, hanging from the clasp, jingled as I walked. Since the sixties lasted well into the seventies in Berkeley, the ethnic pirate look was not unstylish. When I arrived, the door was unlocked, the house already packed. A man with black leather pants and a natural that tripled the diameter of his head was laughing on the sofa with a bald man dressed all in white and a sparrow-like girl wrapped in a gold sari and wearing a ring in her nose. A sophisticated-looking black woman in a slinky red dress leaned against the mantle and nodded her head in time to the speech of an animated little man in blue jeans and a work shirt.

Paul was in the kitchen. I kissed him hello, then went to the dining room to get a glass of wine and something to munch on. With wine in hand and cheese in mouth, I leaned against the doorpost between the dining room and entry hall and tapped my foot in time to "Love the One You're With." Someone touched my shoulder, and I turned to face a man with curly dark brown hair and a large, silly grin. He looked familiar, a little like Abbie Hoffman, who'd recently been in the newspapers and on TV. In baggy gray jeans and a worn cotton knit shirt, he did not appear to have given much thought to his clothes. He said, "You look like you want to dance."

We shimmied and gyrated to the rhythms of the Rolling Stones, Big Brother, and Joe Tex. After each song one of us said, "Again?" and the other said yes. He didn't look at me as we danced. He was a dervish—spinning, twisting, and swiveling his hips in a self-absorbed frenzy. At first I tried to get his attention: I shook my hips like a belly dancer, I twisted so low I was practically kneeling on the floor, and I gestured so broadly that I hit a woman dancing nearby on the side of the head. All to no avail. When I finally gave up, I felt liberated, realizing that to dance with Ben I didn't need to be a good dancer; indeed, I didn't need to be dancing at all.

When we stopped to refuel with French bread, salami, and stuffed celery, I learned that he had a master's degree in physics from the University of Chicago, had been laid off from his most recent job as a high-voltage physicist, and was now working as a substitute teacher. He wrote poetry and was a cofounder of the Berkeley Poets Co-op. I was a graduate student, working on my M.A. in zoology. It was refreshing to meet a man who was neither a student nor a professor. There was no talk of his dissertation or classes, no gossip about campus politics or romances, and no fear of failing his orals. Looking at my left ear, he asked where I'd gone to high school. I couldn't remember the last time anyone had asked me that, and I laughed.

Sitting close on the sofa, we drank wine, then beer. The man in black leather pants kept passing joints our way. I no longer liked marijuana. It made me feel like an Alzheimer's victim, but I took a couple of hits anyhow, because I didn't want Ben to think I was uncool. A slender woman with auburn hair approached us. She was holding the hand of a shorter, older man with round cheeks. "Would you like to dance with us?" she asked.

Cream's "Strange Brew" blasted on the stereo. First I faced Ben, whose eyes still didn't meet mine; then Sena, who smiled mischievously; then Helmut, who was considerably shorter than I and seemed to be staring appreciatively at my flat chest. Then we formed a square, all facing toward the center. Sena's graceful movements contrasted with Helmut's smaller, jerkier ones. Ben was in a frenzy again, swiveling his rib cage and hips and leaning so far backward I thought he might fall over. His energy was impressive.

When the music stopped, Sena smiled broadly, revealing her gums. "Have you ever had a four-way kiss?" she asked. Ben looked at me, just as surprised as I was. We both shook our heads. "Let's try it," she said, lowering her voice. Helmut grinned.

Linking arms around each other's shoulders, we pushed our heads together and stuck out our tongues. With my eyes shut, I couldn't tell Ben's tongue from Sena's or Helmut's. Suddenly Sena pulled Ben toward her and Helmut reached for me. His kiss, more gentle than passionate, ended by his abruptly letting go of me and pushing me toward Sena, who clamped her hands behind my neck and pulled my head toward hers. She felt delicate in my arms, although she was of average height and all hard edges. I'd never kissed a woman before. It was neither sensual nor repulsive. I let go of her quickly and pulled Ben away from Helmut, which, I reasoned, was a legitimate move. We exchanged a brief, electric gaze. His face was flushed from dancing. Cream sang, "I've been waiting so long/to be where I'm going/ in the sunshine of your love." I held him, stroking his back and neck, which were damp with perspiration, and running my fingers through his curls. We kissed for a long time, but when we finally stopped, Sena and Helmut were still waiting for us.

"Would you like to come over to our house? We live right across the street," said Sena. We'd met the sex therapists.

We said we'd take a rain check, then went back to the sofa to continue getting to know each other. We kissed, stopping from time to time to talk about hiking, brain enzymes, or poetry. His kisses were too wet and his mouth didn't fit mine quite right, but I enjoyed kissing him anyhow.

The next weekend we went to the Sea Ranch, an exclusive development about sixty miles north of San Francisco, where Ben owned property. His lot, one of the less expensive ones, was on a forested hillside with no view of the ocean, but he was proud of it and said he wanted to build there someday. When I told him I was opposed to coastal development, he said, "It will all be developed someday whether you like it or not, and the Sea Ranch will be the nicest because they have design regulations and a density limit." He sounded angry, as though I were foolish and uncivilized to object to coastal development.

We slept in his green 1968 Volvo, ate French bread and cheese, and drank sherry from the bottle. The best part of the trip was hiking together in the forest and by the sea and trying to identify plants and birds. When the discussion turned to poetry, he said, in the same tone he might have used if I'd tried to argue that San Francisco didn't have a bay, "All the good rhymed poems have already been written." Another subject to avoid.

As we drove back to Berkeley, we were already talking about living together. I didn't have a crush on him, but I wanted to fall in love with him and be done with the confusion in my love life. I'd had an abortion six weeks earlier, and I felt awful about it. I wanted to get married again and have another baby while Liana, who was now eight, was still a kid. I liked Ben despite our disagreements, and I was physically attracted to him. This seemed like a good enough start.

● ● ●

The outdoor theater by the beach, site of the Spectacular, was surrounded by palms. Ukulele music, playing over a loudspeaker, competed with the surf.

A waiter, tall, dark, and dressed in white like a dental assistant, smiled to reveal a set of large, immaculate teeth. "Good evening, ladies. Your tickets, please."

Yolanda tilted her head. Her hair, teased and sprayed, didn't budge; her eyes locked with those of the waiter. "Where's the fire dancer?" she said. "I hear he's a hot number around here."

I thought she was joking, but after seating us at a long empty table near the stage, the waiter said, "Which would you like first—your drinks or the fire dancer?"

"The fire dancer." She was amazingly decisive.

The waiter disappeared behind the stage door. When he reappeared, beside him stood a short, extraordinarily muscular man, bare chested except for two necklaces of brown and white seeds and wearing a long green grass skirt.

Yolanda leaned across the table. "I'm glad I didn't wear heels."

"Are you kidding?"

"He isn't exactly Tom Jones," she said, "but at least he's a star."

The waiter brought him to our table. "This is Sammy, the fire dancer."

Yolanda and I introduced ourselves. "I'm honored to meet you," she said. "I've heard so much about you! I can hardly wait to see you perform."

"Good to meet you too. I'd like to talk, but the show's starting soon," he said, then slipped away as the lights began to dim.

Strong and agile, he stomped, leapt, and juggled with swords and flaming torches. He threw them behind his back and under his legs, sometimes lying on his back, juggling with both hands and feet. The hula dancers drew enthusiastic applause, but for Sammy the audience whistled and roared.

At intermission he returned to our table. Would Yolanda and I like to join him and one of the other dancers for drinks after the show? She accepted for both of us.

"I'm not interested in meeting men," I said after he left. I was in Hawaii to sleep late, get a January tan, and swoon over cinder cones, macaws, banyan trees, and kihikihi fish.

"This is the last thing I would have expected from *you*. Well, come along for a drink. That can't hurt. I don't want to go alone." She leaned closer and spoke more softly. "I need the experience. I've never even lived alone—only with my parents, my older sister, and now my husband. I don't know what it's like to be free. I love my husband, but I've only been to bed with one other man. That was when I was sixteen. It isn't enough."

As the theater emptied and our dates didn't appear, I wondered if Sammy was having trouble getting another man. When he and another dancer finally emerged from the stage door, Yolanda and I and a young couple gazing into each other's eyes over their drinks were the only people left. Sammy's friend was a good deal taller than he, taller even than me, in fact. He must have been specially selected. Sammy introduced him as Zino.

We walked to a nearby bar where our reflections shimmered in a mirror between aquaria filled with red and yellow fish: two soft-looking, pale women with two dark, muscular Polynesian men wearing Hawaiian print shirts and leis. Yolanda and Sammy decided to go for a ride. I stayed behind with Zino.

As I stirred my Tom Collins with a straw, we exchanged ages and marital status. I was twenty-seven; he was eighteen. I was married; he was single. He did not seem terribly interested in Piaget, information-processing models of problem solving, or how to teach investigative skills in biology.

To keep the conversation going, I asked, "What kind of name is Zino?"

"Made up."

"Does that mean it isn't your real name?"

"Yes."

"What's your real name?"

"It doesn't matter." He paused. "You wanna lay?"

I thought for a moment. "It depends on what kind."

"This kind, of course," he said, smiling for the first time since we'd met and pointing to the lei around his neck.

"Yes, I'd like that very much." He took off the lei and slipped it over my head.

I thanked him. "What kind of flowers are these?"

"What difference does it make?

"I'm just curious."

"The red ones are plumeria; the white ones are ginger. It makes no difference. They aren't special. They're weeds that grow in everyone's yard."

"That doesn't mean they aren't special."

He smiled again and said that he and Sammy were from Samoa, and that Samoan men were the best Polynesian dancers. "Hawaiian women are the worst. They've forgotten everything. They can't move their hips at all without lessons from Samoan men."

I told him about Berkeley and San Francisco and asked if he'd like to visit California. "No, absolutely not. I never want to visit the mainland."

"Why?"

"It's too far from Samoa, and it would be too expensive to go back there. Even here, I'm homesick all the time."

Did his friends or family ever come to Honolulu? No, they were too poor. He'd grown up in a small traditional village and hadn't worn shoes or spoken English until he was a teenager. Now he wished he never had, because he couldn't be happy in the village anymore, although he loved it. He could never be truly happy again.

I sympathized. He invited me to go dancing, for a walk, or to his room. I said I was tired and ready to go back to my own room. He said, "I love you. Let me come with you." Even though I had an unfaithful husband, I couldn't imagine going to bed with a depressed Samoan teenager. I wondered if Ben had told his paramour that he loved her, and if Sammy was, at this very moment, saying it to Yolanda. I said, "It's sweet of you to say that, but no."

It was about three blocks from the bar to my hotel. Many couples were strolling hand in hand or arm in arm. A well-dressed, middle-aged woman staggered down the other side of the street alone. Zino and I walked in silence.

Outside my room I said, "I enjoyed the evening very much. Thank you."

"I'd like to come in."

"I'm sorry, no."

We kissed with our mouths closed. Then he said he loved me one more time.

•••

On a gray Saturday morning about six weeks after Paul's party, I helped Ben pack his books and clothes and take them from his dingy apartment to my hippie pad decked with yellow mirror cloths, fuchsia bead curtains, and a huge Middle Earth poster. His belongings were dusty and disorganized. Moving was easy because the old, worn furniture wasn't his.

Maybe he would be my true love. But maybe not. After we saw *For Promised Joy,* a play about Robert Burns, I said I thought Burns was a great poet. Ben said he was a country bumpkin who wrote shallow poetry. We saw another play, *In the Jungle of Cities,* by Bertolt Brecht. When I complained about the way the characters kept yelling at each other, Ben said I had no appreciation for or understanding of intellectual things.

Whenever we disagreed, he went for the jugular. When I said Sylvia Plath was a genius, he said, "There's no such thing as a genius. She was a bitch who hated men." I didn't like these arguments and asked Ben why he was always attacking me. He said he missed having intellectual arguments with his friends at the University of Chicago, which was a much more intellectual school than Berkeley.

In the past, arguments such as these would have been reason enough to break up with someone, but this time I hadn't started out with fantasies of otherworldly compatibility, so as reality crashed against the shore of my consciousness, there were no sand castles to be washed away.

At first Ben refused to take me with him to meetings of the Berkeley Poets Cooperative, despite my pleas. He said they already had enough people, and that if I wanted to belong to a poetry group, I should start my own. But after we'd lived together for three months, he relented. They didn't have so many people now, he said, so it was a good time to join.

Liana didn't like him. Perhaps it was because we always hugged, kissed, and touched in front of her, and she felt excluded. Or perhaps it was that he wasn't affectionate with her but wanted to discipline her. Or perhaps she sensed that he was different from my previous boyfriends, that he wasn't going to disappear so quickly. Whatever the cause, she defied his commands and wouldn't let him touch her, not even to carry her into our apartment in University Village after she'd been asleep in the car.

Still, on Friday nights the three of us played Clue, Monopoly, Parcheesi, Candy Land, Scrabble, hearts, or checkers. Some weekends we went camping at Point Reyes, other times we went to movies, and sometimes it felt like we were a family.

•••

Back in my hotel room, I began to worry about Yolanda. I could see the headline: "California Housewife Disappears in Honolulu—Last Seen with Fire Dancer." I undressed, turned off the light, and lay on my bed, but sleep was not on the agenda. I got up, turned the light back on, and started pacing. I paced from the bathroom to the balcony, from the balcony to the bathroom, from the nightstand to the dresser, from the dresser to the nightstand, my route the narrow path between the beds. *He might be torturing her with his swords.* Maybe I should call the police immediately. What would I tell her husband?

At four o'clock she came in. "What are you doing up?"

"Worrying what he does late at night with his swords."

"You didn't need to worry. He was really nice. I didn't have an orgasm, though. You won't tell Ben about this, will you?"

I shook my head.

"I felt so guilty I almost didn't go with him, but I figured this was what I came here for, so I might as well do it. I love my husband; I don't think I could ever find a better husband. That's why I wanted to do it here instead of in California. Sammy is really famous. He's worked at both Disneyland and Disneyworld, but his hands got too cold on the mainland. You wouldn't think his hands would get too cold in Florida, would you? He's the grandson of a Samoan chief. In Samoa only the chiefs could be fire dancers. The chiefs taught their sons. His grandfather taught his father and his father taught him, but he doesn't have a son. He's thirty-six. That's really old for a fire dancer, so he'll have to quit soon. He's working on a master's degree in public health at the University of Hawaii."

"It's good he has an alternative career."

"Too bad he doesn't have a son. How did you like Zino?"

"It was interesting to talk to him, but there could never be anything between us. He's just a kid."

In the morning Yolanda fiddled around the room. She spent forty-five minutes applying her makeup. Then she couldn't decide what to wear. I finally went downstairs for breakfast alone. When I came back, she was lying on her bed, dressed in cotton print shorts and a matching blouse. She said she had a headache and wanted to rest. I said I was going to the plaza next door to shop for gifts and would return in about an hour.

I bought a can of macadamia nuts, two leis of Hawaiian liqueurs in little bottles separated by plastic orchids, and three necklaces of koa, elephant ear, and blue marble (a sort of wrinkly brown seed). It was just past noon when I went back to our room.

"Are you ready to see Pearl Harbor?"

"I guess so," she said glumly. "He didn't call or come by. I told him I'd be here all morning."

"You don't want to get involved with him, do you?"

"No, but I want him to want to see me. I know it isn't right, but I want him to be in love with me. What good is it to have an affair if the man doesn't love you? Last night he said he loved me." She stood up, smoothed her clothes, and examined herself in the mirror. "It must have been a bunch of bullshit."

•••

When Ben and I had been living together for about a year and a half, we and two other members of the Berkeley Poets Co-op were invited to read at the Oakland Museum in conjunction with an exhibit of Nathan Oliveira's paintings. We went separately to see the exhibit beforehand. The highlight of Ben's visit turned out not to be the large luminous paintings of figures emerging from the mist, but meeting a woman named Kristy. They started dating, and he seemed more excited about her than he'd ever been about me.

Should we stay together or go our separate ways? I wanted to stay together, get married, and have a baby. We still argued, and he still looked away when we talked or danced. I accepted this. I accepted the imperfections, because I knew that all relationships and all people were imperfect. Prince Charming didn't exist. My choice was to be a spinster or love the toad. But Ben was only half toad. He was also a poet, teacher, and excellent lover. I told him he had to choose between Kristy and me.

He came home after midnight from a date with her. "I've broken up with her. I choose you. I love you. Let's have a baby."

We made love, and I was sure that everything would turn out right. I wanted to start making wedding plans, but he said, "Let's make a baby first. When you get pregnant, then we'll get married." After seven years in Berkeley, I didn't see anything wrong with this. What was important was that Ben and I had a commitment.

Well, we sort of had a commitment. He said he wanted to be free to go out with other women, and I said okay. I didn't think he really was going to go out with other women. Our married friends Charles and Maggie had a similar agreement, but as far as I knew, they'd never acted on it. Maggie said they needed it psychologically: it meant they had their freedom and were faithful by choice. I thought Ben needed the agreement psychologically too.

I went to the student health service to have my IUD removed. The nurse practitioner offered counseling on other methods of birth control, but I said, "No thanks."

•••

On Maui I acquired a nasty sunburn. Back at the hotel I checked my temperature every hour, anticipating the onset of sunstroke. I was going to call the hotel doctor if it started to rise. Yolanda said she didn't see how I could develop sunstroke after being inside so long. I said, "I'm a hypochondriac. Don't bother me with common sense."

By eight that evening I felt pretty confident that I was going to live, so I agreed to go out to dinner in Lahaina. Surrounded by paper lanterns, we sat on a balcony overlooking the sea, where hooks of moonlight were dancing on the water. In the distance we could see the dark peaks and flickering lights of Lanai.

"No offense," Yolanda said, "but I never thought I'd be eating at a place like this with you. I'd like to be in love and be here with my lover."

"What about your husband?"

"I love him, but I'm not *in love* with him. There's nothing passionate or exciting about it."

"It's that way with Ben and me too."

"Do you think you'll ever have an affair again?"

"I don't know, but I'm not looking for one now."

We both ordered chicken Lahaina, the least expensive entrée. We imagined it would come in a sauce with mangoes and pineapple, perhaps topped with a bit of coconut, but it turned out to be dry, leathery roasted chicken, and we spent the meal grousing about how awful it was.

When we got back to the hotel, rock music was echoing through the open corridors. We followed it up stairs and around corners until we reached a nightclub on the fourth floor. Just as we entered, the band stopped playing.

Sitting at the bar was an archetypal handsome stranger, with dark unruly hair and thick lashes surrounding his deep brown eyes. He wore faded blue jeans and a red cotton shirt, open in front to reveal a puka shell necklace resting on a very tan and hairy chest. As I walked by, he grabbed my hand and said, "I'd like to fuck you."

"No thanks, but you can buy me a drink," I said, sitting down beside him. I've always been partial to good-looking men, even the boors.

I ordered a Tom Collins, and he said again, "I'd sure like to fuck you."

"I don't even know you."

"If you'd come earlier, I would have asked you to dance."

"I missed my chance."

"Let's get acquainted," he suggested.

"What's your name?" I asked.

He said the name of a famous artist.

"Pleased to meet you. I'm Emily Dickinson." I held out my hand.

"You're putting me on."

"At least we have something in common."

"I'm not putting you on," he said, taking out his card. Under the name of a law firm, the name of the famous artist was printed, followed by "Jr." "He was my father," the obnoxious handsome stranger explained.

"Is he for real?" I asked the skinny, fortyish man sitting next to him, who wore his hair in bangs, was all dressed in white, including the shoes, and looked like someone who'd be good at golf. He smiled and nodded.

I turned back to Famous Artist, Jr. "What was your father like?"

"I hardly knew him. He died disappointed and half crazy when I was still a kid. A lot of creative people are that way." His eyes had a lusty gleam. "Let's go fuck."

"Let's talk about something else."

"You know, when I was younger, I never had trouble like this with women. Ten years ago I could have any woman I wanted. I must be aging."

"How old are you?"

"Forty-two."

"You look thirty-five."

"But I have no luck with women anymore." He pouted. "Don't you feel sorry for me?

"No."

"Aging is a terrible thing," Memphis, the friend in white, sympathized.

"Yes indeed," I said. "It comes with cross-linkage of macromolecules, cellular free-radical accumulation, and autoimmunity. Some people think there's a genetic program that controls aging."

Memphis and Famous Artist looked startled. I continued, "Lipofuscin, a granular pigment containing oxidized proteins and lipids, accumulates intracellularly with age, particularly in the brain and heart. By age thirty, half of one's brain cells contain lipofuscin."

Memphis rolled his eyes, then looked at Famous Artist and said, "You sure picked one this time."

"How do you know so much?" Famous Artist asked.

"I'm a hypochondriac." Actually, I was quoting from my undergraduate honors thesis on the neurochemistry of aging and a seminar I'd given in graduate school.

"Are you a lawyer too?" I asked Memphis.

"I gather puka shells at Kipahulu and make necklaces to sell in Honolulu. I also make leis."

"You're full of more shit than a septic tank." I'd about had it with these two.

Memphis looked hurt. "I'm a stockbroker," he said. "Do you believe that?"

"Yes."

"Would you like to see my card?"

"No, I believe you. I'm not usually so harsh, but Famous Artist here brings out the cynic in me."

Yolanda, who'd been sitting by me, got up and moved to the empty seat by Memphis. Then the lights came on and the bartender announced that it was closing time. Memphis invited Yolanda for a walk on the beach, and I ran to catch the elevator with Famous Artist, Jr., in hot pursuit. He squeezed in after me, just as the doors were closing. "Let's go for a walk," he said.

"If that had been your first idea, I might have said yes."

"I take back everything else."

"Sorry, this isn't a department store."

He followed me to my room. "Please let me come in. I'm so lonely. I promise I won't try anything. Just let me lie down with my arms around you."

"No, but I'll have breakfast with you. Nine o'clock. Will you be here?"

"Yes."

It's hard to explain why I bothered with this man. No way was I going to bed with him. Maybe I was intrigued because he was so good looking and the son of a famous artist to boot. Maybe I thought he'd be less crude when sober and perhaps even an interesting person.

Yolanda called to say not to worry about her, she was with Memphis and everything was fine. I tried to sleep but couldn't, so I switched on the light to read *The Diary of Anaïs Nin*. I felt pleased with how I'd handled Famous Artist.

•••

Two months after my IUD was removed, I completed my M.A. and
started my doctoral program in science education (I'd decided to get
out of neurochemistry because I didn't like decapitating white mice).
I was two months pregnant. Ben's and my arguments became less
frequent and less intense. When we disagreed now, he was willing
to accept that my opinion was different from his. Still, things weren't
perfect between us. He'd started listening to the radio and watching television a lot, and in our apartment there was no place where
I could find refuge when I wanted to study. I pleaded with him to
lower the volume or to work out a schedule to ensure that he'd get
to listen to his programs some of the time, and that I'd get peace and
quiet some of the time. He wouldn't agree to a schedule, but sometimes he lowered the volume.

The TV and radio issue was a small problem on the scale of things.
The real problem was that Ben had changed his mind about getting
married. He was glad I was pregnant, he said, but he didn't want to
make a commitment. I said, "We don't have to make a commitment.
Let's just get married." His parents were on my side. They begged,
cajoled, and nagged him long distance from Chicago. His father said,
"We never thought we'd have a son who'd do a thing like this." His
mother said, "You'll get a thousand dollars for a wedding present: five
hundred from us and five hundred from Grandpa." Finally Ben said,
"Okay, we'll get married, but I'm not making a commitment."

This was acceptable to me, but not to Rabbi Cahan, with whom
I was studying to convert to Judaism, something I'd wanted to do for
a long time and which I was doing now because I was marrying (I
hoped!) into a Jewish family. At a meeting in his office, when the rabbi
asked if we'd be faithful to each other, Ben said, "I'm not making that
kind of commitment." The rabbi stroked his reddish beard and looked
at Ben, who was picking at a loose thread on the sofa. "Then you're not
ready to get married, and I won't perform the ceremony until you are."

Nevertheless, we set a wedding date, and Ben's parents and
brother and sister-in-law made plans to come to California. I'd read in
the newspaper that in California men and women who'd been living
together didn't need a marriage license. The minister or rabbi could

just file a form afterward to register the marriage. Rabbi Cahan had never done this, but it didn't take him long to get the form and find out what to do with it. He could now marry us on very short notice. It was all up to Ben.

When everyone arrived in California, we met with the rabbi again, and he again asked Ben if he'd promise to be faithful to me. Ben looked at the wall and I looked at Ben, who was wearing bright green pants with zippers that ran all the way down the sides. His curly hair, which now reached his shoulders, was tied in a ponytail. He said no, and Rabbi Cahan said he didn't care how much money people had spent on plane fare: Ben wasn't ready for marriage, and he wouldn't perform the ceremony. We could have had a civil ceremony, of course, but that wouldn't have given Ben's parents much joy. More importantly, it wasn't what I wanted either, so Ben's family went back to Chicago without having attended a wedding.

"Would you mind if I lied to the rabbi?" Ben asked one evening during a commercial. I said no, and we set our wedding date.

On Sunday, June 23, 1974, Ben and I got married in Redwood Regional Park in the Oakland hills. Seven months pregnant, I wore moccasins and a paisley dress from a store called Persian Caravan. Ben was decked out in red velvet bell-bottom pants and a pink-embroidered shirt from Afghanistan. It was foggy when we arrived at the Redwood Bowl, but the sun came out as we took our places under the wedding canopy. A Spanish guitarist, the boyfriend of one of my Biology 1 students, played love songs. Our friends from the Berkeley Poets Co-op read poetry, and Rabbi Cahan recited the traditional blessings. Afterward Ben and I hopped, skipped, and ran in circles with our guests, while an Israeli accordionist played and sang. I believed Ben loved me.

Belden, a poet friend, said he thought all brides should be pregnant. Many guests told me I was the most beautiful bride they'd ever seen, and I believed them. Marie Winston, who'd known my parents since I was a child and had introduced me to Rabbi Cahan, warned me never to go to sleep mad at Ben. "Always let go of your anger and kiss him good night," she said. I thought it would be easy.

Ben gave me his maternal grandmother's wedding ring, which both his mother and sister had worn at their weddings. The ring was now mine to keep and someday give to our child. His mother also brought me a gift from his paternal grandmother—a Star of David necklace. When I'd started studying Judaism, I didn't know if I'd be accepted by Ben's family. Now, the ring and necklace meant I was.

Did I think Ben really wanted to go out with other women? Of course not. I was in love with him, optimistic, and exceedingly happy.

The morning of August 3—exactly nine months and two days after my IUD was removed—I went into labor. Anticipating the work ahead, I ate a large breakfast before going to the hospital. Remembering the anesthesiologist who'd knocked me out just before Liana was born, I refused to even talk to the anesthesiologist. At ten o'clock that morning, propped up on the delivery table, watching between my legs, pushing hard, and squeezing Ben's hand, I gave one final push, and our daughter Tamarind appeared, letting out her first scream when she was only halfway out. Her name meant "Indian date tree." We'd found it in *World Book Encyclopedia*'s article on trees.

The day I married Ben, I thought I couldn't be happier, but the day after I brought Tamarind home, I began to experience true ecstasy. The first time it happened was when I went to the drugstore to get some ointment for Tamarind's bottom, which had begun to look a little red. I started thinking about my two daughters and how much I loved them and how lucky I was to have two lovely daughters, and suddenly I felt so happy I started laughing out loud. I couldn't stop smiling a very broad smile that stretched across my face and kept breaking away into laughter. The clerk at the store looked at me strangely. She must have thought I was high.

Ben and I had to move. Normally students were allowed to stay in University Village for a maximum of four years. I'd used up my four years, plus two one-year extensions, and the university had denied my request for a third one. After searching unsuccessfully for another apartment, we started looking at houses. With a loan from my Aunt Liz and Uncle Bob for the down payment, we bought one by a creek in the Piedmont Avenue neighborhood of Oakland. Built in 1906, it had leaded glass windows, pillars between the entry hall and living room, and lots of woodwork in the living room and dining room. The woodwork had been painted over by previous owners, but I could imagine it restored. Although it had only two bedrooms and one bath, it seemed palatial compared to our apartment in University Village. It was a good thing it seemed so special, because compared to our $75 monthly rent, the $225 mortgage payment was astronomical.

I continued to have spells of ecstasy, but when Tamarind was two months old, they came to an abrupt end. As we cleared the table one evening, Ben said that now that the birth was over and we'd found a place to live, he wanted to start seeing Kristy again. I was dumb-founded. He was surprised that I was surprised. "We made an agreement," he kept saying. What hurt most was that he said he wanted to have another baby, this time with Kristy.

Ben invited her over for dinner. She was a strikingly good-looking woman with pale skin, delicate features, and a thick mane of curly strawberry blond hair. She wore no makeup. Ben's hair, usually a tangled, matted mess, had been washed and combed for the occasion and framed his face in shining waves and curls. He sat at the end of the table; Kristy and I sat across from each other on either side of him. He was entranced by her, which I found both painful and irritating. He hardly looked at me during the whole meal. However, she didn't act flirtatious or return his longing gazes. To all appearances, she wasn't any more enthralled with him at this point than I was.

A few days later she told him she didn't want to have a baby with him, or even an affair. I hoped he'd now make a commitment, but it wasn't to be. He said he needed sex with more than one woman and started going out by himself. He struck up a friendship with a woman he met at a poetry reading, and soon told me he was having sex with her. I had no desire to have an affair myself. I hoped this would be a final fling and that someday soon I'd have a normal marriage.

Ben sank into a dark mood. Days, then weeks, went by, but it didn't improve. There was no card, no gift, no bouquet on my birth-day. He never said I looked nice or that he liked my poems. In fact, he rarely said anything nice to me at all. He seemed to dislike me. He blamed me for his not being a successful poet, not having a Ph.D., and not having a permanent job. We had variations on the same argument, over and over again:

"It's your fault I don't have a job."

"How is it my fault?"

"You don't go to the placement center. You don't look for jobs for me."

"You can go to the placement center yourself. You should find your own job."

"And it's your fault I don't have a Ph.D." Now he'd be scowling and pacing the room, his voice growing louder.

"You dropped out of your Ph.D. program seven years before you met me."

"Ah," he'd wail, "but if it weren't for you, I would have gone back. I wouldn't have you and a kid to support."

"You wanted a kid. Now be quiet, or you'll wake her up."

"I don't want to spend my life slaving to support you." By this time he'd be trembling and breathing heavily.

"No one is asking you to. You can go back to school if you want. You could also spend more time writing poetry." In fact, I had a fellowship and was carrying my own weight financially in this marriage.

"When? When do I have time to write poetry?"

"You could write poetry instead of watching television."

"I can't. I can't write because you suck all my energy away." Now he'd be loud enough to wake the neighbors. "You suck all my energy away so I can't do anything except watch television!"

"You're crazy. I want a divorce!" He was confused and unhappy and taking it out on me. Maybe there was something I could have done to make things better, but I didn't know what.

Divorcing him was my new hope, my dream. I'd divorce him, I thought, after I got my Ph.D. For now, I needed him to help with Tamarind. He'd stuck to his promise of doing half the parenting: he changed as many diapers as I did, gave as many feedings since I'd stopped nursing, and spent as much time playing with her. He was a good father—at least to Tamarind.

Liana was another story. I'd thought they would grow to care for each other. I'd thought any man who loved me and wanted to marry me would love her and want to be a father to her. I'd thought...I'd thought.... In truth, I'd been out of touch with reality. Ben hadn't wanted to marry me, and now he didn't even seem to love me. How could I expect him to love Liana? They routinely exchanged insults and grimaces. At worst, they argued viciously. At best, they ignored each other. When he went grocery shopping, he never bought her favorite foods. I suggested that she give him a list, but he always threw it away and said he lost it. When she did her laundry, she dumped his clean clothes from the washer or dryer onto the basement's dirt floor. I was living in a combat zone.

I felt like a fool for having married him. I should have let Kristy have him. There was a word for people like me: *naïve*. I thought longingly of my ex-boyfriends. Maybe I'm being punished, I thought, for having turned away the men who really loved me. John, who'd proposed before I met Ben, came to visit at the little house in Oakland. He now lived in Indiana and was working on his Ph.D. in chemistry at Purdue. We'd had silly, affectionate names for each other, Ducky Do and Lucy Gosling. I longed for the days when we took physicochemical biology and neurophysiology together and talked about things like the role of antioxidants in aging and why the brain needs sleep. His kisses were a delicious mix of tenderness and passion, and he looked at me when we danced. The arguments that led to our break-up now seemed inconsequential compared to the fights with Ben. After John's visit, I sat on the bank of the creek and wept.

•••

Again Yolanda returned at about four in the morning. She walked slowly to her bed, lay down, and started to cry.

"What's wrong? Did he hurt you?"

"No," she sobbed. "I'm in love. I didn't want it to happen, but now it's happened and I don't know what I'm going to do. He was so sweet, so kind. We walked in the moonlight on the sand. He said,

'I love you.' It was so romantic! Dallas is the nicest man I've ever known."

"I thought his name was Memphis."

"That's right, it is. I'm so much in love I don't know what I'm saying!"

"Are you going to see him tomorrow?"

"No, he has to leave at six in the morning, but I'm going to see him back in California. He's from Sacramento; he gave me his card. Oh, Lucy, I finally know what it's like to really be in love. Did you sleep with...?"

"You've got to be kidding."

"The way you ran off with him made me think it was possible."

"I didn't run off *with* him. I was running *away* from him. I told him I'd have breakfast with him, though."

"Memphis said they were both leaving at six, so I don't think he'll be here."

She woke me up at eight thirty, bouncing around the room like a gas molecule at a high temperature in a small container. "Get up, get up!" she coaxed. "Get ready for breakfast!"

"My God, you're cheerful for someone who couldn't have slept more than a few hours."

"I'm in love! Everything is different when you're in love. You don't need sleep when you're in love."

I got up, showered, and put on shorts and a blouse. My sunburn was beginning to look like a tan. When Famous Artist had not shown up by nine thirty, I decided to call him. Yolanda repeated, "I don't think he's coming."

I felt ridiculous giving the hotel operator his name, and I wouldn't have been at all surprised if she'd said there was no guest listed with that name.

"Would you like Mister or Mister and Missus?" she asked.

"Mister."

"Mister has checked out."

"Then try Mister and Missus."

"Mister and Missus have also checked out."

Famous Artist hadn't been the first married man to pursue me, and I now wondered if it would be possible to find a man who'd be faithful. If I left Ben, what would I have to gain? I had a surge of affection for him. He was not the only unfaithful husband in the world, nor was he the worst one. At least he was honest with me, and he'd been honest with Kristy and the poet too.

On the plane heading back to San Francisco, I kept going to the restroom to look at myself in the mirror and brush my hair. I wanted to be beautiful for Ben. I was looking forward to seeing him and hoped to rekindle our romance. Maybe he could even grow to love Liana, I thought. I felt hopeful.

He wasn't waiting when I disembarked. Yolanda's husband was there, though, and he took her into his arms. As they hugged and kissed, my heart sank to my toes. Ben finally showed up, scruffy and grumpy, at the baggage claim area. He was wearing baggy shorts and a misshapen, dirty T-shirt. His hair looked like a big brown Brillo pad. He said, "Your dad and I managed fine without you. You didn't need to come home." He wasn't saying he wished I could have enjoyed a longer vacation. The message was, "I didn't miss you, and I don't need you." Sometimes we know something. A letter is on its way, a wine will be just right, or the answer is yes. Or a storm is coming, the cake will burn, or the phone won't ring. I knew it was over.

Lucy reading her poetry at the Berkeley Poets Co-op, August 1976.
Photo by Tony Lane.

chapter 10

Starting Over

The plum tree outside the kitchen window was covered with white blossoms, the sun-steeped yard filled with the flutter of monarchs and swallowtails, the buzz of blowflies and bees. The bugs and blossoms had followed long months of gray skies and rain. It was spring, the time of year when things are supposed to happen. Not yet hooked on gourmet coffee, I dissolved a heaping teaspoon of Taster's Choice in a mug of boiling water, then added low-fat milk and a level teaspoon of sugar. Gabe had asked me out! I hoped that, along with the roses and buckeye trees, life would start anew for me.

It had been a whole year since Ben and I had separated, and I'd finally gotten the divorce underway. I took my coffee and cereal to the dining room and sat looking out at the creek. It was Saturday morning. The house, once filled with the cacophony of a toddler, a rebellious teenager, and an incompatible couple, was as quiet and empty as a church on Monday. There was nothing to disturb my thoughts of Gabe. Tonight, I told myself, we'll start over. We'd known each other for nine years, but this would be our first real date in three and a half years, and my first romantic evening with him as a single woman. The thought of it made me giddy. I'd never wanted true love with anyone as badly as I'd wanted it with Gabe, and still wanted it.

I'd met Gabe in 1976, the first time I went to the Squaw Valley Community of Writers, but I'd heard about him even before I got there. With three other women from the poetry program, I'd driven to Squaw Valley, a ski resort in the Sierra near Lake Tahoe, on a stifling Friday afternoon in August. As we negotiated the traffic between

Vallejo and Sacramento with the air conditioner going full blast, Stephanie asked, "Has anyone heard what it's like at Squaw?"

"I think we'll make connections and maybe even some lifelong friends. Just stay away from Gabe," said Frances.

"Who's Gabe?" I asked.

"He's a novelist who's there every year. He tries to get all the girlies into the sauna."

"He rounds them up, five or six at a time," Karen added. "Then he stares at their breasts, puffs up his chest, and says, 'Ladies, may I join you?'"

"Disgusting!" "Outrageous!" "Sexist!" I was the only one in the car who hadn't heard this story.

We stopped for lunch at a restaurant in Sacramento. From the refrigerator into the furnace. Heading for the toilet, I was stopped by my image in the restroom mirror. I took a hard look at myself. My long hair, light brown with blond highlights from the sun, was pinned up with a large barrette. When I smiled, small lines formed around my eyes. I was twenty-eight years old and married. "Don't make a fool of yourself at Squaw Valley," I told myself. "Don't act like a teenager. Don't flirt with anyone, especially not Gabe."

The next morning as I piled scrambled eggs on my plate in the cafeteria, a distinguished-looking man approached me. He had dark hair and a dark beard flecked with gray and appeared to be in his late forties. "You look like a poet," he said.

"You're right. How about you?"

"I write novels. Well, good morning." He smiled, then walked away.

That evening I went to the nightclub, where Gabe was giving the keynote speech, "The Importance of Telling Lies." The man who'd greeted me at breakfast took the stage. "No one wants to hear about your sexual conquests or your unhappy childhood," he told us. "If you want to be a writer, you have to get beyond that kind of self-indulgence. Readers want to be told a good story."

I did not take this to mean that he saw no value in autobiographical writing. My interpretation was that he was advising us to create stories, whether fictional or true, that might engage a reader, as opposed to just recording the incidents and facts of our lives. In nonfiction we have to find theses stories amid all the false starts, dead ends, and unconnected incidents of a life; in fiction we have the luxury of shaping the stories by making things up, or "telling lies." My thoughts then turned to poetry, where I believe different rules apply, although poems, too, must transcend the mere facts of experience. I thought about the truth of Robert Lowell's and Anne Sexton's autobiographical poetry, and of Sylvia Plath's crying out with her own very real pain. In poetry and nonfiction it isn't necessary to "lie," I concluded, but neither is it sufficient simply to tell the truth.

After the talk Gabe came to the bar and started talking to the woman next to me, whose long blond hair was pulled back into a single braid. She disagreed with him about the importance of telling lies, citing Anne Sexton and making some of the same points about poetry that had crossed my mind. She said, "It really is amazing that she wrote *The Death Notebooks* while she was contemplating suicide. She was depressed, yet she turned it into art."

"She wrote 45 *Mercy Street* and *The Awful Rowing Toward God* after that," I said.

Gabe turned to me. "Would you like to join me?"

The band started playing just as we sat down with Page Stegner. "Let's go where we can talk!" Gabe yelled to us.

We went to the empty cafeteria adjoining the nightclub and sat at a corner table as far away from the music as possible. Gabe and Page were the most successful writers I'd ever talked to, but instead of asking questions and listening, I did most of the talking. I told them my story of teen marriage and motherhood, and they told me I should be writing novels. Like many people, they wondered if I were from Kentucky or West Virginia and were surprised to learn that I grew up in the San Francisco Bay Area.

"When I saw you this morning at breakfast," Gabe said, "my first thought was that I wanted to get to know you. My second thought was that you were too young. You look like a kid. I'm glad you're not."

When the band played a slow song, he asked me to dance. We were both wearing jeans and hiking boots. Dancing was a little clumsy, but I put my head on his shoulder and it felt very good there. For the first time since Ben, to whom I'd been married for two years, had told me he wanted to resume his affair with his ex-girlfriend Kristy, I felt truly happy.

Gabe invited me to join him for dinner each night, and I always accepted. I loved to listen to him talk. He was witty and opinionated and knew people like Saul Bellow, Anaïs Nin (whose advances he'd turned down in the 1950s), and Henry Miller, and could talk about his friendships and encounters with them as easily as I could describe my mother's temper and my children's first steps. After dinner he always invited me back to his room, and I always declined. I'd been warned about him, and I didn't want to be the dunce of Squaw Valley. Each night I expected that he'd give up on me the next day and chase someone else instead.

But I was very attracted to him, and on the fourth night I began to waver. It was still light as he walked me to my room, and we stopped to watch a warbler emit a wheezy call from a pine branch. He put his arm around me, and when the warbler flew away he pulled me toward him and we kissed. It was a deep, comfortable kiss without the stiffness or embarrassment that can make first kisses unfortunately memorable.

When I finally pulled away, I said, "Not bad for someone who tries to get all the girlies into the sauna."

"So you've heard the sauna story. It's funny how things get around. What did you hear?"

"That you round up women, five and six at a time, and herd them into the sauna."

"Do you really think I'd try to seduce five women at once? It's ridiculous. I have a friend who owns a condominium at Squaw. He has a sauna, and last year I invited some women from the conference to use it, but I wasn't interested in any of them. I just thought they'd enjoy it. In fact, I didn't want to have an affair with anyone. I was still in love with my wife. We were recently divorced, and I was depressed."

"Do you still love her?"

He hesitated for just a moment. "Yes."

It hurt as though we'd been longtime lovers, although I hardly knew him and we'd only just shared our first kiss.

He held my hand, and we walked in silence the rest of the way back to the condominium I was sharing with three other writers.

The week passed quickly. I formed friendships with the other poets and got helpful feedback on my work. The last night, a Friday, Gabe again invited me to his room after dinner. Since it would now be impossible for him to have sex with me, then ditch me the next night for someone else, having an affair no longer held the promise of embarrassment. He'd been faithful to me all week. I said okay.

Our bodies fit together as perfectly as our lips did, and after we made love, I started laughing. "What's so funny?" he asked. It had something to do with the girlies-in-the-sauna story, something to do with finding what my husband was looking for, and something to do with Gabe's liking me, flat chest and all. But I couldn't articulate exactly what I was feeling. Maybe I was just plain happy.

The next morning at the cafeteria, as I ate oatmeal and a muffin with Karen and Frances, Gabe tapped me on the shoulder. I stood up.

"I'm leaving now," he said, hugging me. "It's been good."

I didn't want to go home to Ben. I wished the week at Squaw Valley could last forever. "I hate saying good-bye."

"This isn't good-bye."

When he left, I sat back down and said, "I liked the sauna." Karen and Frances laughed.

•••

I didn't try to get in touch with Gabe, and he didn't call me. He hadn't even asked for my phone number. He really likes me, I told myself, but he doesn't want to be involved with a married woman. I was tempted to call him but I didn't do it, although he was always on my mind. I had trouble focusing on other things, like my poetry and my doctoral dissertation in science and math education.

Ben had told me about an affair he'd had earlier that year, so I saw nothing wrong with telling him about Gabe. His expression was sullen as he sat on the old mohair sofa in the living room while I gave him an unabridged account of my week at Squaw Valley. He didn't have much to say before we went to bed that night, but at about four o'clock I was awakened by a blasting radio. Ben was charging back and forth through the house, banging each door he passed through.

"What's wrong with you?" I asked.

"You're nothing but a bitch and a whore!" His face was red, his forehead beaded with perspiration, his dark curly hair projecting wildly in all directions.

"What are you talking about? We have an open marriage. You insisted on that, and you've had an affair yourself. Are you supposed to be able to have affairs, but not me? Is that what you want?"

"Yes, that's what I want!" he yelled.

Two-year-old Tamarind had woken up and was crying. Fortunately Liana, now thirteen, was spending the summer with her father in Minnesota. I picked up Tamarind, who was standing at her bedroom door clutching a blue rabbit. I'd been a fool to tell Ben. What I did when he wasn't around was none of his business.

•••

I wanted to see Gabe again, and in November my opportunity arrived. He would be on a panel of speakers at the Celebration of Writers in Oakland, a Saturday afternoon event at the Oakland Auditorium. I feared that Ben, a poet himself, might want to attend, but he wasn't interested.

The day of the event, I washed my hair and put on faded blue jeans, a cotton knit shirt, and a sheer white cotton blouse that tied in front. It was how I always dressed. I didn't want Ben to be suspicious.

Gabe's panel was at the end of the day, and I was so excited about the prospect of talking to him that I couldn't concentrate on what he and the other speakers were saying. I was mesmerized by his penetrating eyes and the deep, resonant cadences of his voice. He was older than he looked, fifty-two to be exact, but as far as I was concerned, our age difference was inconsequential.

After the last speaker made his final comments, I made my way to the front of the crowd. Gabe was watching me. He hugged me and said, "I hoped you'd be here. Don't go away." When he finished answering everyone's questions, he took my hand and led me to a stairwell. On the first landing he swept me into his arms. After a very long kiss, he pulled a piece of paper out of his pocket and said, "What's your phone number? This time we're going to do it right." We stopped to kiss on every landing, and when we got to the ground level, he asked how I was getting home. I would have liked to say, "Who's going home?" But I said Ben was going to pick me up. Gabe said he came by bus, so I told him Ben and I could drop him off at the bus stop.

Ben had presented his lover to me, and I took great pleasure in presenting mine to him. Of course, Gabe didn't know I'd told Ben. When Gabe got out, I longed to go with him.

•••

Every dream I'd ever had of true love was reawakened. I sang love songs as I drove or washed dishes. I knew what I wanted: to divorce Ben and marry Gabe. That was my goal.

Gabe and I next met in his book-cluttered Victorian flat on Russian Hill in San Francisco. It was a clear afternoon, and wind tangled my hair as I stood on the small balcony off his living room, looking at the Bay Bridge as though for the first time. It was a graceful structure, shimmering in sunlight. My home on the other side seemed light-years away.

Back inside, I sat in a rocking chair in the living room, which was decorated with Haitian paintings. Gabe sat on the floor in front of the fireplace.

"What do you want?" he asked.

"To know that whatever happens, we'll always be friends."

"I can give you that. I will. What about Ben?"

"This doesn't concern him. It's between you and me."

"Do you mean you won't tell him?"

"That's right."

He pulled me to the floor, where we made love, then plans to meet again.

•••

We met again and again. We sipped ginseng tea at Gabe's apartment; we strolled, holding hands, at the San Francisco Marina; we ate brownies and hard-boiled eggs amid the Volcanoes, White Knights, and Gypsy Skirts at the Oakland Rose Garden; in the midafternoon we checked into the West Wind Lodge. Ben never asked me what I did in the daytime, and I never told him, but when Gabe started asking me out to dinner, I had to lie. I said I was at a jewelry party with my mother, a movie with my childhood friend Eileen, or a women's poetry group with my friend Mary, whom I'd also met at Squaw Valley. Sometimes I even said I was with Gabe, but I swore that we were no longer lovers.

I became adept at lying. I bought jewelry from the street vendors on Telegraph Avenue in Berkeley and said it came from a jewelry party, I studied reviews of the movies I was supposedly seeing, I fabricated feedback on my poetry. As I drove across the bridge, I'd already be making up details about the evening to tell Ben later on. My parents were my allies. They knew Ben didn't love me and, just as I did, they hoped Gabe would. My mother said, "I'm sure glad you have Gabe, because you don't have any kind of life with Ben."

I lived in a perpetual state of anticipation, waiting for Gabe to say he loved me. My hopes were always high as I drove across the bridge to meet him, but afterward I returned home disappointed.

•••

In the spring of 1977, *Playboy* magazine asked Gabe to write an article about X-rated motels in San Francisco and Los Angeles, and he invited me to check them out with him. We decided to do the L.A. trip in one day, flying down in the morning and coming back that same night. My father drove us to the airport. Liana was at Magic Mountain School; Tamarind was in day care; Ben was at work; and I was skipping my science education seminars to go to the Experience Motel in L.A. I didn't feel guilty, because I thought the circumstances of my marriage justified whatever I might do to find happiness. My only regret was that we couldn't stay longer.

The ceiling and walls were covered with mirrors. A bottle of massage oil stood on the nightstand. We turned on the closed-circuit TV. Lots of group sex, doggie-style mounting, and elephantine penises.

We undressed and headed for the shower. Only a trickle of water came out. Gabe said, "We can skip the shower." More mechanically minded than he, I determined that the showerhead was attached incorrectly and fixed it. After showering, we returned to the gargantuan bed. The mirrors on the ceiling were the best part. Here we were—naked, flushed, touching tenderly or interlocked, sometimes in elegant poses, other times sprawled as awkwardly as kids who'd just fallen from a tree. I thought we looked great together, my hair fanned on the pillow, my long, tan legs wrapped around his white buttocks. He rolled onto his side so that he could see too. This was the real show. He switched off the TV.

Afterward he introduced me to the proprietor as his wife, which I took as a positive omen. Our host asked if we were really married, and I said yes. Then he told me I had eyes like Audrey Hepburn. On the TV across the room, an electric mouse kept darting in to nibble at the crotch of a woman who had her legs open wide and no pants on. It was hard not to laugh.

Gabe had trouble understanding our host's Asian accent, so I interpreted. He said he was a great fan of American literature. Gabe said, "What's your favorite book?" but looked puzzled by the answer. I repeated it: *"The Wind Is Gone."*

•••

Playboy rejected the article. The editors had wanted a first-person piece about Gabe's experiences at the X-rated motels, but his article described a fictitious character's adventures with a long-haired, long-legged woman in king-sized beds in mirrored rooms.

Gabe made me feel beautiful. I needed that, because Ben didn't. In a newspaper article about the Berkeley Poets Co-op, the writer described me as "a willowy young woman with wide eyes and a dazzling smile." Ben, who was always surprised when someone found me attractive, said he was startled when he read that. Gabe described other women who pursued him by saying, "She isn't willowy. She doesn't have eyes like Audrey Hepburn. She isn't you."

Of course, I wanted him to like me for deeper reasons too, and as far as I could tell, he did. At a party in San Francisco, we met an actress/model who wanted to get to know him. She smiled a lovely smile, revealing perfect teeth, and asked what kinds of books he wrote. He said, "Do you read?" She said, "Well, I guess I don't have time to read." He glowered at her and nodded toward me. "She has two children and is working on two graduate degrees, and she reads."

He admired my poetry, and for me this was further evidence that his feelings weren't superficial. "When I read your poems, then ones by famous poets," he said, "I can't tell that theirs are any better. You should be submitting to the best magazines." Ben told me I should be submitting *his* poems to magazines.

About a year after we reconnected, Gabe left to teach a writing course at the State University of New York at Binghamton. As I read at the dining room table one evening, Ben said, "Lady Chatterley is at home tonight. Where is her lover?" Without looking up from my book, I said, "He's in New York." I didn't elaborate, and he didn't ask any further questions, but the unspoken truth was that he knew.

Gabe wrote to me at the Department of Zoology at UC Berkeley, where I worked as a teaching assistant: "Dear Lucy, dear kind friend, The woods smell of cider from all the fallen apples; rain, damp, frost...."; "Dear Lucy, I know I just wrote to you. I can't help it, I feel like writing again...."; "Dear Lucy (more plus kisses), I love the picture....I love even better the letter...." They closed with "Love" or "l.k.l.k.l.k." So much passion and tenderness! He said he wasn't pursuing women in New York. Why shouldn't I believe that he loved me?

•••

Ken—a tall, tan, blond young poet—always sat by me at a poetry workshop at San Francisco State. We liked each other's poetry and had similar opinions on the work of others. Before long we started meeting for dinner before class and became friends. He told me that the first night of class, he hadn't been sure he wanted this workshop, but when he saw the empty chair beside me, he knew that was where he belonged.

Ken started a poetry reading series on campus and invited me to read. It was a small event in a conference room in the student union building. Gabe, recently back from New York, attended. When I introduced him to Ken, they scrutinized each other, exchanging cool hellos.

Back at his apartment Gabe said, "Your friend Ken is effeminate. I don't see how a woman could be attracted to such a *pretty* man. I think he's gay."

I knew Ken well enough to know he wasn't gay. "I'm sure he isn't gay."

"How do you know that?" Gabe snapped.

"Because he flirts with me and he's told me about his past girlfriends."

After the next meeting of the poetry class, as we walked to Ben's Volvo, Ken said, "How's the old man?"

"Who?" I was shivering. San Francisco is always much colder than the East Bay.

"The old man. Gabe."

"I thought you were talking about my father."

"I might as well be. He's old enough to be your father. I don't see how a woman could be attracted to such an *old* man. What you need is a *young* man."

Ken was twenty-one; Gabe was now fifty-three. I knew what young man Ken had in mind.

•••

Despite his warm letters, Gabe still hadn't said he loved me. It had been over a year since our reunion at the Celebration of Writers in Oakland. I still wanted true love. I wanted to live happily ever after with one man, and I was sure it wasn't going to be Ben. I wanted it to be Gabe. I loved him. The missing piece was his love for me.

Over oysters at a restaurant in Japantown, Gabe told me about a dream in which his ex-wife, Melanie, had pink hair: "It was ugly. I wasn't attracted to her. Maybe it means I'm getting over her." Later, as we bathed in his claw-foot tub, he said, "I used to wake up feeling depressed because I wasn't with Melanie anymore. Now I wake up feeling happy, because I know I'm going to see you." Remarks like these made me feel like he loved me. If only he would say so!

Occasionally I told Ben when I saw Gabe. I knew this was risky. The advantage was that it required less lying than saying I was with Eileen, Mary, or my mother. I told Ben that Gabe was giving me feedback on my writing. This worked for a while, but one night when I got home a little later than usual, Ben said, "I called Gabe because I was worried about you."

When Gabe didn't call the next day or the next, I knew something was wrong, because previously he'd been calling me every day. I waited more than a week before calling him. He was cool, but we made plans to get together.

I didn't mention what had happened until after we made love. We were still naked, my head on his shoulder. "You were never going to call me again, were you?" He said no. I was deeply hurt that one phone call from my husband would make him drop me, but I knew better than to make a fuss. If I started complaining, he would drop me for sure. Instead I promised never again to tell Ben when we saw each other.

Friends warned that Gabe was using me, but I didn't think he was (and still don't). He never lied to get what he wanted. If anything, I was the deceptive one, because I wanted more but didn't bring it up. I kept thinking either he would grow to love me, or he already did but wasn't ready to tell me. From his point of view, we were both getting what we wanted and needed: sex and friendship from someone we were physically drawn to and whose companionship we enjoyed. I did indeed want these things, but for me it wasn't enough, so I started spending more time with Ken, and our friendship blossomed. We played tennis (which he did very well and I did very poorly), sang in my backyard, and shared poetry. He was tall, muscular, and golden, with deep-set blue eyes and a high forehead. His poetry was mysterious and poignant, filled with passion, grief (he'd lost his father as a child), and unexpected turns and images. He wanted true love as badly as I did. Sometimes I hoped we'd find it with each other, and I knew he was thinking the same thing.

•••

Ben went into heart fibrillation at work on an August morning after accusing me the night before of trying to kill him by giving him asthma. This was the latest escalation in the accusations he'd been leveling at me throughout our marriage: it was my fault he didn't get his poems published or have the job he wanted, a Ph.D., or his love affair with Kristy. When he called me a murderer, I said I was leaving him unless he got psychiatric help, and I reiterated this the next day, after the doctors at Stanford Medical Center got his heartbeat back on track.

Ken came to see me while Ben was still in the hospital. Sitting on the lawn in the backyard, under the plum tree, I told him everything that had happened, including that I'd told Ben I was going to divorce him if he didn't stop blaming me for everything that had gone wrong in his life. I wasn't consciously hoping Ken would rescue me, but as the breeze ruffled his hair and he stretched out his long limbs, I couldn't help but think how much more handsome he was than Ben, and how much kinder. When he took my hand, it felt completely natural. He said, "I love you." He wanted me to join him wherever he went to get his Ph.D., marry him, and have another baby with him. Too bad I was still in love with Gabe.

I hoped Gabe would react the way Ken did, but as we lay on his bed a few days later, he held me and said, "Divorce is a terrible thing. I've been through it, so I know." I thought, *He doesn't get it. I want to divorce Ben. It isn't a matter of if, but when.*

Later, sitting on the floor in his living room, sipping ginseng tea, I said, "Ken wants to marry me."

Gabe suddenly straightened up. His dark eyes widened. "You'd be crazy to do it."

"I think I'd be happier with him than with Ben."

"That's no reason to get married. How's he going to support a family? He's just a kid."

"He's applying to Ph.D. programs. Maybe I could transfer to the university where he goes."

"What about Tamarind?"

"I'd take her with me. Ben would pay child support."

Gabe's brow furrowed. "He might not. A lot of men skip out. From what I know about Ben, I wouldn't count on him."

"Ken wants to have a baby of our own."

"Why are you even considering this?" He was exasperated. "You'll ruin your career. You'll be stuck with two kids and two ex-husbands (his count was wrong; it would be three of each), one crazy and the other immature. Concentrate on your career. Get your Ph.D. It's your ticket to freedom." He looked away from me, toward the open balcony door. His voice lowered. "Do you love Ken?"

"No, but I think I could if it weren't for you."

"Well, I can't make you an offer. I hope you're not telling me this because he's made you an offer and now you want one from me." His tone had changed from concern to anger. "I don't want to get married again. I don't want to be in love, either, because love leads to marriage. I had love and lost it. I suffered so much I wanted to die. The thought of being in love and getting married again nauseates me."

He'd been married twice and had five children, so I guess he'd given love and marriage a fair shot, but everything he said hurt. I thought, *No, Gabe, I don't love Ken. I love you.* But I couldn't say this. I didn't know what to say.

Gabe broke the silence. "You'd be a fool to marry Ken."

I studied his face, wondering what he was feeling. His expression was distant, his lips set in a hard line. "You'd be a fool to marry Ken," he repeated. Then his face softened. "Please don't do it."

•••

As I removed an escargot from its little well of butter and garlic at a restaurant in North Beach, Peggy, the wife of Gabe's friend Jerry, told a story about a woman she'd worked with at a newspaper in New York forty years earlier. "She was a beautiful blond. Germanic features. Good bones. She was the mistress of a famous playwright when I knew her, and I heard she was the mistress of others later. The newspaper editor worshipped her.

"I was walking near Central Park last week when someone called my name. 'Peggy! Peggy!' I didn't recognize the old woman with a pack of growling dogs pulling her along. 'Peggy,' she said, 'don't you remember me?' Suddenly, I knew who she was. She said, 'I keep the dogs for protection, because THEY'RE after me. They talk to me through the walls. They want to kill me.'

"It makes me sick to think about it. She's become a crazy old woman, living alone, talking to the walls. I remember her as a beautiful girl with the whole office at her feet. All the men wanted her."

"So she never married any of them?" Gabe asked.

"No, she was a bimbo."

"What's a bimbo?" I asked, not sure I wanted to know.

"In those days there were two kinds of women: bimbos and the ones you married."

"There must have been people who fought the stereotypes even then," I said.

"I don't know," Peggy said. "Things were different then." She must have realized what I was thinking. "Of course, we don't have bimbos anymore. Now we have all kinds of possibilities for different kinds of relationships, like the one you two young people have. Things are more complex now. It's not just black and white anymore."

Neither Gabe nor Jerry said anything. I felt terrible. I had never wanted my life to be this way. It just happened. If Gabe had loved me and wanted to marry me, I would have left Ben a long time ago and been faithful to Gabe. But Gabe didn't love me, so that raised the possibility that on top of all my other problems, now I had to worry about whether people were calling me a bimbo.

•••

For Gabe's birthday in 1981, I planned to give him a blue-and-green plaid Indian cotton shirt and a fortune. I'd recently pulled "Your lover will never wish to leave you" from a fortune cookie, and I wanted to share this fortune with him. So I bought a package of fortune cookies and used a pin to remove the fortune from one of them. Carefully I inserted "Your lover will never wish to leave you" in its place and tied the cookie to the bow on Gabe's present.

We met for lunch. It was a windy March afternoon, and he carried the package as we walked the two blocks from his car to a Chinese restaurant on Columbus Avenue. When we finished our mu shu pork and garlic prawns, Gabe picked up the present from the seat beside him. The cookie was gone. I looked under the table and got up to check the floor between our table and the door. I also asked our waiter if anyone had found a fortune cookie. Gabe praised the shirt effusively, but I was crushed because the cookie was missing.

After lunch we retraced our steps, searching the sidewalks and gutters. I imagined a man or woman spotting the cookie and stooping to pick it up. I didn't suppose anyone would eat a cookie found on the street, but since this was a fortune cookie, the person might well think this was his or her lucky day.

"What did it say?" Gabe asked when we got back to the car.

"Your lover will never wish to leave you."

"I wouldn't do that. Why would I want to do that?"

"No, you don't get it. It was supposed be *your* fortune, meaning *your* lover will never want to leave *you*."

"Well, it's okay. Even though I lost the cookie, you don't need to leave me."

I certainly didn't want to leave him. But something finally clicked in my brain, something I'd been denying for a long time. I admitted to myself that he might never say "I love you," and I might want to leave him someday.

•••

That someday arrived just seven months later, when I was in intensive care at Alta Bates Medical Center in Berkeley. Hooked up to a heart monitor and blood pressure machine, I was injected every hour with apresoline, a drug that made my hands and face grow numb and my stomach heave. Every fifteen minutes the cuff on my arm inflated and the machine went click, click, click, then displayed my blood pressure in bright red numbers. When the systolic reading went over two hundred, the machine called the nurses with a series of high-pitched bleeps.

I was too nauseated to sleep. I don't think I could have slept anyhow with the blood pressure machine making its noises and the nurses coming in every few minutes to take my temperature, collect a urine sample, or give me another drug. One of the drugs was a diuretic. To make sure I wasn't completely drying up inside, they weighed me twice during the night by rolling me onto a sling and hoisting me into the air over the bed, where I dangled like a sack of vegetables.

All night long I wondered if I were going to die. There had been times in my life when I hadn't wanted to live to be old, when I'd thought I'd rather check out before I started having trouble finding my way home and my bones became riddled with holes and snapped like twigs when I slipped in my walker, but now the prospect of growing old seemed like good fortune indeed. I'd be delighted to collect Social Security and babysit my grandchildren someday.

Gabe was very much on my mind. I didn't want to die as a liar and adulteress. I'd been having an affair with him for five years now, but he still hadn't said he loved me. Lying in my hospital bed with the blood pressure machine clicking and nurses bustling around me, I concluded that as long as I was with Ben, he never would. Maybe, I thought, there will be hope for Gabe and me when I leave Ben, but until then, there's none. As I watched the sky turn slowly from black to gray, I vowed that if I lived, I'd break up with Gabe.

Just after dawn a young man in a white lab coat entered, carrying a tray of syringes and tubes for blood samples. He smiled and said, "Hi! What are *you* doing here?" I wished I knew. I'd had a headache and heaviness in my left arm the night before, and Ben had taken my blood pressure and found it dangerously high. I'd called my doctor and been told to go to the emergency room immediately. The phlebotomist was followed by a parade of doctors, nurses, interns, and technicians, coming in to say good morning and wish me well. I felt like a celebrity, with my mystery illness. Ben told me I was an anomaly here. All the other patients in the cardiac intensive care unit that morning were elderly men.

After everyone left, I called Gabe. I expected to be at the hospital for several days, so I asked him to visit. He said he didn't want to run into Ben. I told him to come when Ben was at work. He said he didn't think it would be appropriate. Even though I was planning to break up with him, I was devastated. I had an undiagnosed, possibly life-threatening illness, and my lover wasn't going to visit me!

Every day my blood was drawn, my urine collected and analyzed. Gabe called every day, but he didn't visit. Each time we hung up, I wept, reaffirming my decision to break up with him. I didn't think he cared about me. At the same time I fantasized that when I left Ben, Gabe would confess his love for me at last.

Dr. Ballantine, my family doctor, kept adjusting my medications, but he couldn't get my blood pressure under control, so he called in specialists: a urologist, a nephrologist, a neurologist, a cardiologist, a hematologist. My fifth day at the hospital, the nephrologist heard a bruit in my abdomen—a faint gurgle that indicated blood wasn't flowing smoothly through an artery. He thought the main artery to my right kidney was blocked, causing a condition called renovascular hypertension. "It may be hard to believe," he said, "but this is the best thing you can hope for, because it's correctable. Most of the time, we can't cure hypertension."

•••

I didn't see Gabe again until December, about two weeks after I'd had renal angioplasty at Stanford to open the blocked artery. As he did every year, he'd gotten me an application for the Joseph Henry Jackson and James Duval Phelan Awards in literature.

Sitting on the floor, our favorite spot in his living room, I said, "I'm not going to apply this year." I'd been entering my poetry manuscript for the preceding four years, and I didn't want to bother getting rejected again.

"Yes, you are. You'll never get anywhere if you don't try."

I gave in, figuring at least I couldn't be rejected by this competition more than two more times. The award was for writers between the ages of twenty and thirty-five. I'd just turned thirty-four, so this was the next-to-last year I'd be able to apply.

Staring at the fireplace, I started talking about how I'd felt that night in intensive care. This was harder than I'd anticipated. Gabe had been more than a lover, he'd also been a mentor and friend. I was afraid of losing him, but I forced myself to say, "I didn't want to die with my life in such a mess."

"You're not going to die." As he looked into my eyes, I wondered if I could go through with this.

I looked away. "I don't want to live this way either."

At first he didn't believe me. He reached for my hand and held it for a moment. Then he put his arms around me and kissed me. I was thinking of Venice: water in green glass bottles, rickety gondolas, pigeons on the Plaza of San Marco, American tourists huddled on a pier at midnight, singing "America the Beautiful" to the moon. This was like trying to say good-bye without having said hello. I remembered being alone, working my way through a labyrinth of narrow streets, crumbling brick and plaster on either side of me. I never knew where I was going, when I would get there, or how I would find my way back. And there were so many palaces, ancient and deteriorating, with water lapping at doorways. Something beautiful was sinking, something that never existed, something always out of reach.

I caught scraps and phrases of what Gabe was saying, as though from a distance, over a bad telephone connection: "You don't have to...," "...not even a tear...." He was questioning whether I cared about him. I thought the problem had always been that he didn't care enough about me, but the way he looked at me now said that he did. It was confusing. If this wasn't love, it must at least be its seeds. Given the right conditions, the seeds might someday produce an abundant garden.

"I'm sorry," I said. "I want to see you again, but I want it to be when I'm divorced." What I really meant was, "I want to marry you when I'm divorced." Then, and only then, would my life be complete. Of course, other things were important to me too: my children, my career, my poetry. Gabe's love wasn't a sufficient condition for my happiness, but a necessary one.

•••

We talked on the phone every week for the next two years, always agreeing to renew our romance when I left Ben (or so I thought), but we didn't see each other. We didn't even get together to celebrate when I won the Jackson Award, although Gabe was pleased.

The morning after Ben finally moved out, after five years of psychotherapy and having at last agreed that he was responsible for his own life, I called Gabe. "Ben moved out yesterday." Lying on the antique bed in my lavender bedroom, I was dizzy with joy. Ben and I had separated!

"Ben moved out yesterday!" he repeated, astonished.

"Why are you so surprised? I told you more than a week ago that he was moving out this weekend."

"You've been telling me that for eight years."

"I never said before that he'd found an apartment or that he was moving out on a particular day."

"Oh." He was uncharacteristically speechless.

"When can we get together? Let's go out to dinner!"

A long pause. "I think we should wait."

"Why?"

"I don't want people to think you left him for me."

"Why would they think that? We haven't been out together for more than two years."

"I think they might. I think we should wait."

If, in all the years I'd been talking to Gabe about leaving Ben, he had ever expressed a fear of having people think I was leaving Ben for him, it had gone right over my head. I couldn't even recall his having obliquely hinted at this. "You're not the only man I'm hoping to go out with," I argued, but I couldn't sway him. Maybe Ben was the "people" he was concerned about. Maybe Gabe was afraid of Ben. That would explain why he didn't visit me at the hospital and why he stopped calling after Ben called him.

Two months later Gabe called to ask how I was doing. "Terrible," I said. "I had a date last night with a man I corresponded with when Ben and I were together. There's nothing between us."

"Do you want to come over for a bath?"

"Do you want to fall in love with me and live happily ever after?"

"I can't make any promises."

"Then the answer is no." I was still miffed that he hadn't wanted to see me right after Ben moved out. We should have celebrated! It didn't seem that Gabe was any more interested in love and commitment now than he'd ever been.

•••

But after another year passed, he asked me out again and this time I said yes. Tonight Gabe and I would be together again at last. Washing my breakfast dishes, I planned my day: exercise, lying in the sun, lunch, and a few errands. I put on jeans and a T-shirt, but tonight I would wear my denim skirt trimmed with red and yellow piping and the matching jacket with a multicolored *mola* on the back. Gabe had always liked that outfit.

I came home, errands complete, at five thirty. Soon I'd be with Gabe! He'd told me there was a new Southeast Asian restaurant he wanted to try on Larkin Street. After dinner we'd see a movie. In the past he'd usually made the plans for our dates, so I wasn't surprised that he hadn't asked me what I'd like to do.

There was little traffic as I drove across the bridge. Fog was rolling through the Golden Gate, but I could see San Francisco clearly, and the clarity of the city seemed to mirror the clarity of my mind. I knew what I wanted. It was time to begin.

Our table was at the back of the restaurant. The seats were red vinyl, the tables wood-patterned Formica, the floor tile-patterned linoleum. The bottom half of the walls was brick-patterned plastic, the top half wood-patterned plastic. We ordered hot and spicy soup and bean curd beef. The soup contained a new Southeast Asian delicacy: little strips of shredded plastic. Oh, well! Gabe had never been one to indulge in fancy restaurants. We talked about our children and my work. I now had two part-time jobs, one as a technical writer and editor at an electronics company, the other as a chemistry and biology instructor at a community college.

After dinner we walked to the Mitchell Brothers O'Farrell Theatre, where *The Grafenberg Spot* was playing. Gabe had an invitation to the premiere, which had taken place a month earlier. He told the cashier he'd been out of town that night, and we were admitted for free.

The movie had already started: a couple was making love in a swimming pool. By my standards the scene was much sexier than anything we'd seen in the X-rated films at the Experience Motel. Just two people, a man and a woman. That's what I like. Next came a bedroom scene with the same couple. The man was eating the woman. When she came, a high-pressure stream of fluid sprayed from her vulva and saturated his face. Everyone in the theater laughed.

Michael breaks up with Leslie because he can't cope with her urinating in his face. But she isn't urinating: a doctor tells her she's experiencing a female ejaculation resulting from stimulation of the Grafenberg spot. Sex. And more sex. Gabe and I left about halfway through to check out the "New York Live" show down the hall.

Bubbles of colored light circled the room while women in skimpy, black-sequined costumes bounced on men's laps. On stage a woman in a slinky green dress, green cape, and wings was dancing. The dress had slits up the sides. The dancer lifted the flaps of her skirt, showing her nakedness underneath. Then she shed the dress and continued dancing in only the cape and wings.

At the back of the stage was a chest from which she took a red stuffed lobster. She stroked herself between the legs with it as she danced. Next she selected a toy skin diver, a rubber fish, and a thick white stick with a red cap at the end. Sitting on the floor, she turned a key on the diver and held him between her legs as he kicked. Still on the floor, she put the stick into the mouth of the fish, so that the red cap protruded, and rhythmically inserted the device into her vagina. Gabe and I stood at the back of the room, holding hands and giggling. I felt close to him, although this was not the romantic date I'd hoped for. We left when the dancer removed the stick from the mouth of the fish, stood up, and started kissing the fish.

The lady at the front desk said, "The boys are upstairs, Gabe. They'd like to see you." We went through a heavy wooden door and up a staircase lined with old posters for Marilyn Chambers movies. At the top was a cluttered hallway with a picture of Elvis Presley and more Marilyn Chambers posters on the walls. We entered a room, also cluttered, on the left side of the hallway. There was a pool table in the center and, at the far end, a jukebox with a moose head hanging above it. Fishnets containing fake sharks and other sea creatures hung from the ceiling. Papers, books, boxes, and posters were stacked every which way and everywhere.

In his blue jeans Jim Mitchell, short and solidly built, looked like a balding college boy. He said that *The Grafenberg Spot* was made in six days for $160,000. Art Mitchell stopped in to say hello but didn't stay to talk. Gabe told a story about a traveling salesman who always visited the X-rated motels on his circuit. When he finally took his wife to one, a movie came on showing him in bed with someone else during an earlier trip. Jim chuckled appreciatively.

Back at Gabe's apartment we bathed by candlelight in his clawfoot tub, just as we'd always done years earlier. Nothing had changed. A poster showing the funeral procession of Chocolate George, a Hells Angel, still hung on the bathroom door. A photo of a couple rolling on a lawn at Golden Gate Park after the Human Be-In still hung to the left of the sink. It was as though no time had passed, as though I'd just been there the previous week. We washed and dried each other, then went to the bedroom.

There was no change in the way we made love, and no change in anything that was said before or after. Despite our excellent physical chemistry and the fact that Gabe liked me very much, I knew that he didn't love me, at least not the way I wanted to be loved. I'd known this all evening. He wasn't the type to go to the Top of the Mark, but if he were courting me, he'd have planned a different sort of evening. My hurt and disappointment were great, but I knew I'd set myself up for this letdown. Gabe had no idea what my expectations had been or that I was devastated. In the future I would try not to let my romantic fantasies get out of hand, and I would demand more of the men in my life. There would be no more long affairs without love and commitment. I knew all of this as I dressed to head for home (I wouldn't even be spending the night!). As I hugged Gabe at the door, my eyes were already glazed with tears that I knew would shortly be flowing, but I also felt a new sense of power: from now on, I would not settle for anything less than what I wanted and thought I deserved from a man, and I would begin immediately. I expected Gabe to ask me out again, and I planned to say no.

Left: Liana and Lucy in Hawaii, 1990.
Right: Lucy, Liana, and Liana's friend Jamie in University Village, 1973.

chapter 11

Stalked

A photograph of flamingo flowers hung by the dresser. The heart-shaped red blossoms were so shiny they looked like plastic; a long spadix dangled like a scaly yellow-green tail in the center of each one. For the time being, this was as close as I cared to be to the island flora, because a tropical storm was drenching the bougainvillea and amaryllis and whipping the palm trees outside.

This vacation to Kauai was compliments of my daughter Liana, a flight attendant, who was stretched out now on the other bed, reading a book about how to improve your relationship, while I looked in my field guide for the spidery white flowers in the picture hanging over my bed. "We're ready to live together," she said, talking about her boyfriend, Jeff. "We're going to look for an apartment when I get home." My inner sirens wailed when she added, "He's a cocaine addict, but he's promised to give it up for me. When he isn't using cocaine, he drinks a lot, but he's going to try to give that up too."

I took an immediate dislike to him the night we met, at a Halloween party. I was a Hungarian peasant in a kerchief, checked apron, and red-and-black embroidered blouse with full sleeves. Jeff, tall and slender with light brown hair, was a doctor in blue surgical scrubs and a mask. When Liana introduced us, he spoke in a mock Slavic accent, asking about my aches and pains, giving diagnoses, prescribing treatments, and offering to listen to my heart. This was funny at first, but it quickly grew old. I tried dropping the act, but he'd have no part of it: he was an eminent doctor speaking to a Hungarian peasant woman.

He never looked me in the eye; his gorgeous hazel eyes appeared to be focused on my neck. I wondered what he had to hide.

"We're reading self-help books together," Liana assured me. "I think I can help him."

Two of her teenage boyfriends were not just cocaine addicts but also dealers, and two more recent ones were alcoholics. "I'd rather not date drug addicts," she told me as the floral-print curtain billowed in the wind streaming between the closed balcony doors, "but they're the ones I fall for."

They were not the only ones who fell for her. She was tall and tan, athletic, with long golden-brown hair and movie star good looks. She had been courted by many other men, including a TV newscaster.

"They're like your father," I told her. He was already guzzling beer every night at seventeen when I married him. She'd always adored him, although we only saw him a few times while she was growing up. When she was five, I overheard her telling her friend Robin, "My daddy is very rich and he looks like Dean Martin. He lives in a mansion and he has his own airplane and a ranch with horses. Someday he's going to come in his airplane and take me to the ranch and give me my own horse." After Robin left, I asked, "Why did you make up that story about your father?" "I didn't make it up," she insisted. "Yes, you did. He isn't rich, he doesn't have a ranch, and he doesn't have an airplane." Liana became hysterical. She cried so hard I had to struggle to understand what she was saying, but I finally figured it out: "I thought it was true."

She put her book on the nightstand. "I can see how my boyfriends are like my dad, but I still can't change how I feel."

"Jeff could be dangerous," I said, remembering men from my own past: one who had OD'd on downers after threatening to run over my head with his car and watch my brain ooze onto the street, another who had trashed my kitchen in a drunken rage when I was out with another man.

Now the wind was howling, actually howling like an animal, and the room was getting darker. Here I was in paradise, and it was like a scene from a gothic novel.

"I know. He gets agitated when he's drinking. Once he smashed my knickknack shelf. He's okay as long as he stays away from cocaine and alcohol. He's trying really hard now."

I was skeptical. Someone who smashed furniture might also get urges to smash people. I wished all I had to worry about was getting better weather for our trip to the Fern Grotto the next day.

•••

After settling in and painting their apartment a soft shade of peach, Liana and Jeff invited me over. They lived just a few blocks from my house in Oakland, and I joined them for dinner on a clear summer evening. Their two kittens, Missy and Mischief, alternately jumped into our laps and tumbled underfoot. Jeff's hair was longer now (Liana liked it that way), which made him look like a rock star. The three of us laughed, talked, and ate his marinated chicken (I was pleased he could cook!) as the moon rose outside the living room window. Jeff talked about his work in offshore drilling: he didn't like being away from home or helping his supervisors hide safety violations and spills. *Maybe he isn't completely loathsome,* I thought. Like Liana, I wanted to believe he could change.

I took a postcard from my purse and handed it to Liana. It was a picture of the Dead Sea from fifteen-year-old Tamarind, who'd recently left for a six-week tour of Israel. Liana read it and handed it to Jeff.

"Aren't you worried about her in Israel with all those terrorists?" he asked.

I didn't say it: *Not as worried as I am about Liana's living with you.*

Of course, I was no role model for finding Mr. Right. My current boyfriend was Jack, wonderful cook, fantastic photojournalist, but irresponsible partner. When it came to household finances and other matters of conflict, he'd tell me whatever he thought I wanted to hear, like a child who agrees to do his homework from now on and to quit filling up with chocolates before dinner. Fat chance! Although he'd moved out six months earlier, after I threw his engagement ring at him, we still saw each other once or twice a week.

Back home I lay on the queen-sized bed, where I now slept alone, thinking about poetry. I hadn't written a poem for about eight months. The last one came the day after the Loma Prieta earthquake. As I examined the flocked, peach-colored roses on the bedroom wallpaper, my thoughts rolled over from poetry to disasters. The cosmos inflates and stars explode all the time. Catastrophes take place every day: floods, hurricanes, earthquakes. The wallpaper was ugly, like Charlotte Perkins Gilman's yellow wallpaper, and worn and stained in places as well. I wished I'd had it removed a long time ago, but it had been a challenge simply to pay the mortgage, taxes, and insurance. I didn't have any money left over for decorating. I was working as a science administrator at a national laboratory. I'd liked it better being a science writer, but administration paid better. I hoped that someday soon I'd be able to get rid of the wallpaper. Yes, there were bigger things than the wallpaper for me to worry about right now, but in three years in this house, I hadn't even dealt with the wallpaper. It seemed inevitable that the bigger things would escape me as well.

•••

On July 19, the day after Liana's twenty-seventh birthday, my phone rang in the wee hours of the morning. Roused from a dream I couldn't remember, I stumbled down the dark hallway to the answering machine and pressed "Play."

"Mom, please pick up the phone," Liana begged. Then, more urgently, "I need your help! Mother!"

I put on my robe and shoes and grabbed my car keys. When I reached Liana's apartment, a fire truck and a police car with flashing lights were parked outside. Fearing the worst, I parked badly and ran up the front stairs.

Disheveled and terrified, she met me at the doorway. I put my arms around her and we held each other before going inside. Jeff, scruffy and bloody, was sitting on the sofa in the living room. He said,

"Hello, Lucy," in a sinister tone before the police officers led him away.

Liana's blouse, jeans, and face were streaked with blood. On the hallway floor there was a lot more blood, large congealing globs of it, where she'd struggled with Jeff by the phone. In the bedroom the mirrors had been smashed, and there was a hole in the wall above the bed. The floor was cluttered with glass, clothing, and other objects.

Liana said Jeff came home drunk, as he had done many times in the past. This time, when he woke her up, loud and abusive, she spat in his face and said, "It's over. I don't love you anymore."

"So it's over?" he yelled. "Well, then it's really over!" He began smashing mirrors and throwing things against the walls and floor. He pulled out a switchblade knife and held it over her, and she thought he was going to stab her, but instead he slashed his own wrists and said, "I'm going to make you watch me die."

She got dressed and tried to leave the apartment, but he blocked the door. She reached for the phone, but he grabbed it from her and tried to hug her. When she pulled away, he smeared blood on her blouse and jeans, and she started to scream.

"Stop that!" he warned her. "You'll bring the police here."

"That's the point," she said and continued to scream.

While he smeared his blood on her, he accused her of worrying about her clothes because she wanted to look good for her next boyfriend. She told me she was in fact worried about her clothes, but that another boyfriend had nothing to do with it. She was concerned because she didn't have very many nice clothes. *Damn it!* she thought. *I've only worn this blouse twice, and he's getting his blood all over it! And I would have to be wearing my very best jeans!* Of course, she knew that clothes should be the least of her concerns at that moment.

The police took Jeff to the psychiatric ward at Highland Hospital, where he would be held for seventy-two hours, then released. I told Liana that when he got out, I feared he'd get a gun, then get drunk or high on cocaine—or both—and try to kill her. She said, "I'll get a restraining order."

•••

In the morning Liana packed Jeff's belongings and took them to his father's house. Then she brought her own things to my house, where she planned to stay until she found another apartment. She told their friends to tell him she'd transferred to United's Chicago base and was now living in Illinois.

As soon as he got out of the hospital, Jeff started trying to find her. When he called me, I said all I knew was that she was now working out of Chicago. He left several letters for her at my house and my parents' house, and friends told her he was perpetually drunk.

At the end of July, United sent her on a four-day trip to the East Coast and Midwest. The first night she was away, the phone rang in her hotel room in the middle of the night. It was Jeff. When she heard his voice, she thought at first she was having a nightmare. He said he'd told the crew desk that he was our family physician and he had to get in touch with her immediately because of a family emergency. The crew desk gave him her whole itinerary, including the names and phone numbers of the hotels where she would be staying each night. They also told him the date and time she would return to SFO, as well as her flight number. When he asked where she lived, they gave him my address and phone number.

She hung up on him, but the phone rang again immediately. When she answered, he said, "If you hang up again, I'm going to kill you."

She hung up. A few minutes later a bellhop came to say she had an emergency phone call. She declined to take it and asked not to be disturbed again.

For the remainder of the trip, she used aliases when she checked into hotels. She told me she was afraid that Jeff would be waiting for her when she got back to SFO, that he'd manage to get a knife past airport security, and that when she got off the plane, he'd throw his arms around her and stab her in the back.

Tamarind returned from Israel the day before her sixteenth birthday, the same day Liana was due home. She had a deep bronze tan and was ebullient when I picked her up at the airport, but in the car on the way home, her lively dark eyes grew somber as I told her all that had happened with Jeff.

Liana didn't disembark with the passengers that day or go through the passenger terminal. Instead she went underground, through the baggage area. That night she told me she was getting another apartment and the restraining order as soon as possible. In the meantime, she'd continue to stay with me.

The next morning, Tamarind's birthday, Liana called me at work. "Jeff's been shot outside our house!" she said, speaking in a rush. "He tried to break in."

"Jeff's been shot!" I repeated. Tamarind was home too, and I feared for both of my daughters. "What happened?"

"He came around the back and banged on the dining room door, yelling, 'I know you're in there. Your car is out front and your purse is on the table. Open the door!'"

"What did you do?"

"I went upstairs and called the police. He tried to break down the door. When the police came, he pointed a gun at them and they shot him." Her voice was trembling.

"Where did they shoot him?"

"In the chest. It looks really bad." She sobbed, barely able to speak.

"I'll be right home." My own voice was trembling now too.

•••

Three motorcycle policemen were blocking my street. Several police cars and more motorcycles were in front of my house, which was cordoned off with yellow tape. One of the officers at the street blockade motioned to me to pull over, and a plainclothesman in blue jeans and a denim shirt got out of an unmarked car across the street and walked toward me. "We have your daughters," he said. "One of them is in the car. The other is down at the station. Your house is secured. Take your briefcase, lock your car, and get in the car across the street." I was surprised that he was ordering me around like this, but I got into the backseat with Tamarind.

She told me that when the shooting occurred, she was at the Jewish bakery on Grand Avenue, buying a loaf of challah to have with dinner. She came home to find the house swarming with police and Jeff on a stretcher outside.

"I don't want a party," she said. The tables for her birthday party the next day had been delivered that morning and were now in the backyard.

"Don't let him mess up your life. Don't give him his way." I was angry and shaky. I also felt claustrophobic, noticing the absence of door handles and window controls.

The police interviewed Liana, Tamarind, and me separately. The room where they took me was small and windowless, like a closet. The door was locked, the room so stuffy I could hardly breathe. The car I'd just gotten out of seemed pleasant in comparison. This was obviously the same place where suspects were questioned. I tried breathing more slowly to quell my anxiety. There was a small table against one wall, with three chairs. I sat in the middle, an investigator on either side of me. They asked me to tell the whole story of Liana and Jeff's relationship, starting from the beginning. I wondered if I should ask to speak to an attorney, but I couldn't think of any reasons why that should be necessary, since I hadn't done anything wrong. Still, I didn't think the police should be treating my daughters and me like criminals. This feeling was tempered by my gratitude for their arriving at my house so promptly and, I believed, saving Liana's life. Deciding to cooperate, I began my story with the Halloween party where I'd met Jeff. It took about an hour to tell everything relevant that I could remember. Then the investigators left the room. I remained seated at the table (with the door open, thankfully). They returned with a tape recorder, shut the door, and asked me to tell the whole story again.

As I finished telling about Liana's phone call to me that morning for the second time, one of the officers said, "We heard from the hospital during the break. The young man has expired."

"Does Liana know?"

"No. We thought it would be best for you to tell her."

The news of Jeff's death was so shocking that I found myself thinking perhaps it was a mistake. At the same time, I felt relieved, knowing he wouldn't be able to stalk Liana anymore. But there was something else I felt too: sorrow for a young man whose life had careened out of control and sorrow for his parents, who would soon be grieving and, very likely, wondering where they went wrong. My many emotions overwhelmed me, and I started to cry.

The officers said that Jeff's psychological profile was that of a man ready to commit murder and suicide. They called his death a "police-assisted suicide." They also told me I had an exceptionally strong and close family unit. Liana, Tamarind, and I had all been interviewed for two hours each, and we had all told exactly the same story. We had excellent communication and trust with each other, they said, and this would be very important to Liana during the coming weeks.

In the midafternoon Liana, Tamarind, and I were reunited in the officers' lounge, where we ate a late lunch while waiting to be questioned by the district attorney. I let them talk first. Liana said it had made her feel trapped to sit between the two officers in the interview cell, so she asked if she could sit at the end of the table instead. Annoyed, they responded that they had to follow the rules and conduct the interview according to their procedures. All three of us were surprised we'd been treated so much like criminals: whisked to the police station, seemingly without any choice, and interviewed for hours, apparently according to the same procedures used with suspects and convicts. (Later it will occur to me that maybe we were suspects. Maybe the police thought prostitution or drug dealing had been taking place at our house. I will realize that, indeed, I should have asked to speak to an attorney.)

Then our conversation turned to Jeff. "You're lucky to be alive," I told Liana. "Jeff was out of his mind this morning. He might have done anything if he'd gotten into the house."

Nodding, she said, "I have to find another place to live before he gets out of the hospital."

"You don't have to worry about it anymore." I reached across the table and put my hand on hers. "He died this afternoon."

Both Liana and Tamarind started weeping. Part of me felt like crying with them, and part of me felt only anger. The angry part said, *Why should I mourn for someone who came to my house with a gun and might have killed my daughter?* Then, as I let go of my tears once again, I knew I was not crying for Jeff, but for my daughters, whose lives had been forever changed.

•••

It was after five o'clock when Jack brought us home. I noticed a white towel crumpled on the dining room deck and went out to retrieve it. A ribbed towel with a blue band across the middle, it wasn't mine. I picked it up, uncovering a large puddle of congealed blood, its surface scalloped with petal-like forms. Leaping backward, I screamed, then threw the towel back down and ran into the house, suppressing the urge to vomit. The full physical reality of Jeff's death had finally hit me. I was dazed. Someone had been killed at my house! I started to weep.

I assumed that by now someone would have cleaned up the mess on the deck. Who? Jack, the police maybe—anyone. It had never occurred to me that when I got home, a bloody homicide scene might still be there, less than ten feet from my dining room table.

I was really shaking now. Jack put his arms around me and said, "I'll take care of it." I sobbed. I was thankful he was there, although he couldn't change what had happened.

He put the towel in a bag and threw it into the garbage, then started hosing down the deck. I saw this as an act of great love, because Jack had always been more squeamish than I was. Still shaking and crying, I put some Wisk detergent, which was supposed to remove blood stains, in a bucket of water. Even with the Wisk, Jack had to scrub the deck so hard to remove the blood that the paint came off too.

Liana, who'd been alternately crying and trying to console Tamarind and me, called Peggy, her therapist, from the den upstairs. It was the same phone she'd used to call the police that morning. After they talked, Peggy asked to speak to me. "It's no secret that the issue now is guilt," she said. "Liana's recovery will depend on whether she can believe that what happened wasn't her fault."

Calmer now, I said I understood. I was thinking—but didn't add— *If anyone's at fault, I am.* I pictured myself at fourteen, in bed with a boy who liked to drink beer and drive fast and had no use for school. Then again at twenty-six, saying "I do" to a man who didn't want to have Liana tagging along when we went to the movies or to waste his money on her favorite foods. I cringed, remembering the times I hadn't helped with her homework, the night I missed her piano recital, the day I let her take care of herself when she had the flu.

One particular memory played out in detail.

Liana is six years old. I give her a key to our apartment in University Village, and she wears it on a string around her neck. I always try to get home before her, but she needs the key to let herself in when I'm late. This works okay until one night when I'm very late. I'm at the library doing research for a paper, time slips away, and I don't get home until after eight o'clock. I feel guilty about leaving Liana alone, but I'm not too worried. I figure she'll either watch television or go to Robin's house, but when I finally get home, she isn't there and a note on the door says I should go see the head resident. I think Liana has been hurt, and I'm terrified.

In her white blouse and pleated skirt, her hair pulled severely back, the head resident looks older and more conservative than anyone else I've met in the Village. "Your daughter is fine," she assures me, then leads me to an alcove where Liana is coloring at a little table. "I picked her up at your apartment after one of your neighbors called to say a child was screaming outside in the stairwell."

"Why did you stand outside our apartment screaming when you had a key to go inside?" I ask Liana as we walk home.

"I didn't want to be alone."

"Why didn't you go to Robin's house or to one of our other neighbors'?"

"*I wanted you.*"

"*I'll try very hard not to be late again, but I can't promise it will never happen. I'll call you if I know I'm going to be late. You should go to Robin's house or another neighbor's if you get scared.*"

Two months later I'm late again. I call home, but Liana isn't there, so I figure she's with Robin or one of our other neighbors, but when I get home, there's another note from the head resident on the door, and I know I'm in trouble.

"*Liana stood outside your door and screamed again,*" *the stern young woman tells me.* "*Next time I'll take her to the police station.*"

I feel really bad that I've made Liana feel abandoned, but I don't think I'm a terrible mother. I want to say, "*Liana obviously isn't used to being left alone, or she wouldn't have been so scared when it happened.*" *But I don't expect any sympathy, so I just say,* "*I'm sorry. It won't happen again.*"

In truth, my mothering left much to be desired. This had nothing to do with Jeff's being disturbed, I thought, but a lot to do with Liana's falling in love with him. Sure, her father's absence while she was growing up and her stepfather's inability to take his place helped shape her expectations of love too, but even their lousy (or nonexistent) parenting didn't let me off the hook, because I had chosen to be with these men despite many early warnings of their shortcomings. None of this is to say I thought Liana's childhood experiences led inevitably to Jeff's death on our dining room deck, only that they made her attraction to someone with so little capacity to love more likely.

After dinner I told Liana and Tamarind they needed to decide whether to cancel Tamarind's birthday party. Liana spoke first: "I think we should have the party." Tamarind looked at her questioningly. Liana said, "I mean it. I think it would be better for all of us to get our minds off Jeff. We have to put this behind us, starting now." Tamarind said, very softly, "I think we should have the party too."

They felt the same way I did—that we had to drive Jeff's spirit from the house, and we had to do it immediately. The party would be a ritual to rid our home of him, like driving a silver stake into the heart of a vampire.

Our family came. So did Tamarind's teenage friends. We gathered in the backyard for a vegetarian potluck buffet. What great fortune to be eating frittata, macaroni and cheese, green salad, French vanilla ice cream, and chocolate cake! When Tamarind and her friends started throwing ice cream, at first I was annoyed, but then I joined in the laughter. There would be more tears later. I wished I could make the world right for my daughters, but I knew I couldn't even protect them from the dangers of their journeys. Jeff would always be there, lurking around the next corner or standing in the shadows in the worst of our dreams.

Top: Evelyn and Dick, 1993
Bottom: Evelyn and Ethel, eight years old, 1920

chapter 12

Time-Out!

My mother was sitting in the living room in her favorite chair, an
overstuffed plaid rocker, the TV table in front of her cluttered with
tissues, pills, and a teacup. My father sat a few feet away in his tweed
recliner. Between them was an end table covered with lace doilies on
which animal knickknacks had been neatly arranged. Sunlight slipped
through the leaded glass windows behind them, illuminating dust
particles in the air. The room smelled musty, of illness and age. It was
noontime, but my mother wore her nightgown and floral-print cotton
housecoat. A pink nightcap covered her head, bald from chemotherapy, but she had on nylons and red shoes, as though she really should
get dressed because she was going somewhere that day.

My mother was not going anywhere. She had late-stage lymphoma;
a walnut-sized, red-and-purple tumor bulged under her chin. The next
day she was supposed to begin a new course of chemo with a stronger
drug. I was there that Sunday afternoon because she was too weak
to cook dinner and had asked me to bring over two Nancy's frozen
quiches, a meal that my culinarily challenged father could prepare.

"Did you order the anniversary cake?" she asked. Her anniversary
was still two weeks away, but she'd rather be two weeks early than a
minute late for anything.

"Yes."

"Is it a carrot cake? Did you tell them it should say, 'Happy Anniversary, Evelyn and Dick, Fifty-Seven Years'?" They'd married in Reno in
1940 and honeymooned at Yosemite, fed deer from their hands.

"Yes. I ordered it from Just Desserts."

My mother looked me over, as she always did, before passing judgment on my hair and clothes. "I like your dress," she said. "Is it new?"

My sleeveless beige cotton dress, printed with clusters of rust-colored flowers, was from a discount store. "I got it a couple of months ago at Ross." I was pleased my appearance could give her some small pleasure, though I remembered how, as a teenager, I'd loved to outrage and embarrass her by ratting my hair as high as possible, rolling the waistband of my skirt to make it as short as possible, and outlining my eyes with thick black bands of eyeliner and rainbows of blue, green, and lavender eye shadow. My mother never talked about those days anymore; she never mentioned the past, either her own or mine. She was eternally rooted in the present and future, never looking back. I wished I could look back with her, to examine the layers of her life and mine.

The dress I wore now was not the one foremost in either my mother's mind or mine. It was a big day for dresses, because I was about to go shopping for one to wear to Liana's wedding, which was two weeks and six days away. "Why did you wait so long to look for a dress?" my mother asked. "I've had my dress for two months. You're the mother of the bride!" Scolding was her normal mode of interacting with my father and me. When I was a child, I thought her scoldings meant she didn't love me, but now they amused me. It was touching, even, that she was so obsessed with my appearance.

"I work full time. It's hard to find time to shop. Can I see your dress?" I was worried that she might not be well enough to attend the wedding, but pretending she would be there seemed like the right thing to do.

"Dick, I'm too weak to get up. Show Lucy my dress. It's the pink one in the closet in the front hall."

My father and I looked through the closet, but we couldn't find it, so he went to look in the bedroom closet, while I returned to the living room. "Where's your father?" Her voice had turned querulous.

"He went to the bedroom to look for your dress."

"I told him it was in the front hall, not the bedroom."

"I couldn't find the dress," he said when he came back.

"That's because you weren't looking where I told you to look," she yelled. "It isn't in the bedroom. It's in the front hall."

"We looked there," he protested. "We couldn't find it."

"It's in the garment bag. Don't you two nincompoops know enough to look in a garment bag?" She continued at full volume: "I know where I put my dress. I may be weak, but I'm not senile." She scowled. "With all your degrees, I'd think you'd know how to find a dress in a closet."

I suppressed a laugh. My mother always yelled over trivial things. It was impossible to please her. As a child, I'd wanted to get away from her. This was one reason I married for the first time as a teenager. After hearing it for almost fifty years, though, I was no longer fazed by her yelling. I didn't feel anger, hurt, or even embarrassment when she screamed at me or anyone else, at home or in public. My father had never seemed to be affected by her tirades.

My father took the dress from the garment bag and held it up for me to see. It was rayon, hot pink, and looked like it would fit a twelve-year-old. My mother, only five-one, had lost a lot of weight during the past year. Her once ample figure had been reduced to loose skin and bones, and she now weighed only ninety pounds. "I'm going to wear black patent leather shoes and a black patent leather purse with it," she said. Her closets were stuffed with dresses, her bedroom stacked high with boxes holding shoes and a purse to match each one. Shopping for dresses, shoes, and purses was one of her favorite pastimes. The others were shopping for jewelry, playing bingo, and watching quiz shows on TV.

"It's lovely," I said. "I'd better get going. Call me later if there's anything you need."

I didn't share my mother's passion for shopping. I would much rather spend a Sunday afternoon reading, writing, or hiking, but I enjoyed wearing nice clothes, especially for important occasions, and my daughter's wedding was certainly that.

When Liana, now thirty-three, was born, I'd wanted to prove I could be a better mother than my own, someone my children could talk to about anything. As a teenager, however, Liana was as resentful and rebellious as I had been. I only confirmed that teenagers do not make great parents.

I thought of her father, with his stunning blue eyes, greasy brown hair, and penchant for drinking beer, and of Ben, who didn't like to comb his wild curly hair. Emotional canyons gaped between my husbands and me. Maybe I was attracted to men whose hair would offend my mother. I might have been wiser if I'd had a mother I could talk to. Then again, maybe I was too bullheaded to listen to anyone. Liana and her fiancé had been together for almost six years, so I was hopeful they'd bridged any canyons by now.

●●●

I use my key to enter my mother's house. "I'm here," I call out. It's February 1977, and I am twenty-nine. My mother has summoned me to show off the new display case she has purchased for her figurines with some of her inheritance from Mary Zenner, an elderly neighbor she'd kept company and helped with cooking and housework. Entering the living room, my mother points out the case in the corner. It's trimmed with oak and has six glass shelves on which sit her Royal Doulton figurines. "It lights up," she announces, plugging it in.

As a child, I'd hated the figurines—all those nineteenth-century girls and women with their billowing red and pink dresses, their parasols and bouquets. They seemed so prim and old-fashioned, not just by looking prim and old-fashioned themselves, but also by being objects that, in my opinion, only someone prim and old-fashioned would want to own. I'm still not sure I'd ever want to have them in my own house, but now, for the first time, I see their charm. I open one of the glass doors and take out a young woman seated on a green loveseat, her long red dress flowing around her.

"Don't drop it," my mother warns.

The bone china lady in my hand holds a fan in one hand; a bonnet with a pink ribbon rests on the seat beside her. I turn her over and read "Sweet and Twenty."

"'Sweet and Twenty'—that's from a Shakespeare poem," I say. "It ends, 'In delay there lies no plenty;/Then come kiss me, sweet-and-twenty!/Youth's a stuff will not endure.'"

My mother smiles. "Well, he's sure right about that." Without pausing, she adds, "I want to give you something too. I know you want to go to Europe. I always wanted to go myself, but you know your father. It was hard to get him to go any farther than the TV. Now that he has a remote, he doesn't even go that far. Ben's no traveler either, it seems." She goes to the mantel, picks up a slip of paper, and hands it to me. It's a check for two thousand dollars. "Go to Europe," she says. "I always wanted to go shopping in Paris. Bring me back a purse or scarf."

•••

Driving down College Avenue from Oakland to Berkeley, I stopped whenever I spotted a store with dresses in the window. The area had become gentrified over the preceding twenty years, the five-and-dimes replaced by upscale boutiques, diners like Paul's Grill giving way to gourmet restaurants with European-inspired names like Citron and Garibaldi.

I tried on long dresses, short dresses, silk dresses, satin dresses, cotton dresses, print dresses, plain dresses. Shopping for dresses had been more fun when I was younger and everything looked good on me, but I found a dress I liked. It had white roses embroidered on a peach background and a matching waist-length sheer jacket. I wouldn't need a real coat. The wedding would be in Petaluma, where the weather in July runs from very warm to roasting.

When I got home, the phone was ringing. "I want you to come back over," my mother said. "I'm too weak to move. Your father is going to call 911, and I want you to be here."

•••

I rushed into their house—the same one I'd once shared with Ben, a post-Victorian cottage with a dormer window and pillars on the front porch. My mother had never liked living there, but my father did because it was similar to the house where his parents had lived, just a few blocks away, when he was born. Still in her nightgown, house-coat, and red shoes, my mother hadn't moved from where I'd left her at noontime. "Did you find a dress?" she asked.

Describing it, I was sorry I hadn't brought it to show her. She listened, asking questions about the dress, the price, and the store where I bought it. "You'll have to take me there when I'm better," she said, then turned to my father. "You can call 911 now."

After he hung up, she said, "Bring me a bowl. I'm going to vomit."

"I don't think you need to vomit," he said. "You haven't had any-thing to eat or drink today." He looked haggard, tired from taking care of my mother and from battling his own illness, myasthenia gravis, an autoimmune disorder that causes progressive weakening of the muscles. His shoulders were stooped; his head leaned forward. He could no longer straighten to his former height of six-two.

"You can't tell me what to do," she roared. "I'll throw up whenever I want to. Now get me a bowl, goddammit, or I'll throw up on the rug."

My father shook his head. "Before I got my hearing aid, your mother was the only person I could hear. Now I know it was because she was always yelling at me."

He brought a large green bowl from the kitchen. She coughed into it a couple of times, but as he had predicted, there was nothing in her stomach to throw up.

A siren announced the ambulance's arrival, and I got up to open the door.

Two burly young men burst in. They took my mother's pulse and blood pressure, and asked questions about her illness. One of them took notes on a clipboard. "Have you taken any medication today?" he asked.

"Yes. Vicodin." Her doctor had prescribed it for back pain. He thought the cancer might have spread to her spine.

My father, standing in the dining room, said, "She didn't take it because it upsets her stomach. She doesn't remember."

"I know what I've taken," she yelled.

"Evelyn, I've been with you all day and you haven't taken any medication." He spoke as though to a child whose behavior is innocent but annoying.

"Don't listen to him. He's a liar," she shrieked. When my mother was angry, she had the most unpleasant voice I've ever heard, and it appeared she was going to exit this life screaming every step of the way.

The paramedics exchanged surprised and worried glances. They didn't know she yelled like this every day. The darker one, who looked like he might be Italian, rallied his conflict resolution skills. In a loud baritone he called, "Time-out!"

My father, who still stood in the dining room with my mother's back to him, pointed his right index finger at his head and traced several circles in the air. My mother was the one who was lying. Because her doctor had prescribed the pain medication, she thought she was obligated to take it and didn't want him to find out she hadn't. She wasn't always clear on the difference between prescriptions that are necessary to control or cure an illness and those that simply treat one's symptoms. There was no use trying to explain this to her, because she wasn't a good listener. Throughout my childhood and for much of my adulthood, I'd thought she wasn't very bright. Then I read an article on attention deficit hyperactivity disorder in adults. My mother had all of the symptoms. She was the most talkative person I'd ever met. She couldn't even be quiet during movies, so even before I started school, my dad stopped taking her and took me instead. At home she would never leave me alone so I could read or do my homework without interruption, and at dinner parties she could never wait her turn to speak but would just start talking, usually on a totally different subject from the other guests.

The paramedics lifted her onto a gurney. As they carried her out the door, still wearing her red shoes, she called to me, "Be sure to bring my red purse to the hospital. It matches my red shoes."

I started looking for the purse, but my father stopped me. "Go home," he said. "Get yourself something to eat. It's going to be a long night in the emergency room. I'll take the purse to her, and I'll call you tomorrow."

•••

On Monday I didn't go to my job at the health museum, but I didn't visit my mother, either. Instead I absorbed myself in unreality by working on the libretto for a science fiction opera called *Eighteen Months to Earth*. Earlier that year I'd agreed to write it at the request of the composer, who liked my poetry. The opera was about a young man who was born on a spaceship. The only people he'd ever known were his parents, who were now dead, and he was on his way back to Earth, eager to meet other people but also worried about how he'd react to them and they to him. That day the songs describing his return to Earth became my escape.

Before work on Tuesday I stopped off to see my mother. She was in the intensive care unit at Kaiser Hospital, at the corner of MacArthur and Broadway, across from a grimy mall where the yuppie area meets the inner city. By then I felt guilty that I hadn't come on Monday. I knew I should be spending as much time as I could with her. She didn't have much longer.

She was attached to monitors and an IV line, her pink nightcap still covering her head. "I couldn't start the new chemotherapy yesterday, because I was too weak," she said. "I hope I can soon, so I can get better."

She'd handled chemo amazingly well, often going directly from a treatment to dinner and bingo. Although the chemo weakened her, she'd resisted letting either it or her illness interfere with her life. Since her hair had fallen out, she'd continued to see her hairdresser every week to have her scalp washed and massaged. The previous week she'd gone to dinner and bingo on Tuesday night, had lunch with me in downtown Berkeley on Thursday, and had dinner at Aunt Ethel's apartment on Friday—an impressive schedule for an eighty-five-year-old woman with advanced cancer. She'd only stopped babysitting about a month earlier. There had been many times when I didn't want to be like my mother, but I certainly wanted to be like her when I faced my final illness.

I wanted to tell her how brave she was and that I was proud of her, but before I could say anything, she blurted out, "I don't know what they did with my red shoes." She looked all around the room, then pointed to the nightstand. "Lucy, look in that cabinet and under the bed. They were in a bag with my clothes. I don't want to lose my red shoes."

I opened the nightstand. I got down on my hands and knees and looked under the bed. I looked in the bathroom. I looked behind the curtains. I looked in every corner of the room. No bag of clothes. No red shoes. "Maybe they have your things at the nurses' station. Don't worry about it. We'll find them."

•••

On Wednesday morning she was in a regular room. Liana had brought her a bouquet of white carnations, pink roses, baby's breath, and ferns. I never gave my mother flowers because she always complained about them, saying they were a waste of money. Maybe Liana, who was completing her M.A. in psychology, knew better than I when it was appropriate to defy my mother. Now I felt guilty, because I'd come without a gift. "Is there something I can bring you? A book or magazine? Something special to eat?"

"A new cap. I'm getting tired of this one."

"Okay." I wanted to try to get closer to her, to understand each other better while there was still time, but first I decided to reassure her about the shoes. "Dad took your red shoes home with your bag of clothes."

"I know. He already told me." Her voice took on an edge of annoyance. "Where is he? He ought to be here by now."

"Mom, it's only nine fifteen. He'll be here soon." My dad had been coming to the hospital three times a day. He came after breakfast and spent most of the day with her, leaving only for lunch and dinner.

Helping people was central to his character. He helped his own
mother through a debilitating illness that lasted sixteen years and
ended with her death when he was thirty-four. Now there was not
only my mother to take care of, but also Aunt Ethel, who'd been
widowed since age fifty, and Betty Sink, a neighbor for whom he was
legal conservator, chaperone, and friend. Since his retirement, my dad
had made a full-time job of doing chores and errands for my mom,
Aunt Ethel, and Betty. He fixed their leaking sinks and broken chairs
and took them shopping, to medical appointments, to church, and out
to dinner and bingo. They were a foursome, and he called the three
women his harem. He also did a lot of errands for me, particularly
going to the post office and dry cleaners and picking up my prescriptions. As his own health deteriorated, I felt guilty about asking for his
help, especially since he already had his hands full with his harem,
but if I didn't ask him to do anything for me for a couple of weeks, I
always received a cheery phone message: "Dr. Day, don't you have
any errands for me?"

"Call him," my mother shrieked. "Right now! Tell him this is no
way to treat me."

I dialed his number. "I'm at the hospital. Mom's upset because
you're not here yet." He said, "Tell her I'll leave right after breakfast." Loudly, she kept saying, "Tell him this is no way to treat me,"
until I hung up.

"He's never treated me right. Fifty-seven years. Never took me on a
trip. Never knew how to make money, only how to lose it." It was true
that he'd lost a lot of money gambling, even though he was the casino
owners' worst nightmare: the man who could count cards and calcu-
late odds in his head. Fortunately for them and unfortunately for my
mother, he also liked games of pure chance. Ironically, when I once
tried to talk to him about his gambling days, he said he did it for my
mother, that he didn't make enough money at Bank of America to buy
everything she wanted. I guess that's what he needed to believe. But
all of this seemed irrelevant to me at this moment. He was being good
to her during her illness. I wanted to feel only love and sympathy for
her and have no deception between us, but there was no way I could

tell her what I was thinking: *Why can't you go a day without complaining?* I thought she was lucky to have found a husband at all, that one or two dates would have been more than enough for most men.

I kissed her. "I have to get to work now. Dad will be here soon."

•••

I'd just settled at my desk at the museum when her oncologist called. I'd never met him, and I wished now that I'd gone with her to see him the preceding week, as she'd asked me to. In a calm, gentle voice, he asked if I was free to talk. "There's nothing more we can do for your mother," he said. "Her cancer is too advanced for further chemotherapy. It would only weaken her and hasten her death. There's no reason to keep her in the hospital. She can either go to a nursing home or go home with help from hospice. She only has about two months."

My eyes welled up and I felt like all my breath had been sucked away. "Do my parents know?"

"Not yet. They'll have decisions to make. I thought you should know first, so that you'll be ready to help them."

Usually I turned to my daughters when something was troubling me, but now I needed to be the one both they and my parents could turn to. I hoped I was up to it. Right now, just breathing was a difficult chore.

•••

My mother had a miserable childhood. Her mother, Emma, an orphan, was raised by a contractor and his wife, Frederick and Mary Hazard, near New Bedford, Massachusetts. Against the wishes of the Hazards, she married a man named Ebenezer, who worked in a shoe factory. She gave birth to eight children before she died during the flu epidemic of 1918–19. My mother and her twin sister were seven years old. The four surviving children went to live with various relatives. My mother was taken in by the Hazards, Aunt Ethel by Ebenezer's parents. When my mother and aunt were twelve years old, the

Hazards decided to move to California, and Ebenezer let them take both twins.

The Hazards didn't allow my mother and Aunt Ethel to have friends in the house, play games, or visit friends' homes after school. They were allowed out only to go to school, attend church, and run errands. At home they did all of the housework and cooking. My mother said Aunt Ethel didn't do her share, though, and my mother ended up doing all the chores herself. Aunt Ethel told me their grandparents were mean and favored my mother. There was never a birthday party in this home, never a Christmas tree, and never any presents. My mother and aunt were not allowed to write to their father. They must have been in bitter competition for what little affection their grandparents had to offer, and my aunt, who'd lived happily with her father's parents, must have blamed her later plight as much on my mother as on the Hazards.

This was all I could remember being told about my mother's and aunt's childhoods, except that during an argument when they were five years old, my mother pushed my aunt into a pigpen. I wanted to know more. What were their brothers, Raymond and Frederick, like? Their father? His parents? Surely there were some family stories to be told. I hoped that during the last two months of my mother's life, she would finally talk about the past. What was school like for her? How did my father court her? How did she feel watching the world around her change throughout the twentieth century?

•••

It's Thanksgiving morning 1918, in Acushnet, Massachusetts, Land of the Cushenas, which the Pilgrims bought from Massasoit in 1639 for thirty yards of cloth, eight moose skins, fifteen axes, fifteen hoes, fifteen pairs of breeches, eight blankets, two kettles, one cloak, two pounds in wampum, eight pairs of stockings, eight pairs of shoes, one iron pot, and ten shillings. Lately the grown-ups have been talking in low voices about the terrible flu that's sweeping the world, but Evelyn doesn't think this is anything she has to worry about. She is happy. She and her twin sister, Ethel, just turned seven and their parents gave them each a doll with an alabaster face and brown curls. These are the most beautiful dolls that the twins have ever owned. Evelyn's has a pink dress, Ethel's a blue one. If they switch the dresses, no one will know. Like Evelyn and Ethel, the dolls are identical. Ethel is outside under the maple tree, which has already lost most of its red leaves. She's playing with their brother Fred, who's a year older. Out the kitchen window Evelyn can see Ethel chasing Fred around the maple tree. She doesn't think Ethel will catch him, because his legs are longer. Fred likes to play tag and have races with the twins, because he usually wins. Evelyn, who doesn't like to lose races with Fred, has chosen to stay inside and help her mother make pumpkin pies to take to her grandparents' house, where they will soon be going to dinner. Her father is outside chopping wood. Ray, her little brother who just turned two, is playing with a wooden spoon on the floor.

She and her mother have already rolled the dough, patted it into the pie pans, and trimmed the edges. While her mother removes the pulp from the pumpkin slices that she boiled in a big iron kettle, Evelyn carefully breaks four eggs into a bowl and churns them with an eggbeater. Her mother says, "That's enough," as soon as the yolks are blended with the whites to make a frothy yellow mixture. Evelyn adds the milk and spices her mother has already measured and beats a little more. Then her mother hands her a spoon to stir in the sugar and pumpkin pulp. The filling is too thick for Evelyn to mix well. Her mother takes over, but not before Evelyn dips two fingers in the bowl and licks them clean. She has no idea she will move to California, a place as far-off and exotic as Mexico and France. She has never imagined living with anyone other than her parents, Ethel, Fred, and Ray, whom she tickles now in the pumpkin-scented kitchen, so warm from the stove.

•••

On Thursday morning my mother was sleeping when I arrived. I sat on the chair at the foot of her hospital bed and watched her. She wheezed and made little jerking motions in her sleep. I hoped she'd wake before I had to leave because I'd brought her a new nightcap, a yellow one just like the pink one, and a card I'd selected carefully, rejecting the ones that said "Get well soon." This one had flowers on the front and said "Hope you're feeling better today."

I knew she loved me. Throughout the years, she'd given me all she could financially and had always helped with my children and household chores. I loved her too. I placed the card and nightcap on the chair and left for work. My long-awaited conversation with her would not begin today.

•••

A social worker from the hospital called me that afternoon. "We need your help," she said. "Your parents are in denial, and we have to make arrangements either to transfer your mother to a nursing home or send her home with hospice."

"What does she want to do?"

"Neither. She says she isn't going to do either, and she's quite adamant about it. She wants more chemo."

"What does my father say?"

"That he doesn't tell your mother what to do."

"I'll talk to them." I understood my mother's attitude. She was using a strategy that had worked for her four years earlier. A young doctor in Kaiser's emergency room had told her that there was nothing further that could be done for her heart condition. She said, "What about surgery?" He said, "You're not a good candidate. You're too old and too nervous." "I'll show them old and nervous," she told me. The next day she called her cardiologist and demanded that she be scheduled for bypass surgery as soon as possible. Six weeks later she had the operation, and it was a success.

•••

I knew something was amiss even before I entered her room on Friday. My father was sitting in the chair at the foot of her bed, holding her medical chart, shaking his head. Once inside the room, I could see why he was troubled: she was sitting up, her head hanging forward, bobbing. Her breathing was rapid and shallow, and each time she exhaled, she made a small moaning sound. Her eyes were closed, and she did not appear to be conscious.

My father looked up. "I don't like this," he said. "Her blood pressure is up. I don't like it at all."

"I'm going to find out what's wrong with her," I said, exiting quickly.

"What's wrong with my mother?" I asked a heavyset African American nurse.

"We gave her more Vicodin for her back pain. She asked for it."

Back in her room I asked my father, "What did you decide about taking her home or sending her to a nursing home?"

"She's going to be transferred to a nursing home this afternoon."

"Does she know?"

"She said yesterday she wasn't going."

My mother was in no condition to put up a fight, and the thought crossed my mind that perhaps the medical staff had sedated her to make her more cooperative. I would understand this.

"She's wearing the cap I brought yesterday."

"Oh, she loves it," my dad said. "She put it on right away, and it looks so pretty on her."

I'd read that even people in comas can hear, so I moved closer to speak to her. "Mom, do you feel any pain? You shouldn't feel any pain now, and if you do, I'll tell the nurse."

Her eyes remained closed, but she shook her head. My father looked startled that she could respond.

"I have to leave now, but Dad is here with you. You're not alone."

"Just drop me off, just drop me off," she said.

"I love you very much, and I wish I could take you home, but you're not well enough. Dad will stay here with you."

"Good-bye," she said softly.

My father nodded. I kissed my mother's cheek and left.

•••

At one o'clock a group of stroke patients came to the museum. The volunteer docents who gave presentations on the human body were used to talking to children, so I decided to do the presentation for this group myself. I had just placed the torso model on its stand and welcomed the group when Ann, a volunteer, said that my father was on the phone.

"Tell him I'll call after the presentation."

"He said it's very urgent."

I thought my mother must be refusing to go to the nursing home and I'd deal with it after the talk. "Tell him I'll call him back."

Ann left but returned to the auditorium a few minutes later. "Your father said he has to talk to you now. Please take the call," she pleaded. "I'll do the presentation."

I picked up the phone at the front desk. "I have some bad news," my father said, his voice breaking. "Your mother is dead."

•••

My father was in a small unmarked room near my mother's hospital room. From the hallway it looked like a closet, but it was a comfortable little living room with a sofa, chairs, a table, and a phone. I'd never thought about it before, but I realized now that hospitals must have many such rooms tucked away where people can go to weep and hug and carry on without disturbing anyone.

Adele Valdez, a friend of my mother's, was with my dad. She'd come to visit Mom but had arrived just after she died. I was glad Adele had been there while my dad waited for me. After hugging them, I went to say good-bye to my mother.

I scarcely recognized her. Toothless, lying on her back with the contours of her skull and ribs clearly visible under her slack, yellow skin, she looked a hundred years old. I took her hand, which was already stiff, and kissed her cold, waxy cheek. I thought her death was an act of will. She hadn't wanted to go to the nursing home. I admired her for having had the courage to let go, but I wished she'd waited to see me again. I told her I was sorry I hadn't stayed longer on Wednesday, that I'd had no idea it would be our last visit. "I'm glad you're no longer in pain," I said, "but I'll miss you immensely." Then I removed her watch, although it was valuable only as one more small memory of her.

That evening the family gathered at my house for Chinese take-out, and my dad reminisced about my mother: "She was *soooo* pretty—the cutest little girl you ever saw. She looked like a movie star." When he told the story of their elopement to Reno, Aunt Ethel, who was losing her mind, turned to me and said, "Were you there?" We looked at old pictures of my mother and aunt in their twin dresses and fabulous hats, and for the first time, it hit me that they'd been beautiful, with their high cheekbones, dark hair, and hazel eyes. I pictured my mother in the kitchen when I was a child, fixing dinner in a floral-print dress and lace-trimmed apron, trying to be pretty even as she worked. Why hadn't I noticed at the time?

•••

It's the summer of 1939. Evelyn and Ethel live on Cambridge Way in Piedmont, California, in a house with a bay window and pink snapdragons in the front yard. The twins, now twenty-seven years old, have not seen Fred, Ray, or their father since they left Massachusetts in 1924.

Evelyn took care of their grandparents until their deaths in 1935 and 1936. She is still the housekeeper and cook. Ethel works for an insurance company in San Francisco. They have never been close to anyone except each other, but now something exciting has happened that is about to change both of their lives: Evelyn has met a man. His name is Dick Lang. He is tall, blond, and blue-eyed, twenty-one years old, and lives with his parents less than half a mile away, on Boulevard Way. He has invited Evelyn to the World's Fair on Treasure Island. She asked if her sister could come too. She has never been out on a date.

A bouquet of red and yellow roses from Dick is in a crystal vase in the center of the dining room table. Ethel and Evelyn are systematically trying on every dress they own. They must look their best for Dick and the fair.

When he arrives, Evelyn is wearing red shoes and a navy blue dress with white polka dots, Ethel a green skirt and jacket with a white blouse that has a row of tiny black pearl buttons down the front. All three squeeze into the front seat of his blue Ford, with Evelyn in the middle, close to Dick.

The fair, on a manmade island in the middle of San Francisco Bay, is a wonderland of pyramids, towers, and fountains. Evelyn, Ethel, and Dick stroll amid silver trees, orange trees, and palms, past sculptures of Incans, Polynesians, and prehistoric beasts. Orchids and hibiscus bloom everywhere. As they head for the Gayway—where they'll try to muster enough courage to try the cyclone coaster, rocket ship, and giant crane—Dick takes Evelyn's hand. A thrill runs through her body. It's the happiest she's been since before her mother's death in February 1919. She hopes he'll propose. She has already decided to say yes.

•••

On Saturday morning Dad and I went to Chapel of the Chimes to arrange for interment and complete my mother's death certificate. The only customers there, we were ushered into a large, darkly furnished room with plants, urns, and a desk and chairs. The slender, ashen-faced man who met with us wore a gray suit. Perhaps the staff considered it in poor taste to outshine the dead.

He asked questions about my mother, starting with the date and place of her birth. My father answered until he was asked the names of her parents. When he hesitated, I said, "Emma Hazard and Ebenezer Bumpus."

"How do you know that?" my dad asked.

"It was on papers she gave me. Also, she told me."

"She was adopted by the Hazards," he protested.

"They raised her but never legally adopted her." I knew this because a stack of papers she'd given me to put in my safe deposit box included correspondence showing that there was no record of an adoption in either California or Massachusetts. My mother's birth certificate, also with the papers, identified her as Evelyn Ellis Bumpus, daughter of

Emma Hazard and Ebenezer Bumpus. But I'd known this before seeing the birth certificate. She'd told me her parents' first names when I was a child. Then, when I complained to her that I hated my name, Lucille Lang, because the other kids called me Blue Seal Langendorf and Lou the Seal, she said, "How would you like to be called Evelyn Bumpus and have all the fat bullies crash into you, saying 'Bump us! Bump us!'?" She added, "Don't tell anyone. It's just between you and me." That was the only time I ever heard her say her parents' last name. She took the Hazards' name after moving to California.

"Where were her parents born?" asked the ashen man.

"Her mother was born in Massachusetts, her father in Scotland," I said.

My father said, "I thought he was born in Massachusetts." He sounded a bit gruff, like someone who knows he's right but expects to be overruled.

"She always told me he was born in Scotland," I insisted. We put Scotland on the death certificate, but years later I would have to get it corrected after serendipitously finding information about her father on the Internet. The name Bumpus came from Edouad Bompasse, a Huguenot who arrived on the *Fortune,* the first ship after the *May-flower,* and was called Edward Bumpus in Plymouth. Ebenezer, who went by Eben, was an eighth-generation descendant of Edouad, and he was born in Acushnet, Massachusetts.

My mother always denied knowing anything about her father's ancestors, although Aunt Ethel once told me he was descended from the Pilgrims. I said, "But my mother says he was born in Scotland." "I don't want to contradict your mother," Aunt Ethel said, then told me no more.

Mom never wanted me, or anyone else, to know much about her parents. She was loyal to the Hazards, the people who raised her; that she was their adopted daughter was the story she told. I know now that her biological mother, Emma, was the illegitimate daughter of a Caucasian woman, a housekeeper, and a Wampanoag man. The Hazards, I'm sure, impressed upon both Emma and my mother that this was a background to hide.

"Did she graduate from high school?" the undertaker wanted to know.

Simultaneously, my dad said yes and I said no. "She graduated from Piedmont High School," Dad said.

"I looked for pictures of her and Aunt Ethel in the yearbooks at the Piedmont High School library, but there were none and no mention of their names. I asked her about it, and she said they dropped out in eleventh grade to take care of their grandparents."

My dad shook his head. "She always told me she graduated."

The undertaker looked perplexed. I guess he didn't think we had very good communication in our family.

When the subject turned to interment, Dad said, "My wife wanted to be cremated." This wasn't true. My mother had told me on several occasions that she wanted to be buried in a casket in her grandparents' plot. However, I didn't want to contradict him again. Also, I had been mentally tabulating the death expenses. With the urn and cremation fee, the expenses were already up to thousands of dollars. A casket, embalming, and full burial would cost even more. Contradicting my dad again would have been both embarrassing and expensive for him. His feelings took precedence now; my mother would be cremated. We selected a bronze urn and a container to hold it. I'd never known before that a container for ashes needs its own container, but this was the ashen man's area of expertise, and he said the second container was required. On Wednesday we would bury my mother's ashes in her grandparents' plot.

•••

When the phone woke me on Sunday morning, my first thought was that it must be my mother. She called me several times a day. Then I remembered.

"Lucy," Dad said, "I'm going to tell you something that's just between you and me. I'm not going to tell anyone else because I don't want them to think I'm crazy, but I want you to know because I don't want you to worry about your mother. She was here this morning when I got up, and she was happy. This wasn't a dream or hallucination. She was sitting in her chair in the living room. She said the cancer was gone and she was fine. I asked if she'd like some breakfast, but she said she didn't need anything, that she was just stopping by to let me know she was okay. Then she disappeared."

As I listened, I was happy for my dad. Although I thought it was a dream, I hoped my mother would visit me too.

•••

The flowers for the interment service have mistakenly been delivered to my house. Complicating matters further, my mother calls to say she needs a ride to the cemetery. I put the flowers onto the backseat of my car. One of the arrangements is not what I ordered: it's a bouquet of pink roses in a vase rather than a spray of roses for the container holding the urn. When I point out the error, my mother says, "Don't worry about it. It doesn't matter."

We're not allowed to drive into the cemetery, so I look for a parking place outside. Unable to find one nearby, I park several blocks away. My mother says she needs my help to walk, so I leave the flowers in the car and put my arm around her. She leans on me as we walk.

When we're still a couple of blocks from the cemetery gates, she says she needs to rest. We sit on a bench at a bus stop and put our arms around each other. I feel guilty because I know my father is waiting at the cemetery. He trusted me to get the flowers, and I have not only failed to deliver the flowers, but I am late myself. Still, it seems more important to take care of my mother. I start caressing her and stroking her hair, which is brown again. She's growing younger. She strokes my hair too, and I whisper, "It's okay. We don't have to go." Just as my mother didn't go to the nursing home, she's not going to the cemetery. We'll bury her ashes, but she won't be there. I hold her very close; words are unnecessary. I know her better than anyone, and there is nothing left to say.

Top: Ada Peckham Lang and Dick, ca. 1922
Bottom: Mariam Gertrude Peckham and Henry Harrison Peckham,
undated photo

chapter 13

The White Swan Motel

My father loved to tell the story of the White Swan Motel. To be inspired, he needed at least several listeners, so he told it at family gatherings—a birthday, anniversary, Christmas, Thanksgiving, or Fourth of July party. He didn't tell it too often, maybe once every five or six years. No one ever complained about having heard it before. Maybe some were being polite or had forgotten it, but I believe that, like me, most of the people in our family enjoyed the story and didn't mind hearing it again. Dad usually told it when the conversation turned to ghosts, horror movies, or serial killers, but the last time, the subject was writing.

It was an Indian summer afternoon near the end of the millennium. We'd gathered at my Aunt Liz and Uncle Bob's house in Napa for their birthdays and anniversary, which we always celebrated as a single event because all three occasions occurred between August 31 and September 15. My dad, Uncle Bob, and I were sitting at the scarred redwood picnic table in the backyard—Uncle Bob and I in the sun, my dad across from us, shaded by the ranch-style house. Aunt Liz and Aunt Ethel were a few feet away in the lawn swing—a big swinging sofa whose plastic floral-print upholstery was faded and ripped. Liana and Tamarind were there, but my mother had been dead for two years. We were eating stuffed eggs and crackers and cheese and drinking mediocre white wine. Although my aunt and uncle lived in California's Napa Valley, famous for its wineries, they had never learned the difference between Chardonnay and cheap Chablis.

My father was past eighty, and his myasthenia gravis was worsening. He never complained, though: he just took his medicine and went on with his life. Many people with myasthenia end up in wheelchairs, but he didn't expect that to happen to him.

We'd been talking about the coming millennium—the Y2K problem, doomsday fanatics. I don't remember how the conversation turned to writing, but my father said, "I have a story for you. If you want to be a successful writer, this is the story you should write."

As a young man, he'd hoped to be an actor or writer. Growing up in the 1920s, he'd met Charlie Chaplin, Jackie Coogan, and other actors at a hotel in Pasadena where he and his parents often stayed. Chaplin said, "Yes, you can be an actor too." After graduating from high school, he drove to Hollywood and visited the studios, saying he was a friend of Charlie Chaplin's, but no one even offered him a screen test, let alone a part in a movie. Then he wrote some stories, including memoirs of his encounters with Chaplin and Coogan, and sent them to *Reader's Digest,* but he only got rejection slips. Ultimately his form of creative expression became photography. He was a fine nature photographer, but it was a private passion. He took tens of thousands of 35 mm slides—flowers, animals, landscapes, sunsets, night lights, clouds—over about forty years but never published or exhibited them.

Although he never went to college, he always unabashedly claimed to be a near genius, and he did indeed have a phenomenal memory. Now, while his peers were having trouble remembering the events of their own lives, he could still recall in detail the plots and casts of every movie he'd ever seen, even the silent ones that had first inspired him to consider a career in acting.

As far as creative pursuits were now concerned, though, he was ambitious for me, certain I could be a best-selling author and eager to offer advice.

He launched into his story, hands in motion. Loss of muscle tone had begun to limit his facial expressions, and his skin was pale from avoiding sunlight, which interacted badly with his medications, but his blue eyes were lively, his voice animated. "This is a true story. It happened a long time ago, in the nineteen forties, before you were born. Your mother and I had only been married a few years. I was still in my twenties. Your mother, Aunt Ethel, and I had been to Pasadena to visit my cousins, the MacQuiddys. Back then it took two days to drive from Los Angeles to Oakland. They hadn't built Highway 5 yet. You had to take 99 through the valley, which always smelled like an outhouse because of all the fertilizer the farmers used, or drive up the coast, which was more scenic and had some fresh air. It was slow, but I liked the coast route. Before we left Pasadena, I looked at a map and figured we could make it to San Luis Obispo before nightfall. We planned to spend the night there and continue on home to Oakland the next day."

I'd driven the coast route with him myself five times between the ages of eight and twenty-three, always on the way to Disneyland, which for my dad was second only to Reno as a favorite destination. We always drove south on the coast and came back home through the valley. Since my mother's death, he'd often said he'd like to visit Disneyland again, but neither of my daughters had children yet, and all of us had places we'd rather go.

"We started out after lunch," he continued. "Almost right away, things started going wrong. First I had a flat tire. Then traffic got backed up because there was an accident. No sooner had it got going than we were stuck again, this time because of roadwork."

Aunt Ethel, who was eighty-seven and had appeared to be snoozing in the lawn swing, opened her eyes, recognizing the story. Everyone was listening to Dad.

•••

In 1935 my father is seventeen years old. His mother, Ada Peckham Lang, wants to inspire him and his brother, Bob, who's four years older. She isn't satisfied with her own accomplishments. She did oil paintings at her finishing school, Chamberlain Institute, but kept only one, a still life of decaying peach-colored roses. She doesn't particularly like it; it's too dark. She has already destroyed all of her other paintings because she didn't think they were good enough. Her husband insists that she keep this last one.

She was a schoolteacher in the San Joaquin Valley before her marriage. She has always wanted to do more with her life, maybe return to painting, maybe become a writer, but she hasn't been able to mobilize herself. In 1918 her eldest son, Billy Jr., died at age eight in the great flu epidemic, and she has felt like a bug stuck in glue ever since. Ada herself would not attribute this to Billy's death, but to her own inadequacy. In her opinion, she is inferior to her mother, Mariam Jones Peckham, who was born in 1846 and became a political activist and feminist writer. It occurs to Ada that by writing a family history and telling her mother's story, she can inspire her sons. She writes: "My mother was the most ambitious woman I've ever known.... All her life, she was a great worker both in public and private life. I often think how little I have accomplished compared with her great achievements"; "When she attended school, she won distinction by being the best essayist in her class and received prizes for her splendid work in literature. She wrote more or less during her entire life on various political and social problems of her day"; "I can best describe my mother as a 'new woman.' She advocated coeducational colleges, professions for women, and the ballot for the so-called 'weaker sex.' In other words, she wanted equal rights for men and women."

•••

"It was already dark by the time we got to Santa Maria. We stopped there for dinner at a roadside café and talked about getting a room there for the night, but we decided to drive on to San Luis Obispo. I figured we could make it by nine o'clock.

"Then a heavy fog rolled in. I'd never seen anything like it. Thick as whipped cream. I couldn't see a thing. Your mother begged me to stop." His voice became high-pitched as he imitated a frightened woman: " 'Dick, Dick! We can't go on. You can't see the road. We'll all be killed!' I said, 'I can't stop here, Evelyn. There's nowhere to stop. When I find a place to stop, I will. Someone will crash into us for sure if I stop here.'

"I thought things couldn't get worse, but instead of getting to San Luis Obispo, we came to a wooded area. Through the fog you could barely make out the shapes of densely packed trees. It was as though I'd driven right out of California and into a fairy tale. At that point, I wouldn't've been surprised to see a witch's cauldron bubbling under one of the trees. I don't get scared easily, but by then I was scared, so you have to understand what great relief I felt when I thought I saw a sign ahead." He let out a deep sigh, as though he'd just spotted the sign. "Because of the fog, I couldn't read it until we were right up close. It was just a painted sign, no lights or anything. It said White Swan Motel in large black letters. Above the lettering was a picture of a swan." As he spoke, he pointed in the air. "The driveway was gravel. This was no fancy motel, but we'd've taken anything then."

He spoke mostly to me, but he looked around periodically to make sure that the rest of the audience was with him. "It was a small place, just three cabins. One of them, the office, was on the right as you drove in. They put us in the cabin at the far left, the one furthest from the office," he said, showing the positions of the cabins with his hands. "There was a bedroom for your mother and me, a smaller adjoining room for Aunt Ethel, and a shared bathroom. The first thing I noticed was that everything was covered with dust. That seemed odd, but I just figured the White Swan Motel didn't get much business. Then I noticed there were no pictures on the walls— no flowers, no seashores, nothing. It was a queer place. Bleak.

"We were tired, so we didn't waste any time getting to bed, but we didn't get to sleep long. A little after midnight, noises started coming from the cabin next door." His voice became more ominous. He relished scaring us. "There was banging, sounds like furniture crashing, and the clattering and dragging of chains."

"Ghosts!" said Uncle Bob with a chortle. "What I want to know, Dick, is did you see any ghosts?" Although he'd heard the story before, he was playing along. His tone was that of a worldly twelve-year-old speaking to his superstitious eight-year-old brother.

"There might have been ghosts there, but I didn't see them. This story isn't about ghosts," Dad said indignantly.

"What's it about then?" asked Tamarind, who was twenty-five and the youngest among us. I was curious too. Some of the past tellings had indeed been about ghosts or aliens, and it had seemed that the main point was to scare us.

He paused only a few seconds, stroking his chin, then said, looking at Tamarind and drawing out each word, "It's about saving your own life."

•••

In 1936, the year my father graduates from high school, my grandmother starts having spells of weakness. Her legs grow rubbery and collapse beneath her, and she becomes reluctant to go out. Because she has difficulty swallowing, she subsists on milkshakes, juice, and soup. Her doctors say nothing is physically wrong with her, that she's suffering from depression. My father, who had planned to attend the University of California at Berkeley, puts his plans on hold and takes care of her for the next four years instead.

She stays home for the better part of sixteen years, growing progressively weaker, writing in her diary each day. By 1952 she is bedridden and can't even swallow liquids. Myasthenia gravis is not a genetic disease, but one can be genetically predisposed to it. Her doctors, however, have not thought of myasthenia. They recommend institutionalization and electroshock, the best treatment they know of for depression. Seventy-six years old, she's carried weeping from her home. The first treatment kills her.

•••

Turning toward me again, Dad said, "Your mother was scared by the noises. She said, 'Dick, what's that?' I said, 'I don't know. Let's just try to get some sleep. We'll get out of here first thing in the morning.' I was scared too, but I didn't want to show it."

"This is one of Dick's tall tales," announced Aunt Liz, who never wanted anyone to think she was gullible. I thought she was wrong, that the story was mostly true, but that Dad embellished it.

"This is no tall tale," Dad said. "This really happened."

"It sure did," Aunt Ethel concurred. "I was there." Her short-term memory was pretty much gone, but she could still be clear about the past.

•••

It's 1957, and I am nine years old. My family is seated around the dining room table at Aunt Liz and Uncle Bob's house. If my cousin Jan were here, I'd have to sit with her in the kitchen, but she isn't, so I get to sit in the dining room with the adults. Aunt Liz, Uncle Bob, and Dad are discussing my grandmother's self-published family history, in which she claimed that her mother, Mariam Peckham, was descended from William Floyd, who signed the Declaration of Independence, and that her father, Henry Harrison Peckham, was descended from the Pilgrims who came over on the Mayflower. *My dad and Uncle Bob are very proud of these ancestors, so I've heard about them many times before: they are people I should live up to and sources of my "good genes." "How do we know these things are true?" I ask. "Grandma's book just says them. She doesn't show the family tree." "Your grandmother would never say anything that wasn't true," Uncle Bob assures me. "I guarantee you that you are a* Mayflower *descendant," my father adds.*

My mother, who was born twenty-five miles from Plymouth, says nothing. "Who were your ancestors?" I ask her. "I don't know and I don't care. What you do with your own life is all that matters."

•••

"Tell us what happened next," said Liana. We all knew what happened next, but the story never lost its suspense.

"Your grandmother and I held each other close, listening to the awful sounds. It must have gone on for more than half an hour."

"How do you think I felt?" said Aunt Ethel. "I was all alone in the other room."

Dad took a deep breath, shaking his head and apparently looking off into a neighbor's yard, though in truth he must have been looking deeply inward. He continued, speaking more softly, as though we were at the White Swan Motel and he didn't want the people in the next room to hear him. "Then a woman screamed. It was a long, high-pitched, blood-curdling scream. I switched on the light to look for a phone to call the police, but there was no phone in that room." He was silent a moment. "There were two more screams." His voice, which had been nearly a whisper, rose to a loud wail. He screamed twice. "Ethel came running into our room and slipped on a throw rug in the hallway. 'I think there's something wet under the rug,' she said. The screaming and other noises had stopped. Everything was silent, spooky. Your mother said, 'Dick, I think someone just got killed over there.'

"I nodded, scarcely able to believe this was happening. Then I went to the hallway and picked up the rug where Ethel had slipped. The substance underneath it was red and moist, but starting to congeal. I thought, 'My God, someone's been killed in here too!' I told the girls, 'Pack up fast as you can. We have to get out of here!' "

"At that point, I pulled back the curtain enough to peek out the window. My heart was already hammering, but when I looked out, it became a percussion band: a pickup truck was parked behind me, perpendicular to my car. Another car was parked to the left. I didn't know if I could get out. Still, I ordered, 'Ethel, Evelyn, get your clothes on now and throw your stuff into the suitcases. Don't waste a minute!'

"Ethel looked under the rug herself. She gasped, turning pale, and looked like she was going to scream. I didn't often tell the twins what to do, but I said, 'Ethel, don't scream. It's not going to help us.' "

"I knew not to scream," she said. "I thought Evelyn was going to scream."

"Outside the fog was thick as ever. We got into my '36 Ford, and I started the engine. That truck didn't have to park behind me; someone had deliberately tried to block me. I backed into it, then pulled forward, and as I angled out, I also hit the car next to me." His hands gripped and turned an imaginary steering wheel, and he looked over his shoulder as he described backing up. "The truck was blocking the driveway, and to get around it, I had to drive under the trees. When I made it to the road, I drove as fast as I dared in that fog."

"It was just a few miles to San Luis Obispo. I considered looking for the police station, but I had no idea where to find it. I didn't dare stop at a phone booth. Everything was in darkness, and I was afraid that someone from the White Swan Motel might be following us. I just kept driving. I told the girls to get some sleep, but they were too scared. I was still scared too. I would've been scared even if we hadn't been at the White Swan Motel, because the whole coast was enveloped in that fog, all the way to Monterey. At Monterey I headed inland toward Salinas, and only then did we get away from it. It was well past dawn when we reached San Jose, but even then I didn't stop. I kept driving, all the way to Oakland.

"It was late morning when we got home. Your mother and Ethel went straight to bed, but tired as I was, I couldn't sleep. I knew I was lucky. I saw we were in danger and I got us out of there. But the trouble is, there are a lot of White Swan Motels in this life, and sometimes you're at the White Swan Motel and don't know it. I'm not just talking about vacations."

I wondered if he was also talking about gambling. Through the years, he'd lost a lot at keno, slot machines, and horse races, though he claimed to have been a winner at low ball, which he'd played several nights a week at the Key and Oaks Clubs in Emeryville while I was growing up. And how about his mother and her illness that was never properly diagnosed? Not to mention the jobs in banking that he'd worked at unenthusiastically for more than thirty years. Then there were bad marriages and ill-conceived affairs, which he had not experienced as far as I knew, but which I was well acquainted with. Maybe those, too, were White Swan Motels.

Aunt Liz said, "We can go inside now."

"That's not the end of the story," Dad said, annoyed by the interruption. "Let me finish."

"Make it quick," Aunt Liz said. "I don't believe a word of this."

"I wanted to call the White Swan Motel to report what had happened to the manager or owner, but the operator said it wasn't listed. So I called the San Luis Obispo Police Department and gave them the basic information. They told me to put everything I could remember into writing and send it to them. I also wrote to the local newspaper, the San Luis Obispo Chamber of Commerce, and the Better Business Bureau. I covered all the bases. I thought someone had been killed that night and I might be a key witness."

Because I knew what was coming, the skin was already rising all along my arms, even though I was sitting in the sun.

•••

I look for my father's Mayflower ancestors, but I can't find any. Perhaps they don't exist. Mariam Peckham's great-aunt was married to William Floyd, so she was not his descendant after all. John Peckham, her husband's earliest known ancestor in America, was a British nobleman and religious dissenter who arrived in Boston around 1634, joined the Anne Hutchinson party in 1639, and was one of the earliest settlers in Rhode Island. I learn, however, that my mother and Aunt Ethel are descended from fifteen Mayflower passengers.

•••

"About a week later I started getting replies. Everyone but the newspaper answered, and they all said the same thing: 'Dear Mr. Lang, Thank you for your letter. We have looked into your claims but have been unable to take any action, because there is no White Swan Motel.'

"God as my witness," he said, as the believers and nonbelievers among us thought about where he and my mom and Aunt Ethel might have been that night and what could have happened there. "They all said, 'There is no White Swan Motel,' so you see, you have to figure it out if you're stuck there and get out on your own."

Left: Bob and Liz Lang on their fiftieth wedding anniversary, 1986
Right: Aunt Liz with her mother, Frances, ca. 1920

chapter 14

Aunt Liz

It was not a desire to see her so much as family responsibility that made me drive from my house in Oakland to Napa that day to visit ninety-three-year-old Aunt Liz, my father's brother's widow. The drive took more than an hour under the best of circumstances, and circumstances on Bay Area freeways were rarely the best. I was never especially fond of Aunt Liz, nor was she of me as far as I could tell, but I needed to help my daughters, on whom the burden of Aunt Liz's errands, housework, and gardening had fallen. By choice, Aunt Liz had never had children. My father said she'd had two abortions in the 1940s. When my second daughter was born, Aunt Liz told me she'd been afraid of childbirth. When she was younger, she'd told others she was more interested in making money than making babies and was going to become a millionaire. She and Uncle Bob did do well in real estate for a while, but they sold all of their property in the early 1970s, before prices in California shot really high. Now she resisted hiring people to help her. When she fell or had a bout of illness, she'd get someone to stay with her, but as soon as she was back on her feet, the helper was dismissed.

Before leaving home, I called to say I'd stop for groceries. Aunt Liz gave me a short list, saying she didn't want to put me to any trouble, but after driving fifty miles to do errands for her, I'd have preferred to stock her kitchen well. She said she'd fix lunch for me and that she had something she wanted to talk about. She'd been hinting at this "something" at all of our family gatherings for the preceding year or so. I said okay, imagining she was going to say she'd decided to cut me out of her will.

Aunt Liz was not affectionate with me when I was small. When I was a preschooler, my parents sometimes left me with her and Uncle Bob when they went to Reno for the weekend to play the slot machines. Even on those sleepovers Aunt Liz never hugged me. She always kept her distance, as though I had a cold. Even Mabel Johnson, the neighborhood old maid and another of my babysitters, let me undo her braided bun after my bath, just for the joy of it, and held me close as she dried me.

Nor was Aunt Liz charmed by my childhood pranks. Whenever my parents took me to visit her and Uncle Bob at their Tudor-style house a few blocks away from us in Piedmont, my mother warned me to be very neat and quiet. She said, "If Aunt Liz were your mother, you'd really have to toe the line."

While the adults talked politics and money in the dining room, my cousin Jan and I always ate by ourselves in Aunt Liz's kitchen, where our chatter wouldn't interfere with their conversation and there was no Persian carpet on which we might drop our food. Sometimes I ventured into the dining room and tried to join in the discussion, but one of the adults always said, "Little pitchers have big ears," or "Children should be seen and not heard."

After dinner there was always a poker game. Ever so quietly, one night when I was about seven, I went upstairs to Aunt Liz and Uncle Bob's bedroom after the poker game started. On the dresser were old pictures of them. Uncle Bob was tall and slender with dark wavy hair and a mustache. In one Aunt Liz was on a horse, her auburn hair tucked into a cap. Now they'd both gained weight and Aunt Liz didn't ride horses anymore. I wished she did, so she could teach me. Aunt Liz's wedding ring, gleaming by the picture with the horse, caught my eye, and I slipped it into my pocket.

Later that night I watched as the adults rushed around the house and crawled on the floor, looking under furniture. Sometimes they stopped to ask me, "Have you been upstairs?" or "Are you sure you haven't seen a diamond ring?"

When a policeman arrived, my mother explained to me, "A burglar was here tonight and stole Aunt Liz's wedding ring."

The policeman noted that a burglar could have come in the open bedroom window, but he thought it more likely that the ring had been misplaced. "Most burglars wouldn't enter a house filled with people," he said.

The next morning my mother shook me to wake me up. "Do you have Aunt Liz's ring?"

I shook my head.

"Tell the truth. Aunt Liz is brokenhearted."

Feeling sorry for Aunt Liz, I took the ring from my nightstand drawer and handed it to my mother. "April fool!" It wasn't April. I just wanted my mother to know I'd played a joke, not committed a burglary.

When my mother returned the ring, Aunt Liz didn't think it was funny. "You should give the brat a good whipping and take her to a psychiatrist," she said. For years I was sorry I hadn't kept it.

•••

Aunt Liz was born in Chicago on September 15, 1910. Her mother, Frances, was an aspiring actress, her father a piano teacher. Frances used to tell the story of Aunt Liz's birth at family gatherings: she was born prematurely between Frances's convulsions and weighed only three pounds. The midwife put her in a shoebox, then placed it on the open door of the oven, which had been lit to provide warmth for the tiny baby. No one expected either Frances or the baby to survive. Aunt Liz's older brother, also premature, had died shortly after birth.

When Aunt Liz was still too young to remember her parents' ever living together, they divorced and Frances came to California to try to make it as an actress. While her mother traveled, performing in shows and plays, Aunt Liz stayed with her maternal grandmother in Reno. Although Aunt Liz adored her grandmother, she resented her mother's leaving her for extended periods. Even as an adult, she described her mother with bitterness: "She was too starstruck to be bothered with a child." My dad told me that during the 1930s and 1940s, Frances responded, "When you're a mother yourself, you'll understand."

Aunt Liz had been christened Maude Elizabeth, but she hated the name Maude because her schoolmates called her Maude the Mule. After marrying Uncle Bob, she had her name legally changed to Elizabeth. She told me she later realized that if her name had been Liz in elementary school, the other children would have called her Liz the Lizard.

She wanted to go to college, but there was no money for it, so after high school she went to work. By then her father was in California too, and he became a chess buddy of my paternal grandfather. The men soon discovered that one had an unmarried daughter, the other an unmarried son, both in their twenties, and the fathers arranged for the two to meet.

Aunt Liz and Uncle Bob married in 1936, shortly before her twenty-sixth birthday. From the start, she was adamant, my dad said, that she didn't want children. My uncle was a dockworker, but Aunt Liz had greater dreams for both of them. Starting with a modest bungalow, they bought houses, repaired and remodeled them, then sold them at satisfying profits. Aunt Liz loved to say, "I laughed all the way to the bank." By the 1950s they were buying, selling, and managing apartment buildings.

•••

It was a sunny day with enough of a breeze to keep the smog washed away. The oak-dotted hills were still green from spring rain. The drive would have been pleasant if traffic hadn't been backed up behind the toll plaza for the Carquinez Bridge. Slowed by the tie-up and my stop at the grocery store, I arrived at Aunt Liz's ranch-style bungalow in the wine country about two hours after leaving home.

After a perfunctory hello kiss, I asked how she was feeling. "As well as can be expected." She was a survivor of breast and colon cancer as well as a broken hip. Once a hefty 170 pounds, she was now down to 1 1 0 and able to wear my old sweaters, but she was tough and still very much alive.

I recalled visiting her in the hospital after her surgery for colon cancer when she was in her late eighties. She told me she knew she wasn't going to die yet, then described a dream she'd had before waking in the recovery room. She was playing a bingo-like game with God. The board stood upright, was as big as the side of a house, and had large illuminated red and green squares. The goal was to illuminate a row of green squares. If she did that she'd live, but if she got a row of red ones she'd die. God was questioning her, and each time she answered, either a red square or a green one would light up. When she answered the final question, a red square came on, completing a row. She thought she was going to die, but God said, "Don't worry. It isn't your time yet. I'm going to let you win," and a row of green squares came on instead.

The house was stifling. Although it was April, all the windows were closed and the heater was on high. She always kept her house this way now. I put her frozen dinners and peanut butter away, then sat down on the pastel floral-print sofa in the living room, under the gloomy painting of a sailboat drifting near shore on a cloudy night. She sat nearby in her antique rocking chair. I decided to ask her about the home movie of my second wedding, which I was more concerned about than the will.

Aunt Liz and Uncle Bob had never wanted my father to put me in his home movies. He'd first done so on a trip to Canada when I was six. When he showed this film at a family gathering in the rumpus room in Aunt Liz and Uncle Bob's basement, Uncle Bob said, "That's not Canada! All I see is Lucille."

My grandfather defended the movie, but Aunt Liz said, "Everyone thinks their kid is the most interesting thing in the world. What they don't understand is that no one else thinks so."

When I was eight, my dad, Aunt Liz, Uncle Bob, my friend Diane, and I drove to Disneyland. On the way Dad announced that he'd bought a roll of Super 8 film and was going to make a movie of our trip. "All you want to do is make a movie of Lucille," said Uncle Bob.

When Dad protested, Uncle Bob said, "I'll bet you five hundred dollars you can't resist putting Lucille in that movie."

There are a few quick glimpses of me: at the back of a crowd, spinning in a teacup, or on the Jungle Cruise in Adventureland. Mostly, though, my dad documented the fake hippopotami in the river, the Indian dancers in Frontierland, and strangers entering Sleeping Beauty's castle. Still, when Uncle Bob saw the movie, this time in my parents' living room, he roared, "I see Lucille! You lose."

Aunt Liz said she thought including me in such movies might give me an inflated sense of self-importance, and Uncle Bob bet my father that he couldn't resist putting me in his movies for the duration of my childhood. As it turned out, there would be little opportunity to do so, because Aunt Liz and Uncle Bob traveled a lot and had my dad's movie camera most of the time. They developed their own brand of child-free home movies with lots of buildings, trains, and jumpy landscapes shot by Aunt Liz from the window of their moving car.

My dad only made two more home movies. One documented another trip to Disneyland when I was eleven. I secretly disposed of it when I was sixteen, because again there were just a couple of quick glimpses of me, but many long, loving shots of my dad's cousin Beulah and her daughter Marg. I wish now that I had that movie, but as a teenager I found it so painful to watch that I wanted to make sure I'd never have to see it again.

Later the year I was sixteen, he made one more movie, in which he included me along with a half dozen or so other family members and friends. When Uncle Bob saw it, he said, "You're not supposed to film Lucille!" This time my dad protested mildly, saying he didn't see anything wrong with the movie.

All of this came back to me decades later, the last time my dad showed me his movies. I started crying, not because I wasn't in a lot of home movies, but because I'd been rejected by my aunt and uncle. They didn't even want still photos of me in their house and instructed my mother early on not to give them copies of my school pictures. "Why did Uncle Bob hate me?" I asked.

"He didn't hate you. He was jealous of me, because I had a child. Elizabeth never wanted children, but my brother would have been a good father." Maybe and maybe not. My dad got up from the tattered chair where he liked to sit, sat down beside me on the uncomfortable white Victorian-style sofa my parents had inherited from a neighbor, and put his arms around me. "I loved you when you were a little girl, and I love you now," he said. "My brother never had that."

I understood then that something far deeper than a battle over home movies had been going on throughout my childhood. Uncle Bob had wanted children. To his credit, he never wavered in his devotion to Aunt Liz or left her for a woman who would give him a family. On the contrary, he remained passionately in love with her his entire life. After he had heart valve surgery in his eighties, I took Aunt Liz to visit him. She told him, "I won't stay long. I don't want to tire you." He said, "You don't tire me, Liz. You energize me! Come hold my hand." She took his hand, and I went to get lunch. When I returned an hour later, they hadn't moved. They were gazing into each other's eyes like two teenagers, still holding hands.

The pain Uncle Bob felt watching movies of me must have been far worse than what I felt watching the Disneyland movies. For him, the missing children were dead; for me, the missing child was in the mirror. Of course, it would have been kinder of him not to take his grief out on me. Perhaps he wasn't even conscious of doing it, although I think my father understood it all along, and that's why he gave in.

Uncle Bob partially redeemed himself by creating a lovely home movie of my second wedding. This was my second marriage to Mark, and two-year-old Liana was also there. The movie included great close-ups of all three of us, and I always thought it would someday be mine.

When Aunt Liz was cleaning out her garage after Uncle Bob's death, she called to tell me she'd found the movie of my wedding and asked if I wanted it. I said yes. Then she argued that because it was so old and I was no longer with that husband, she should throw it out. "No," I insisted, "please don't throw it out. I'd really like to have it."

It wasn't just the movie itself that mattered. Like the one I threw out at sixteen, this one represented something bigger: it meant my uncle could look at my daughter and me without wishing we'd disappear.

The next time I saw her, I asked for it. She said she didn't know where it was but that "it must be around." Now, more than two years later, it still hadn't turned up.

"I'd like to have the movie of my second wedding," I said now. "You told me you had it after Uncle Bob died."

"It should be in the box in the dining room," she said. "It's labeled."

There was indeed a box of home movies in the dining room, but my wedding movie wasn't among them. The ancient wooden clock over the mantel chimed the hour, proclaiming that time was not on hold for me. Deciding to save further looking for another occasion, I went to the kitchen. Aunt Liz had fixed ham-and-cheese finger sandwiches and stuffed zucchini. It must have been a lot of work for her, given her state of health and the difficulty of getting around in a walker. When I saw her preparations, I was surprised. It looked like someone special was expected. I heated the stuffed zucchini according to her instructions and set the table.

We sat across from each other. Thin, with straight white hair and a face as deeply etched as the bark of a tree, she was wearing a turquoise-and-black sweater that had been Liana's, then mine. She looked very different from the robust woman I'd known growing up. Everything about her seemed smaller. Even her nose was tiny. It was as though she was dissolving and would soon disappear.

I remembered meals I'd had with her as a child, including one at my friend Diane's grandparents' house when I was four. After loading up her plate at the buffet, Aunt Liz placed it to my right on the dining room table just as I sneezed without covering my nose. "You have no manners," she yelled, slapping my face. I started screaming. "She's just a little girl," Diane's mother, Thelma, said. "She doesn't know about germs. You have to teach her." Aunt Liz turned toward me and hollered, "Don't you dare ever spray your germs on my plate again."

On another occasion, when I was in second grade, at a family dinner at Aunt Liz and Uncle Bob's house, my father started bragging about how well I was doing in school. Uncle Bob said, "I don't want to hear about how brilliant Lucille is." Aunt Liz said, "Everyone thinks their kid is the most intelligent kid in the world, but it is really boring for other people. Please don't bring this up at the dinner table again."

I didn't feel angry so much as sad and hurt about these incidents and similar ones. My mean joke with Aunt Liz's wedding ring was my only attempt to fight back, to make her and Uncle Bob feel bad. In fact, through the years, I tried to win their hearts. I didn't even know I was doing it. I danced and sang for them, wrote poems, and gave them drawings in which rainbows, hearts, and flowers sprouted everywhere. Aunt Liz said I sang off-key.

At thirteen I stopped trying to please my aunt and uncle and even my parents. All that mattered was pleasing boys. I don't blame anyone for the wild ride of my adolescence, certainly not my aunt and uncle. Still, I think it might have made a difference if they had been more caring.

Whenever I complained to my mother about Aunt Liz and Uncle Bob, she said the same thing she said whenever I told her my elementary school classmates had thrown dirt clods at me: "Just don't think about it. If you don't think about it, you'll forget it, and it will be like it never happened. On the back side of time, no one will remember and it won't matter anymore."

But I had a knack for remembering things. I didn't purposely try to do it. I especially didn't try to remember bad things. It just happened, like the sun rising or a river flowing to the sea, so here I was on the back side of time, remembering how Aunt Liz had slapped my face when I was four and demanded that my father stop bragging about my achievements when I was in second grade.

Even my memory itself became a source of insults from Aunt Liz. When I was small, she started telling people I had no real intelligence, just a photographic memory. When I was in high school, she and Uncle Bob advised me to take shorthand, advanced typing, and other business classes, in case I didn't get into college. Even after I was accepted at Berkeley, according to Jan, Aunt Liz continued to tell people I had no real intelligence, that my photographic memory might get me through high school, but I would never make it in college.

I no longer felt bitterness about any of this as I ate Aunt Liz's finger sandwiches and stuffed zucchini, but I can't say I'd grown to love her, either. I watched as she ate, each movement slow and deliberate. It was sweet of her to fix the food for me, I thought. I complimented it, for lack of anything else to say.

Aunt Liz started to thaw after my first year at Berkeley. She hadn't spoken to my mother for ten years, since a dispute following my grandfather's death. Suddenly she wanted all of us to be together as a family for Christmas dinner at her house, and I secretly took credit for it. I was doing well in college and beginning to earn Aunt Liz's respect. I thought that her respect for me made her feel more warmly toward my mother too.

Although I never forgot the early insults, in later years there was no use in bringing them up, because it seemed that Aunt Liz and Uncle Bob forgot they'd ever disliked me. My parents, aunts, and uncles never discussed family problems openly, and I think confronting Aunt Liz and Uncle Bob would only have produced anger and denial. As it turned out, I was the closest thing they ever had to a child of their own, and their sense of ownership grew stronger through the years. They fully claimed my daughters as their grandchildren, and the last time I called them before Uncle Bob died, Aunt Liz called out to him merrily, "Bob, it's your baby! It's Lucille! Your baby is on the phone!"

I didn't know it that day as I ate the finger sandwiches at Aunt Liz's stuffy house, but this would be our last visit. She didn't bring up the "something" she wanted to tell me, so I asked, "What is it that you wanted to talk about?"

"I've wanted to tell you this for a long time," she began. "When you were little, I always wanted to hug you. I felt bad for you, because I didn't think your mother was physically affectionate enough. Ethel was much more affectionate with Jan. I thought your mother might not want me to interfere, though, and I didn't know if you would let me hold you. Do you remember? Would you have let me?"

She looked frail and helpless on the other side of the table. My turn to thaw had finally come. I was long past any need to get even. "Yes, I would," I said, "and it's not too late." We were almost through eating, and I got up and went to her. She stood up, and we wrapped our arms around each other. I was holding her up, because she was too weak to stand on her own. She started to sob. I remembered the box of trinkets she kept for me to play with when I was small, and I imagined her coming across some pretty little thing and putting it in the box, thinking, "Lucille will like this." Maybe there were other acts of kindness I'd forgotten. I tried to hold my own tears back but couldn't do it. With her head on my shoulder and mascara running down my cheeks, I held her until her cat began to cry for food.

Top: Lucy, a.k.a. Geronimo, age four
Bottom: Tamarind, Lucy, and Liana, 1994

chapter 15

On Being Bad

When I say, "I was a juvenile delinquent and teen mother," my husband always argues that I wasn't a juvenile delinquent. "But I ran away at thirteen, was suspended from school for cutting at fourteen, had a baby at fifteen, shoplifted, hung out with bikers, drank, smoked pot, and dropped bennies. I think that's the real deal," I counter. "It's not who you are now," he protests. "It's not the person I know." But it is who I was, and I believe who I am now is as closely related to that person as a tree to its inner rings or the Earth itself to its molten core.

Rebellious kids are strong willed, have their own take on experience, and will feed convention to the piranhas if they see fit. As far as I can tell, our species has been producing a new crop of such kids every generation since the days when menfolk were throwing spears at woolly mammoths to provide dinner. One might ask why. Maybe in the early days kids who went out against their parents' wishes sometimes found new caves (housing for the whole community!), and maybe those who turned up their noses at what mom offered for dinner sometimes discovered new edible plants. Perhaps such kids have been nudging social practices in unexpected and occasionally helpful directions through the ages.

My will manifested itself long before adolescence. My father liked to tell me about an incident that took place when I was three or four months old and couldn't yet sit up or crawl. He said, "I was changing your diaper on the bed upstairs when the phone rang. I thought it would be safe to leave you for a few minutes. I wasn't gone five minutes, but you rolled off the bed, down the hallway, and down the stairs.

You knew what you were doing. You followed my voice and landed screaming at my feet, as though to say, 'How dare you leave me! You can't do that!' I thought, 'My God, what have we created?' "

My earliest memories are of being in my crib, watching dancing points of light in the darkened room. They swirled and glittered, or fell like rain. Usually they were red, blue, or green, but once a swarm of yellow ones arrived. I watched, holding very still, afraid they were bees. If my parents put me to bed before I was tired, I stood at the end of my crib and cried. Sometimes my mother or father would come back, pick me up, and sing a lullaby; other times they let me scream.

Delighting in mischievous behavior, I liked to hide my empty bottle from my father. I usually threw it under the crib. Once I reached down as far as I could between the slats and threw it under the bed next to the crib. My father acted really baffled as he looked for it. I watched excitedly and was disappointed when he found it. The next time I put it underneath my pillow, inside the pillowcase. He looked all around the room, in every corner, under every piece of furniture as I watched from the crib. Finally he came back and pointed to the pillow. Shaking my head, I picked up the pillow to show him there was no bottle underneath.

He left the room, calling, "Evelyn, did you take Lucille's bottle?"

When I heard my parents coming up the stairs, I pulled the bottle out. As they entered my room, I waved it for them to see. They looked at each other quizzically, and I was pleased.

Whenever I wore my coveralls as a toddler, my mother explained to people that my grandmother had bought them for me. Previously my mother had always dressed me in party dresses and warned me not to get dirty when I went outside. The other kids in the neighborhood always made fun of the frilly dresses and dared me to make mud pies. I knew my mother would be mad, but I eagerly complied.

When my mother was hospitalized for a nervous breakdown when I was two, my father enrolled me in nursery school. Promising to come back later, he left me bawling the first day, and I went to an area where children were working with clay. Some of their handiwork was on display: cats, dogs, cows, horses. I noticed that nobody had made a pig, so I started working on one.

A teacher said, "What are you doing?"

"Making a pig."

"Are you sure you want to make a pig? Don't you want to make something prettier than a pig?"

"No! I want to make a pig." I wanted to be different, a principle that would drive a lot of my behavior in coming years.

The day my mother came home, she stayed in bed. A no-nonsense lady with gray hair was there to cook for us and watch me. When she came into my mother's bedroom with biscuits and jam, my mother took one and offered one to me. When I accepted it, the lady scolded, "That's not for you. That's for your mother," and reached to take it back. I took a bite. She said, "Your mother has been very sick. You should be good to her." With my sticky hand I took a swipe at her dress.

At three I loved the excitement of getting lost. Karen Mickens, who lived across the street and was ten months older, was always willing to join me, but her little sister, Patsy, needed some coaxing before she'd come along. The Piedmont police soon knew all of us by name and where to take us home. Whenever we played outside, Mrs. Mickens would periodically stick her head out the window and yell, "Don't go on any of Lucille's famous walks!" All too soon, though, I found I could no longer get lost. No matter how far I walked, I could remember how to get home.

On the corner of Karen and Patsy's block, there was a shiny red fire alarm box with a little handle inside a compartment covered with glass. Oh, how I longed to pull that handle and bring the fire engines to my neighborhood. I told Karen and Patsy, and Karen dared me to do it. She crouched down, and I stood on her shoulders and used a rock to break the glass. Then I pulled the handle and we ran as fast as we could to hide behind the nearest garage. As the engines came screaming down the hill, we crept out of our hiding place to get a closer look.

"Did you see who pulled the alarm?" asked one of the firemen.

We shook our heads.

It was so much fun we decided to do it again a few days later. This time we didn't even hide. We waited on the corner, but the engines didn't come. Instead a man in a red car arrived, followed by a policeman who knew us, and they told us we were breaking the law. The Mickens girls said in unison, "Lucille did it!"

A fireman and a police officer came to my house that night. They sat in the living room with my parents while I played on the floor with my Raggedy Ann doll and Evelyn, my blue stuffed cat. My mother kept saying, "How could she reach it?" and "I don't see how she broke the glass."

"Why did you do it?" our visitors asked.

"I wanted to see the fire engines."

"On Saturday your father can bring you to the firehouse," the fireman said. "We'll give you a special tour." At the Piedmont Fire Station that weekend, I got to climb on a fire truck and even sit in the driver's seat, while my father yelled, "Fire! Fire! Fire!"

My mother always said I was worse than a dozen kids. Maybe she was right.

Fifteen years later, when I was eighteen, I had my own three-year-old child, Liana, and it terrified me whenever she wandered off. Whatever survival value existed in her ability to find her way home was more than counterbalanced by the danger of her being kidnapped or hit by a car. By the time my younger daughter, Tamarind, started walking, I knew better than to leave her alone outside even briefly. Once, though, she got away from me during a peekaboo game when her father and I were shopping at Macy's. A security guard found her and brought her back about fifteen minutes later. Those were the worst fifteen minutes of my life.

Perhaps it was payback time for my own contrary behavior. As a toddler, I refused to go to bed at eight o'clock, wouldn't drink milk without chocolate in it, and once cut a brand-new dress to shreds to protest getting my hair cut. When I couldn't get my way by arguing, I screamed. My Uncle Dick started calling me "Geronimo" and "the wild Indian" before I started school, and my parents threatened to give me back to the Indians if I didn't behave. I said, "Good. I want to see the Indians," and answered "Geronimo" when anyone asked my name. (I would learn many years later that my mother was one-quarter Wampanoag. She kept this to herself, apparently cowed by the Hazards, who raised her, into believing that Native American ancestry was something to hide.)

In those days my best friend was Diane, whose grandparents lived on Fruitvale Avenue next door to my Aunt Ethel and Uncle Dick. She was Swedish and Danish, with blue eyes and long blond hair. We met while playing out front when I was three years old and she was eight, and she invited me inside to see her dolls. We had a great time until a policeman knocked on the door, looking for me because my parents had reported me missing. Given my history, I don't know why my mother took a chance on leaving me alone outside.

When Diane and I played house, we made real cookies; when we played school, she taught me to read, write, add, and subtract. She also taught me how to play games like Monopoly, Clue, Candy Land, and canasta. And early on she taught me, literally, that I wasn't the center of the universe. We were playing at her grandmother's house when she told me she thought her cousin Claire, who was a little younger than I, thought she was the center of the universe and every-thing existed for her. I said, "I thought everything existed for me." Diane said matter-of-factly, "It doesn't. All children start out think-ing that." I started crying. "She's just a little girl," Diane's mother, Thelma, said. "You shouldn't make her feel bad." Later I asked my mother if what Diane had said was true, and she said it was. I was disappointed, but I didn't cry.

The day I started kindergarten, many of my classmates were scared and cried for their mothers, but I was glad to be at school. I walked home almost every day with towheaded Ken, who wore jeans a couple of sizes too big with suspenders and rolled cuffs. One day as we poked along Lake Avenue, he said, "My big brother could beat up anyone in the world."

"He couldn't beat up my daddy."

"Oh yes he could. My big brother could beat up your daddy any day."

"Oh no he couldn't, but I could beat you up!" I said, pushing him into the gutter as we turned the corner from Lake onto Greenbank. I kicked him until he fell down. Then I started hitting him with a stick. I wanted to put him in his place for bragging and insulting my daddy. When he started to cry, I dropped the stick and ran the rest of the way home.

That afternoon Ken and his mother came to my house. His mother told my mother that I'd beaten him up and ought to be punished. I said it wasn't true. She said, "My son never lies. He knows he'd get his mouth washed out with soap and water if he did."

After they left, my mother asked again, "Did you do it? If you tell me the truth, I won't punish you."

"Yes," I admitted. Then she whipped my behind.

Playing follow-the-leader as we headed outside for recess one winter morning, I had a sudden urge to kick Peggy Toby. I knew it was wrong, but I felt like being bad. I did it, and Mrs. Minor, our kindergarten teacher, benched me. I pretended I knew a game to play with the leaves on the ground by the bench, and many of the kids hung around the bench, asking me to teach them, until it was time to go back inside.

I identified with the mischievous kids in the Beverly Cleary books that Mrs. Minor read to us, but none of the grown-ups seemed to understand. However, they needn't have been concerned about my "aggressive behavior," as I once heard Mrs. Minor refer to it when she was talking to my mother. In fact, I'd felt guilty after beating up Ken and kicking Peggy, and had decided not to do things like that anymore.

In first grade I grew bored with *Howdy Doody* and *The Mickey Mouse Club*; I preferred *Your Hit Parade*, which I'd first watched with Diane. It was also that year, at the age of six, that I bought my first popular record: Teresa Brewer's "Let Me Go, Lover!" The song made me think of Ricky Schiller, on whom I'd had a crush ever since the music teacher paired us for a dance our class was to perform for the open house at our school. When I was captain of the kickball team, I always chose Ricky first; when he was captain, he chose me. Hand in hand, we walked to the auditorium for assemblies; as we read, "Oh, oh, oh. See Dick run!" I tried to catch his eye.

I wasn't the only girl who liked dark-haired, dark-eyed Ricky, the only Jewish child in our class and the class clown. Each day at recess a group of four or five girls would chase him around the playground and try to kiss him. Once I caught him, wrapped my arms around him, and kissed him on the lips with a pucker and smack. "I let Lucille catch me," he told our astonished classmates, "because she was the one who tried the hardest, like she really meant it."

Toward the end of the year, Miss Clydesdale took us on a tour of the post office. Between the bins of mail, I said, "Ricky, I love you."

"I know," he replied.

I joined the Everly Brothers Fan Club in second grade. On the application I said I was sixteen and attended Piedmont High School. As the first member from Piedmont, I received a letter from the national president, asking me to be president of the local chapter. I tried hard to get the other girls in my class to join, and some of them wanted to, but their mothers, who didn't approve of premature adolescent behavior, wouldn't give them the money for dues.

When I was eleven, I talked my mother into becoming an Avon lady. Since she didn't use makeup, she wasn't enthusiastic, but I promised to help. I went through the training with her, and when we went door to door, I did most of the talking. The housewives were friendly, but most of them didn't buy anything.

My real fun came when it was time to send in the order, which my mother never even looked at. I ordered one of each of the perfumes and dusting powders in pretty containers, with names like Cotillion, Topaz, and To a Wild Rose. When the package arrived COD, my father wanted to send it back, but my mother insisted on paying, saying that it would save her the trouble of Christmas shopping. But I was not about to give my booty away as Christmas presents, and as soon as we opened the package, I took everything up to my room.

On our second order, I ordered every color of nail polish and lipstick and every fragrance of cream sachet. My dad said he was going to put an end to my mom's Avon career, but before he did anything about it, she received a letter saying she was fired for misusing her position and failing to work her territory.

One morning in sixth grade, I decided to cut school. I wrote a note to my mother, saying, "Don't worry. I just need a feeling of freedom and wind in my hair." After putting the note in our mailbox, I set out for Aunt Ethel and Uncle Dick's house, about three miles away. When I got there, Uncle Dick put me into his navy-blue Oldsmobile and drove me home.

My mother was hysterical.

"What's the matter?" I asked.

"I was worried about you. Why did you do it?"

"Like I said in the note, I just needed to feel free."

"Don't give me that crazy talk!" she screamed.

That was the year my father told me I couldn't play anymore with Jackie, the only black girl in Piedmont. He took me out for a drive and said, "All the neighbors are talking about it. I don't want you ever to see her again." I said, "She's a nice person. She's my friend." He said, "She may have a heart of gold, but she's not your kind." I cried, because I knew my father was wrong. He was afraid to stand up to the neighborhood busybodies, and I'd have to defy him. It was the first time my rebelliousness would be put to genuine good use.

I sowed the seeds of rebellion throughout my childhood. When I was twelve, they were ready to take root and grow. I could hardly wait to smoke, drink, have sex, and cut school some more. It seemed like this was what I'd been preparing for all along.

•••

Being bad felt good when I was a teenager. It felt delicious. It was one great adventure, but by the time I was twenty-seven, I had my own rebellious twelve-year-old daughter, and then kids' bad behavior wasn't fun anymore. I was surprised when Liana started cutting school, coming home drunk at dinnertime, and hanging out with nine-teen- and twenty-year-old men. I thought my mother's incessant nag-ging and puritanical outlook had driven me to such behavior. I didn't nag Liana, so why was she doing this?

I called social service agencies to get psychotherapy for her. The first place said they didn't treat adolescents without seeing the whole family. Kids like her, they said, almost always came from dysfunc-tional families, and the whole family must be treated, not just the adolescent. I resisted and called another agency. They said the same thing. Again I resisted and continued down the list. When the third agency said, "We don't treat adolescents without...," I knew what was coming. "Okay," I said, "my husband and I will come with her."

Liana didn't want to see the therapist. She insisted that Ben, her stepfather, was the one who needed therapy, but I talked her into it, and the three of us started seeing Barbara, a reserved young woman who had a sandbox and little plastic figures in her office for work with children. Liana was bored, because we spent most of the time talking about Ben's and my relationship. Soon she stopped coming, but Ben and I continued to see Barbara and gripe about each other. It didn't worry Barbara that Liana wasn't with us. Liana was a normal adolescent, she said, and her rebelliousness was normal: "I've seen a lot of emotionally disturbed children and teenagers, and Liana isn't one of them."

One night she didn't come home. I called the police, who were not terribly concerned that a rebellious twelve-year-old was missing. The officer who took the report at about midnight told me he expected that she'd turn up within forty-eight hours.

I couldn't sleep. At about four o'clock in the morning, a car pulled up in front of the house. Then I heard footsteps and a thump on the porch. The doorbell rang, and I got up to answer it. The car was gone. Liana was lying facedown on the porch. I felt her pulse, then tried to rouse her, but she was unconscious. I woke Ben up, and we took her to an emergency room.

A blood test showed she'd been drinking heavily. The doctor told us to take her home and let her sleep it off.

She continued to cut school and come home drunk. When she did go to school, she spent her time with the parkies—the kids who gathered in the park behind the school to smoke marijuana. Her grades were terrible. She fought with Ben, shunned me, and complained often and bitterly about having to share a room with Tamarind, her two-year-old sister. "You should keep Tamarind in your room," she said. "*You're* the one who had the baby." Ironically, all her friends now called her Happy.

Where had I gone wrong as a parent (other than starting too soon)? I thought maybe I hadn't told Liana often enough how wonderful she was: I hadn't helped her build a positive self-image. So I started telling Tamarind several times a day how sweet and smart and pretty she was. I called her "my good girl," hoping to make her believe in her own goodness.

I wanted to be Liana's friend, but the more I pressed it, the more she pulled away. When I asked about her feelings, experiences, and plans, she said, "What's your trip?" or "Cut the interrogation." She refused to discuss sex and birth control with me. Once I broached these subjects when she was looking at herself in the bedroom mirror, preparing to go out, combing her long wavy golden-brown hair. "It's important to talk about these things," I insisted. "You have to think about what you're doing and make conscious choices, or you could get pregnant." She looked at me with her large hazel eyes, so similar to my own. "I'm not going to get pregnant," sneered the daughter I conceived at fourteen. "I'm not that stupid!"

Even though it went against my better judgment, I let her stay out late (even all night) and hang out with other troubled kids. In therapy I told Barbara how resentful Liana was, although I was extremely permissive. Barbara thought I was too permissive. She said I identified too strongly with Liana, that when I let her go out at night, I was letting myself out as an adolescent. Barbara thought she needed boundaries.

I couldn't provide them. It was probably true that I identified with Liana and was giving my younger self permission to be bad, but it was also true that I couldn't deal with the consequences of trying to tell her what to do. She was frequently absent from or late for school. I knew it was my motherly responsibility to get her up for school, but when I shook her and said, "Liana, get up, or you'll be late for school," she screamed, "Get away from me, you fucking bitch." It was easier to let her sleep.

Every encounter became a confrontation. At dinnertime one night she came swinging and banging through the house in her tank top and patched blue jeans. "Yuck! What's that stink?"

"Chicken curry soup."

"Make me a hamburger."

"I think you ought to fix your own dinner if you don't want what I'm cooking."

Many decibels higher: "It's YOUR JOB!"

I gave her money for a hamburger. Should children get to choose what they eat? I recalled having once believed this. I gave Tamarind a choice: she could eat what I ate or she could starve.

At fifteen Liana started tenth grade at Maybeck High School, a small private school in Berkeley, but she was unmotivated and her attendance was spotty. Her friends included dropouts, adults who hung out with teenagers, and undirected kids like herself. Once I came home in the middle of the day and found her sitting on the back porch, talking on the phone and sipping red wine with a girlfriend. I picked up the wineglasses and smashed them onto the cement patio below. Of course, this hurt me more than it hurt her: they were my wineglasses.

Her boyfriend, Eric, was a roadie for an obscure rock band. In her second semester at Maybeck, she dropped out and moved in with him and his mother and stepfather. I felt I had no more control over her than I had over the orbit of the moon or the rise and fall of the tides.

I often berated myself for having given birth as a teenager, but I told myself things could be worse. At least there were adults in the household where Liana was living. Her boyfriend's mother ran a bookstore, and Liana was working there, so I knew she wasn't going wild twenty-four hours a day. *It could be worse, it could be worse.* That was my mantra.

•••

When Tamarind was eleven, as I drove her to Hillcrest Elementary School one morning, she told me she didn't want to go to Bob and Susie's house anymore after school. When I asked why, she explained that their daughter, Willow, made fun of teen magazines and irritated her by acting babyish. Tamarind was entering adolescence, I realized, but Willow, two years younger, was not. I didn't want Tamarind to lose Willow's friendship. Also, Bob and Susie had been good to Tamarind, and I didn't want to lose their friendship, either. Not to mention the peace of mind that came with knowing she was safe after school. I told her I'd talk to Bob and Susie to let them know how she felt. I said I was sure she'd be able to continue going there. "Nothing you say and nothing they say can change how I feel. I don't want to go there, and you can't make me go there," she said. "If you take me there, I'll leave."

This was a side of Tamarind's personality I hadn't seen before. She'd always been sweet, loving, and agreeable. Now I could see that she was also strong willed like her sister, like me. Perhaps I could have said, "You have to keep going to Willow's house for now. It isn't right to drop a friend without trying to work things out." But I didn't feel I could tell her what to do any more than my mother could have told me what to do, or I could have told Liana what to do. I identified with Tamarind, just as I had identified with Liana. Maybe Tamarind would have been more cooperative than I had been as an adolescent, but I will never know, because I gave in to her.

She had another surprise for me. Ever since her toddler days, when Liana started rebelling, I'd been calling her my good girl. On our way to Hillcrest, just a few days after telling me she wasn't going to Willow's house anymore, she said, "Don't call me your good girl anymore. It sounds like I'm such a goody-goody. I hate it. I'm not your good girl. I'm not perfect. I have bad thoughts sometimes like everybody else." I was hurt and embarrassed. Even more strongly than I did when she told me she wasn't going to Willow's house anymore, I realized that her childhood was over.

When Tamarind was fourteen, I let her and her friends cover her bedroom walls with graffiti. In very large letters above the dresser, she wrote, "I AM NOT PREPPY." What else is new? When I took her shopping at Hilltop Mall, I was acutely aware that the other teenage girls were not dressed all in black and did not have purple-black hair. I was forty years old. The thought crossed my mind that perhaps I carried a gene for this.

I really began to worry when Tamarind started ninth grade at Oakland Technical High, a large public school. Her grades plummeted. She told me she didn't think her teachers cared whether she went to class or did her homework; as far as I could tell, none of her new friends were headed for college.

In tenth grade she went to Maybeck, the high school Liana had briefly attended, and did well there, but she wanted to go to Berkeley High, another large public school, for her junior year. Neither her father nor I lived in Berkeley, but friends of ours agreed to put their utility bill in her father's name. He also had our friends' address printed on his checks and a phone line with an answering machine installed at their house. Tamarind lasted at Berkeley High for about six weeks. She told me she didn't like the cliques, how you had to wear a certain kind of jeans and a certain kind of lip gloss to belong to a group. She thought the social scene was stupid, and she stopped going to school. Officials from the Berkeley School District started calling me at work, threatening to send a truant officer after her and also to have me arrested. I told them she would be returning to Maybeck in January. In actuality, she had to reapply and hadn't yet been accepted, but I was hopeful they'd take her back. They did, and that's where she graduated. I don't believe she would have graduated if her only options had been the public high schools.

A lot of Liana's rebellion was directed against Ben and me. Tamarind's was more aimed at creating her own identity. My own rebellion was similar in some ways to Tamarind's and in others to Liana's. Like

Tamarind, I was trying to establish my individuality. Like Liana, I was rebelling against my family, particularly my mother. Also like her, I would give just about anyone the benefit of a doubt. (According to a newspaper story, Eddie, who stood me up at Chicken Delight in 1965, is now an ex-convict who "nearly pulled off the perfect bank robbery." And then there was the man who admitted on our first—and last—date that he'd murdered his wife.)

•••

Shortly after she dropped out, Liana passed the California High School Proficiency Exam and started taking community college courses. By the time she was eighteen, she was back in school in earnest. She ultimately earned a bachelor's degree in dramatic art and a master's in psychology, and she's now a marriage and family therapist. In addition to seeing private clients, she runs anger management workshops for men and women and specializes in helping families affected by domestic violence. In honor of her work, she was selected in 2002 to be one of the relay runners who carried the Olympic torch for the winter games in Salt Lake City.

After graduating from high school, Tamarind studied for a year at the California College of Arts and Crafts, then transferred to UC Santa Cruz, where she earned a degree in biology and environmental studies. She later earned an MBA and is now an accountant.

Maybe motivation was also part of my genetic bequest. By the time I was fifteen, shoplifting was permanently off my to-do list. By nineteen I had no desire to be an alcoholic, drug addict, or convict. Instead I was obsessed by the desire to garner knowledge and do worthwhile things in the world.

Yet I believe that the person I am now is related to the wild adolescent I once was, and that my contrariness has paid off. As an example, when I was a senior at UC Berkeley, I took an upper division course in quantum mechanics. It was part of a physical chemistry sequence for chemistry majors, and I enrolled because the sequence for biology majors conflicted with classes I wanted to take in dramatic art and sculpture. In the quantum mechanics course, all of my classmates were men. This was 1971, and a great many people still thought that men were innately better than women in math and science. (Some still do, but thankfully their numbers are dwindling.)

I sat at the back of the class because I didn't want all of the men staring at the back of my head during the lectures. I'd prepared for exams in previous physics and chemistry courses by reading and rereading the textbook and my lecture notes, and by going over the homework problems again and again. Before my midterm in quantum mechanics, I tried something different: after reading the text and lecture notes only once, I did all of the problems at the end of the chapters we'd covered, including those that hadn't been assigned. It worked. I sailed through the exam like a cliff swallow on an ocean breeze, finished early, and got the highest grade in the class.

The day the exams were returned, Professor Jura followed me out of the classroom. He said, "While I lectured, I always looked at you and thought you didn't belong there, didn't understand what was going on, and were going to flunk. I'll never think that about a student again." He also said he'd give me a recommendation anytime for any reason, because he thought I could do whatever I wanted. The point here is not that I'm a mathematical or scientific genius (I'm sure I'm not). The point is that I thought the idea that women weren't as good as men at math and science was a bunch of baloney, acted accordingly, and won Professor Jura over. Later, hoping to win more people over, I would coauthor a book entitled *How to Encourage Girls in Math and Science: Strategies for Parents and Educators.*

As a child, I didn't take dance or art lessons, play a musical instrument, or participate in sports. Maybe activities such as these could have provided an outlet for my willfulness and urge to think differently. Although there's no way to know for sure, intuitively I believe this is so. When Tamarind was a teenager, she was deeply involved in art. It was a way to defy convention, and I believe this prevented her rebelliousness from becoming self-destructive. Now, whenever my daughters ask for money for lessons for their children, I say yes. Yes to soccer. Yes to swimming. Yes to piano. Yes to gymnastics. Yes to drama. Yes to camp. So far, my grandchildren are very well behaved. So what if I'm broke!

In 2006 artist Nancy Mizuno Elliott was commissioned by the Alameda County Arts Commission to create four works of art for the new Alameda County Juvenile Justice Center, the facility where I was incarcerated when I ran away from home at thirteen. One of the works, *Bee Wisdom*, "asks the viewer to live passionately and forsake 'coolness.' " In *Bee Wisdom* Elliott incorporated the last stanza of "To an Artist," a poem that I wrote for Tamarind when she was a teenager:

To an Artist

"Fuck the real world. I'm an artist!"
your button announces. Your room
is strewn with paint, palettes and brushes.
Crumpled clothes hang every which way
from open drawers; more are heaped
on the floor with your paper and glue.

A young man's eyeball rolls down his cheek
like a huge bloody tear. He offers
his other eyeball, which is stuck
on his finger like an olive, to the tongue
of a gaunt green man with pointed ears.
Your paintings are surreal, weird.

And you are lovely. Your hair is dark
and tangled; your skin is smooth.
I have lived with you for eighteen years—
ever since I pushed and grunted,
and you slid from my pulsating womb
into the obstetrician's hands.

Why not make love with the real world?
Wrap your arms and legs around it;
give and take as much pleasure
as you can. Smile at the neighbors,
give your boss a daisy, laugh often, cry
if you have to, caress the new-mown grass.

Michelangelo's David *(1504), Galleria dell'Accademia, Florence, Italy*

chapter 16

Visit to David

In the summer of 1977, en route to Israel to study Hebrew at Tel Aviv University, I arrived in London eager to see and do as much as possible before my classes began. This was my first trip abroad, so not to waste even a moment, I signed up for a tour that promised to show me seven countries in two weeks. The guide, Pierre, was a dapper little Frenchman with thinning hair. He loved to give orders, but at twenty-nine I had no more use for his authority than I'd had for the principal of my junior high school when I stuffed my school uniform into a Dumpster in seventh grade. A woman from Wisconsin, her adult daughter, and I were the only people on the tour who chose not to eat dinner at the hotel with the group every night. In addition, I sometimes chose to explore a city on my own. Pierre needled me every day about the diseases I might get by eating at restaurants he wasn't familiar with, and he kept telling me that he knew the interesting sites. No need to strike out on my own! Although he claimed to speak six languages himself, he said of my interest in Hebrew, "You're wasting your time. People everywhere speak English."

What he showed us mostly was the inside of the bus. (What did I expect with two days per country?) I dreaded the sound of his voice, calling out at the Cologne Cathedral or the Eiffel Tower, "Okay, ten minutes, then back on the bus!" Before he could speak at the Colosseum, I called out, "Okay, time's up, folks. Just stay put!" Everyone laughed except Pierre.

I confess I did have one moment of fondness for him. Outside the Tivoli Gardens near Rome, a pack of about a dozen teenage boys followed me, alternately chanting in Italian and calling in English that I should go with them. Maybe they targeted me because I was alone. They didn't pay any attention to the twenty-two college girls on my tour, who were traveling with their professor and exploring the gardens in groups of three or four. When I walked faster, the boys walked faster. I started to run, and they ran after me. I ran all the way back to the bus, where some of my tour mates had already gathered. Even after I got on the bus, the boys kept yelling that I should come back out and go with them. They didn't leave until Pierre told them off in Italian.

According to the brochure, in Florence we were supposed to visit the Accademia di Belle Arti to see Michelangelo's twice-life-sized marble sculpture, *David*, the pièce de résistance of Renaissance sculpture. I wanted to see the tension in David's face, the twist of his body, the bulging veins of his lowered right hand. As we approached Florence, Pierre announced that the Accademia was already closed and he was taking us instead to the Piazza della Signoria to see a bronze replica of *David* and have a group photograph taken by his friend "Fellini." Later that afternoon, after we checked into our hotel, Laura, the daughter from Wisconsin, picked up a guidebook in the lobby and looked up the Accademia. It said that the museum's closing time was two hours later than Pierre had claimed, but by now the museum really was closed.

I figured Pierre had lied to us so that he could get his cut on sales of Fellini's photograph. When we got back on the bus to go to Santa Croce—the church that holds the tombs of Michelangelo, Galileo, Machiavelli, and Rossini—I told Pierre what the guidebook said, adding that he should have let the group decide whether to go to the Accademia or the Piazza della Signoria. He neither looked at me nor answered, but after I sat down, he got up and started pacing the corridor of the bus.

"It's a lie," he bellowed, his face red, the bulging tendons in his neck reminding me of the marble veins in David's hand, which I hadn't gotten to see. "You are a liar! The hours of the Accademia have changed. I told you the new hours." Still pacing, his scalp shining under his sparse hair, he yelled, "I have brought hundreds of groups here. I know the hours of the Accademia. I am the tour guide. I have great dignity. You are nobody. You are only a passenger. You have no dignity. I can throw you off the bus anytime I want to, suitcase and all."

When his tirade ended, I said, "I don't give a damn," without raising my voice.

Pierre returned to his seat, but a few seconds later he jumped up and rushed back to me. He was trembling all over, and for a moment I thought he was going to hit me.

"I am not going to let you have the last word," he screamed. "I am going to have the last word." I didn't think he could get any louder, but he did as he yelled, "I don't give a damn, either!"

I said nothing. Pierre sat down, and the driver started the bus.

When we got off at Santa Croce, one of the men in the group approached me and whispered, "He's afraid of you." Many of the other passengers, all of whom had remained silent during Pierre's tantrum, quietly offered support. After examining the frescoes, carvings, and tombs of the illustrious at Santa Croce, I walked to the Accademia while the group went shopping for leather goods. A fine mist made the pavement and gray stone buildings glisten. The hours posted were exactly as specified in the guidebook.

•••

For nearly thirty years this was what I remembered about my visit to Florence. When anyone asked what I did there, this was the story I told. I do not consider myself a negative person, but, yes, I also remember when my first husband, who didn't want me to graduate from high school, threatened to have me committed to the state mental hospital because my studying so much was a sure sign of insanity; when my second husband told me at the Inverness Inn that he'd rather be there with Kristy, his ex-girlfriend; and when my lover of several years told me that the thought of love and marriage nauseated him. But wouldn't anyone remember these things?

I might have gone the rest of my life thinking that the story of my nonvisit to *David* covered pretty much everything I saw and did in Florence, but in 2007 my third husband, Richard, bought a DVD course entitled *Great Artists of the Italian Renaissance*. The first photos of the Brancacci Chapel in Florence, with its two tiers of frescos, enraged me. Oh, the exquisite beauty of Masolino's *The Temptation of Adam and Eve*, Filippino Lippi's *Disputation of Simon Magnus and Crucifixion of Saint Peter,* and Masaccio's *The Expulsion from the Garden of Eden, Baptism of the Neophytes,* and *Saint Peter Healing the Sick with His Shadow!* I had been to Florence, but I hadn't seen Saint Peter upside down on the cross, the naked neophyte being doused with holy water, or the red-clad, sword-wielding angel driving the fallen couple from Eden. That boor, that lout of a tour guide, Pierre, had not shown these to me.

Gradually, as the lecturer explained the fresco technique of painting on wet plaster with water-based pigments that penetrate into it, a sense of déjà vu came over me. A memory rose as inevitably as a gas bubble in water and finally broke through the surface of my brain: I recalled standing in the middle of the chapel, looking up at *Saint Peter Healing the Sick with His Shadow* on the left. The painting is based on Acts 5:15, which describes believers who "carried out the sick into the streets, and laid them on beds and pallets, that as Peter came by at least his shadow might fall on some of them." In it, the sick in front of Peter are still lying by the street, but those behind him have risen and are now well. Then I'd looked up at *The Temptation* on the right. I was startled by the serpent, which I had never before envisioned as having a woman's head and blond hair. I kept staring and staring at the paintings and told an Australian woman on my tour that I hoped to burn these images into my brain, to remember them always.

Pierre said, "This is what everyone must see in Florence. The *David* is not nearly so beautiful. The replica is almost the same, but there is no replica of this." He was trying to appease me, but it was true that, given a choice of seeing just one of these, I would choose the chapel.

Why had I forgotten something I'd so fervently resolved to remember? Why do I remember things I've made no attempt to remember, such as my Aunt Ethel and Uncle Dick's old-fashioned round washing machine with the external wringer; the words of the Colgate toothpaste jingle that Buffalo Bob Smith sang on *The Howdy Doody Show* in the 1950s; and the gorgeous neon-blue-and-orange markings of a sea slug, *Hermissenda crassicornis,* glowing in a sunlit pool on the mudflats of Bodega Bay on a summer morning in 1972? How does seeing a picture or being reminded of something bring back a whole scene that one might never have thought about again? I think we all have our own internalized Pierres as we go through life. Memory is a fallible, bossy guide that tells us which experiences we're allowed to revisit, which ones we aren't, and which ones we'll have to take the guide's word on.

As I watched the DVD, more memories came back: I'd first heard of the Brancacci Chapel from a boyfriend in college who'd visited Florence before he met me. Like Pierre, he told me that when you go to Florence, the chapel is something you must not miss. From his trip he brought back a brooch with a floral mosaic—three bell-shaped white flowers, a bud, and two leaves on a black background—framed in a lacy oval of Florentine silver. He'd bought it for a girlfriend, but when he got home, he realized that he didn't love her, so he never gave it to her. A few years later he gave it to me. I wondered now where I had put it and what else I had forgotten.

Top: *Richard and Lucy in Mexico, 2001*
Bottom: *Lucy and Richard with their family, 2010. Front row, left to right: Sabine, Brandon, Autumn, and Tamarind. Back row, left to right: Liana, Chase, Lucy, Richard, and Phillip holding baby Devlin.*

epilogue

I Feel Carnelian

I am a Californian. If you say *tree*, I will think *redwood*. If you say *winter*, I will think *rain*. If you say *ocean*, I will think *Pacific*. When the temperature is below sixty-five degrees, I feel cold. In 2002 I married a foreigner: a man from New York. Richard is a journalist who grew up on Long Island and spent much of his adult life in Manhattan. When our romance began, he lived in his dream home: an apartment with a view and lots of light. I lived in mine: a four-bedroom house with a family room and a backyard. He read *The New York Times* from back to front every day; I skimmed the *San Francisco Chronicle* from front to back. We found that our worlds could intertwine.

Our matchmaker was a mutual friend, Herb, a novelist. When Richard moved to California in 1991, he had lunch with Herb. When the conversation turned to single women, Herb told him about me, but wouldn't give him my phone number because I'd been involved with another friend of his, and he didn't know if it was on or off. It was off. Richard, enterprising, called me at Lawrence Berkeley National Laboratory, where I worked at the time.

We made plans to meet for lunch at La Val's, a pizza joint on the north side of the UC Berkeley campus. He said, "I'm tall, with wavy brown hair and hazel eyes." I said, "So am I." We recognized each other easily. The only discrepancy was that his hair was beginning to turn silver. He was forty-eight; I was forty-three. We liked each other, and he invited me out on a real date.

We had dinner at Lalime's, a romantic restaurant in Berkeley. Over delicious things such as soft-shell crab with watercress and mandarins, he told me what he hoped to find with a woman: marriage and a child. He had never had either. Many women would have swooned right then and there, that this dream of a man, who had worked for national magazines and written a best-selling book, who had sparkling hazel eyes and a charming way of tilting his head when he smiled, who could talk about so many things with wit and ease, wanted marriage and a child. But I had survived three unhappy marriages, two to the same man, and I had two daughters, eleven years apart. I was in my twenty-eighth year of raising children, and I was almost done. I did not think I was the right woman for him.

We went out a few more times. When he came to my house, he found it too dark. It was night; the drapes were closed. He didn't like the drapes, and he didn't like the dark paneling in the dining room or the dark wainscoting in the living room. He didn't like the wallpaper. He didn't think he could ever live there.

We stopped going out. We stayed in touch, but we only saw each other twice during the next nine years. He took me out to lunch once in downtown Berkeley, and he came to one of my poetry readings. That was all.

In December 1999 my off-and-on romance went off again. This time it was really off. The handle broke and I threw it away. It was off for good.

I didn't usually work on Saturdays, but sometimes I did if there was a special event at the Hall of Health or I didn't get my work done on Friday. On Saturday night, April 1, 2000, I stopped at the Berkeley Bowl for groceries on my way home from work. As I approached the entrance to the store, Richard came out. We started talking. Since he was doing his grocery shopping at seven o'clock on a Saturday night, I figured it was a safe bet to ask, "Are you still single?" He was, and he seemed glad that I was too. He tilted his head in that charming way and smiled.

He called the next morning and asked if I was free on Friday. Yes! We went to Café de la Paz, a tapas restaurant, and nibbled the night away. We have been together ever since.

While I had been going through my on-off romance, he had one of his own, with some of the same kinds of problems. On all of the issues that had caused the breakdown of those romances, we were perfectly in tune with each other.

The first time I spent the night at his condo, he put his arm around me while he slept, and it felt good, like I was home. I thought, *This is my husband.*

Five months into our romance, we attended a wedding on Nantucket. In the lodge the night before the ceremony, the bride and groom gave moving speeches declaring their love. Afterward I whined, "Richard never says anything like that to me." I thought I was making a joke, but Joan, a good friend of his, said, "He will. He just needs more time."

On my birthday he told me to bring a scarf. Was he taking me to a Muslim restaurant? An orthodox Jewish one? He used it to blindfold me, then took me careening through the streets of Berkeley. At least that's how it felt. When you can't see anything, every bump and turn is amplified. He was very sweet about it, worried that he was truly scaring me, but he didn't let me take the blindfold off until we were inside the restaurant. It was Lalime's.

The following year we celebrated his birthday in Oaxaca. I hoped he'd say "I love you" in a courtyard overflowing with impatiens and bougainvillea, over mole at a restaurant on the zócalo between maria-chi songs, or on the corner of a cobblestone street lined with pale blue and orange houses. Instead he surprised me with it when we returned home, as we waited at a taxi stand at the San Francisco airport. His love is good news, any place, any time!

I was madly, passionately, over-the-top in love with him. They called me Rucy at a Thai restaurant where we often ate, and we started calling each other Rucy and Litchard. We took walks on the beach at Point Reyes, watched French movies on his VCR, took a cooking class together, and had "study dates," when we would simply read together in his living room as he sat in his rose-colored leather chair and I lay on the sofa. He made a fabulous omelet every Sunday morning.

Before the year was out, we were talking about marriage. I said, "I want a real proposal." He said, "You'll get one." I waited. We told people we were going to get married. They asked when. I said, "After he proposes to me." While I was waiting for the proposal, we had dinner at a Thai restaurant. I didn't think it unusual when the waitress brought out two Chinese fortune cookies with the check. He said, "You go first." I broke a cookie open. The fortune said, "Rucy, will you marry me?" I kissed him and said, "Yes, yes, YES!"

He suggested that we write wedding poems to each other, based on the then-recent scientific finding that if the universe were put in a box and observed from a distance, it would appear beige, not turquoise as had been originally reported. We agreed to read the poems during the ceremony without showing them to each other beforehand.

We got married at my house in Oakland. We moved the furniture out of the living room, erected a wedding canopy decked with roses at one end of the room, and set up chairs for our thirty-five guests. The rabbi looked young enough to be a bar mitzvah boy. He'd been concerned at first because I had only a civil divorce from Ben, not a *get,* a Jewish divorce decree, but he decided to let it slide. Independently, Richard and I had decided to write villanelles about the color of the universe. Also independently, both of us had chosen to start with the same epigraph from *The New York Times.* I thought it was a good omen:

Color of the Universe

The universe is really beige. Get used to it.
    John Noble Wilford, *The New York Times*

To Richard

I can't believe the universe is tan,
not red or green or lavender or blue.
I feel carnelian when you take my hand—

not beige, like lima beans from a can,
but a splendid, electrifying hue.
I can't believe the universe is tan.

Rose and gold are what I understand
when I think of waking up each day with you.
I feel carnelian when I take your hand,

and like the universe my love expands,
surrounding us with turquoise and chartreuse.
Can you believe the universe is tan,

a color desolate as lunar sand
and homely as a peanut or cashew?
I feel carnelian when we're hand in hand,

listening to Perahia play Chopin.
The stars all turn cerulean on cue.
I don't care if the universe is tan:
I feel carnelian as you take my hand.

A Blessing in Beige

The universe is really beige. Get used to it.
    John Noble Wilford, *The New York Times*

To Lucy

Some stars burn brighter as they age
like maple leaves and apple trees flaming up from green.
Alas, the color of the universe is beige,

not peach or pearl or the palest shade of sage,
not turquoise, as they once thought—so serene.
Some stars burn brighter as they age.

The love that we have is harder to gauge,
but it too burns brighter the later it seems.
Does it matter so much if the universe is beige?

As a poet breathes sound onto a silent page
your love bathes my days in aquamarine.
Some stars burn brighter as they age.

Let them light up our lives as we leave this stage
and fill our hearts with their triumphant sheen.
Who cares if the color of the universe is beige?

A bird in flight outshines its silver cage.
If the sky's too bright the stars shine unseen.
May our stars burn brighter as we age.
Hurray, the color of the universe is beige!

•••

Our wedding bands are white gold. Richard's has "Like the universe my love expands" engraved on the inside; mine has "Some stars burn brighter as they age." We had the poems printed as a broadside to give to our guests. Our reception was in the backyard. We had round tables with beige tablecloths and a different color of napkin on each one. Our wedding cake was chocolate with mocha frosting and decorated with colorful stars and planets. Friends and family read poems and blessings. A trio called Cascada de Flores played Cuban and Mexican folk songs while we ate.

I would have gotten pregnant if I could. We went to two fertility clinics and a doctor of Chinese medicine who specialized in fertility.

We considered adoption, in vitro fertilization with a donor egg, and a surrogate mother. Then a wonderful thing happened: we started having grandchildren. The first one arrived eight months after our wedding. The next one came two years later, the third one a year and a half after that, and the fourth after another three years. Two boys and two girls: Brandon, Sabine, Autumn, and Devlin. Brandon and Sabine are the children of Liana and her husband, Chase. Autumn and Devlin belong to Tamarind and her husband, Phil.

Richard and I babysit often. We take the kids to the zoo, the park, and the Bay Area Discovery Museum. They call us Grandma Lucy and Grandpa Richard. We read to them and play ball in the backyard. We have learned to play Zingo and have become acquainted with Thomas the Train and reacquainted with Chutes and Ladders and Candy Land. We have watched many Curious George videos. We feed the kids, bathe them, and put them to bed, then go home exhausted ourselves. Richard's sister tells him that he's skipped a crucial stage that usually precedes having grandchildren, but he doesn't seem to mind.

The first year we were married, we lived in North Berkeley in Richard's sunny condo with a panoramic view of the Bay Area. My office was in a corner of the bedroom. There was no room for most of my clothes, let alone my other possessions. We started looking at houses, but when we saw the price tags, he started liking my house in Oakland more and more.

Richard said that since I'd tried his place, he'd try mine. Tamarind and Phil had been living there, but wanted to move. It worked out. Before moving in, we got rid of the wallpaper and drapes and, on a whim, bought a dozen colorful rugs of various sizes at an auction, all of which fit perfectly where we'd imagined they would go. Since then, we've built a library and a deck and filled the house with paintings and sculptures, mostly by friends. Both of us now feel completely at home for the first time.

Of course, we argue. Sometimes I get my way, sometimes he gets his, and sometimes we compromise. When we were planning the library, we scared off a prospective carpenter with our bickering about how far apart the shelves should be. We decided to make them adjustable.

Here's one more poem I wrote for Richard:

Birding: A Love Poem

I offer you the tundra swans
rising in my hazel eyes, each
with a yellow spot on its black bill,
heading toward the horizon,
honking all along my auditory nerves
with long necks outstretched.

I give you my heart, its wings
beating like a flock of snow geese
to send blood through my aorta.
They shimmer in morning light
before turning east and drifting
to earth like a rain of gems.

Please take my fears, frenzied
as a hundred red-winged blackbirds
swooping in chaotic patterns
as they fly from my amygdala,
singing their squeaky song,
and land in a stand of tall reeds.

My obsessions and sorrows,
those awkward ducks that waddle
on islands in my mind, quacking
and whistling, are yours also. Each
has its beauty: a blue wing patch,
a white crown, an emerald head.

Nor can I withhold from you
my vanity, preening itself
like a sandhill crane at the edge
of my retina. You'll find it in flocks,
alternately gliding and flapping,
its rattling call filling my throat.

My anger—that red-tailed hawk,
perched on a tree in my cerebrum,
I offer more reluctantly. Its talons
are sharp, its call a high scream.
I confess that even I dislike it
as it circles, then dives for its prey.

My love is yours for the taking,
of course—a meadowlark on a rock
on a grassy hill in early December,
its yellow breast and black bib
pulsing softly. It won't stray far:
this is its year-round range.

I surrender my molecules too,
swirling in flocks, layer upon layer,
in my cells, like so many birds
with hollow bones and rapid hearts,
heading south, the air full of wings,
dazzling, alive with offerings.

About the Author

Photo by Richard Levine.

Lucille Lang Day has published creative nonfiction in *The Hudson Review, Istanbul Literary Review, Passages North, River Oak Review, Willow Review,* and many other journals. She is a recipient of the *Willow Review* Award in Creative Nonfiction and a Notable Essay citation in *Best American Essays.* She is also the author of a children's book, *Chain Letter,* and eight poetry collections and chapbooks, including *The Curvature of Blue, Infinities,* and *The Book of Answers.* Her first poetry collection, *Self-Portrait with Hand Microscope,* received the Joseph Henry Jackson Award. She received her M.A. in English and M.F.A. in creative writing at San Francisco State University, her M.A. in zoology and Ph.D. in science and mathematics education at the University of California at Berkeley. The founder and director of a small press, Scarlet Tanager Books, she also served for seventeen years as the director of the Hall of Health, an interactive children's museum in Berkeley.

HEYDAY

into California

About Heyday

Heyday is an independent, nonprofit publisher and unique cultural institution. We promote widespread awareness and celebration of California's many cultures, landscapes, and boundary-breaking ideas. Through our well-crafted books, public events, and innovative outreach programs we are building a vibrant community of readers, writers, and thinkers.

Thank You

It takes the collective effort of many to create a thriving literary culture. We are thankful to all the thoughtful people we have the privilege to engage with. Cheers to our writers, artists, editors, storytellers, designers, printers, bookstores, critics, cultural organizations, readers, and book lovers everywhere!

We are especially grateful for the generous funding we've received for our publications and programs during the past year from foundations and hundreds of individual donors. Major supporters include:

Acorn Naturalists; Alliance for California Traditional Artists; Anonymous; James J. Baechle; Bay Tree Fund; Barbara Jean and Fred Berensmeier; Joan Berman; Buena Vista Rancheria; Lewis and Sheana Butler; California Civil Liberties Public Education Program, California State Library; California Council for the Humanities; The Keith Campbell Foundation; Center for California Studies; City of Berkeley; Compton Foundation; Lawrence Crooks; Nik Dehejia; Frances Dinkelspiel; Troy Duster; Euclid Fund at the East Bay Community Foundation; Mark and Tracy Ferron; Judith Flanders; Karyn and Geoffrey Flynn; Furthur Foundation; The Fred Gellert Family Foundation; Wallace Alexander Gerbode Foundation; Nicola W. Gordon; Wanda Lee Graves and Stephen

Duscha; Alice Guild; Walter & Elise Haas Fund; Coke and James Hallowell; Hawaii Sons, Inc.; Sandra and Charles Hobson; G. Scott Hong Charitable Trust; Kendeda Fund; Marty and Pamela Krasney; Kathy Kwan and Robert Eustace; Guy Lampard and Suzanne Badenhoop; LEF Foundation; Kermit Lynch Wine Merchant; Michael McCone; Michael J. Moratto, in memory of Ernest L. Cassel; Steven Nightingale; Pacific Legacy, Inc.; Patagonia, Inc.; John and Frances Raeside; Redwoods Abbey; Robin Ridder; Alan Rosenus; The San Francisco Foundation; San Manuel Band of Mission Indians; Tom Sargent; Sonoma Land Trust; Martha Stanley; Roselyne Chroman Swig; Thendara Foundation; Sedge Thomson and Sylvia Brownrigg; Tides Foundation; TomKat Charitable Trust; The Roger J. and Madeleine Traynor Foundation; Marion Weber; White Pine Press; John Wiley & Sons, Inc.; The Dean Witter Foundation; Lisa Van Cleef and Mark Gunson; and Yocha Dehe Wintun Nation.

Getting Involved

To learn more about our publications, events, membership club, and other ways you can participate, please visit www.heydaybooks.com.

ECO-FRIENDLY BOOKS
Made in the USA